Whatever Happened to Monetarism?

Modern Economic and Social History Series

General Editor: Derek H. Aldcroft

Whatever Happened to Monetarism?

Economic Policy-Making and Social Learning in the United Kingdom since 1979

MICHAEL J. OLIVER

Routledge
Taylor & Francis Group

LONDON AND NEW YORK

First published 1997 by Ashgate Publishing

Reissued 2018 by Routledge
2 Park Square, Milton Park, Abingdon, Oxon, OX14 4RN
52 Vanderbilt Avenue, New York, NY 10017

Routledge is an imprint of the Taylor & Francis Group, an informa business

Publisher's Note
The publisher has gone to great lengths to ensure the quality of this reprint but points out that some imperfections in the original copies may be apparent.

Disclaimer
The publisher has made every effort to trace copyright holders and welcomes correspondence from those they have been unable to contact.

A Library of Congress record exists under LC control number:

ISBN 13: 978-1-138-36264-2 (hbk)
ISBN 13: 978-1-138-36266-6 (pbk)
ISBN 13: 978-0-429-43194-4 (ebk)

Typeset in Sabon by Manton Typesetters, 5–7 Eastfield Road, Louth, LN11 7AJ.

Contents

Contents

Modern Economic and Social History Series
General Editor's Preface

Economic and social history has been a flourishing subject of scholarly study during recent decades. Not only has the volume of literature increased enormously but the range of interest in time, space and subject matter has broadened considerably so that today there are many sub-branches of the subject which have developed considerable status in their own right.

One of the aims of this new series is to encourage the publication of scholarly monographs on any aspect of modern economic and social history. The geographical coverage is world-wide and contributions on non-British themes will be especially welcome. While emphasis will be placed on works embodying original research, it is also intended that the series should provide the opportunity to publish studies of a more general and thematic nature which offer a reappraisal or critical analysis of major issues of debate.

Derek H. Aldcroft

Manchester Metropolitan University

List of figures

List of tables

Preface

Throughout the 1970s, the economic policy of the Conservative Party became increasingly influenced by many of the monetarist arguments emanating from the United States. After winning the General Election in May 1979, the Conservatives came to power with the intention of conducting economic policy along monetarist lines. This book will examine why this resolve faltered and how the demise of monetarism in the United Kingdom since 1979 can be explained through a social learning model.

While it is not disputed that there were inevitable complexities resulting from the model developed in the 1970s, the real failure of the Thatcher macro-strategy can be traced from the abandonment of monetarism in the mid-1980s. The deleterious nature of policy from 1985 (when the government finally deserted monetary targeting) was destabilizing by 1988 and, following an unwise monetary expansion, the economy underwent a boom. Consequently, this study will argue that the monetarist strategy was rejected for a number of reasons over the 1980s. This included the recession of the early 1980s; the rise in unemployment; the change in attitude to the role of the exchange rate; the effects of financial liberalization; and disagreements between politicians and policy-makers.

This last point is of particular importance as an explanation for policy failure. Too often, economic historians tend to neglect or downplay the importance of the politician in the policy-making process. Given that some members of the Conservative Party were embracing monetarist doctrines during the 1970s and early 1980s, it is surprising that not only did they abandon this new macroeconomic strategy with indecent haste when teething problems arose, but they seemed to learn little from their experiment by the end of the 1980s. This study will seek to emphasize the important role that Nigel Lawson played in dismantling key parts of the monetarist framework during the 1980s.

One of the problems which is encountered when examining a subject so near to the present is trying to obtain primary sources. This is made less of an issue with the availability of so much diverse secondary literature on the 1980s. Nevertheless, there is still a problem with obtaining internal memos, letters and papers which will be unavailable for another 30 years. During the course of writing the book, I undertook a number of interviews with Treasury and Government officials who argued that, while such documents will ultimately shed more light on the mechanics of policy-making, they will add little to explain what motivated policy-makers and politicians to adopt certain policies.

In this respect, the task of examining economic policy in the 1980s has been made much easier with the publication of Nigel Lawson's (1992a) autobiography. The two volumes of memoirs from Margaret Thatcher (1993, 1995) are a useful reference work, although Geoffrey Howe (1994) adds less to existing economic knowledge than Nigel Lawson. The problem with such autobiographies are that, typically, the authors have a particular 'story' with a distinct slant. Indeed, while it is clear that Howe, Lawson and Thatcher are all from the Conservative Party, this study will highlight some of the contradictions which surface in the written memoirs of these three protagonists. Moreover, although Lawson's account is the more detailed of the three, his work also suffers from irregular coverage on some issues.

Other autobiographies have been used from former Cabinet ministers (Gilmour 1992; Ridley 1992; Tebbit 1988; Walker 1991), although they contain less economic substance than those mentioned above. Although the Civil Service has been relatively silent on economic policy-making in the 1980s, the contributions of Burns (1994), Middleton (1989) and Pliatzky (1989) have been useful.

Various Bank of England articles have been cited in the text, along with HM Treasury press releases and evidence from Treasury Select Committees. The Treasury Select Committee reports are invaluable to the economic historian because they provide an excellent critique of policy and events post-1979.

Aside from the secondary sources, a series of interviews conducted between 1991 and 1995 provided valuable information for this study. Over this period, I selected 18 politicians, government advisers and economic commentators, many of whom were directly involved with policy formulation in the 1970s and 1980s, and wrote and asked them if they were willing to be interviewed by me. Of these, five were unwilling or unable to see me (Margaret Thatcher, Brian Griffiths, Brian Walden, John Major, Norman Lamont), one agreed to be interviewed but later died before being interviewed (Keith Joseph), one did not reply (John Biffen), nine agreed to see me in person (Sir Samuel Brittan, Sir Terry Burns, Professor Tim Congdon, Sir Terrance Higgins, Will Hutton, Peter Jay, Sir Peter Middleton, Professor Sir Alan Walters, David Willetts) and two agreed to respond to written questions (Nigel Lawson and Geoffrey Howe).

All of those who agreed to be interviewed in person were recorded, with the exception of Will Hutton. The interviews ranged in length from one to two hours. I felt that it was important to approach each interviewee on the understanding that I wished to incorporate their spoken evidence into the book. The interviewees agreed to being sent a transcript of the interview, whereupon they made minor amendments (mainly grammatical changes) to their original answers. All but Sir Terence Burns were happy to be cited, where appropriate, directly in the text. Although Geoffrey Howe had agreed to co-operate, his autobiography came out as I was formulating my questions. After examining his autobiography (which followed the publication of both Margaret Thatcher's and Nigel Lawson's) I decided not to question the former chancellor.

With the objective of obtaining the most accurate answers, I sent a list of questions to each candidate a week before the interview to give the interviewee time to prepare. Because the interviews were attributable, the reader can form their own judgements about the credibility of the sources when I have quoted anything at length. Where possible, I tried to standardize my questions, although there were slight variations according to the context in which they were being interviewed. For example, I asked Samuel Brittan and Peter Jay when they thought that fatal policy mistakes had been made in the 1980s, even though my primary questions to both concerned the role of the press in introducing monetarism to a wider audience.

It became clear after several interviews that many of the discussions between policy-makers and officials were not accurately documented (if they were at all). Indeed, one senior Treasury official recalled that during the late 1980s, Chancellor Lawson would disappear 'in a huddle' with one or two officials without any secretarial support and discuss economic policy. This was told not to imply that all important economic decisions are made in such a clandestine, 'conspiracy theory' environment, but to illustrate how policy-making is often considerably ad hoc – as will be shown in the 'shadowing the Deutschmark' period and when the pound left the ERM.

I wish to register here my thanks to the following people who have participated in discussions with me during the course of writing this book: Sir Samuel Brittan (*Financial Times*); Sir Terry Burns (HM Treasury); Professor Tim Congdon (Lombard Street Research); Professor Larry Dodd (University of Florida); Sir Terrance Higgins; Will Hutton (*Guardian*); Peter Jay (BBC Television Centre); Chris Kelly (HM Treasury); Dr Frank Longstreth (University of Bath); Sir Peter Middleton (Barclays Bank plc); Chris Patten (Governor of Hong Kong); Professor Sven Steinmo (University of Colorado at Boulder); Professor Sir Alan Walters (AIG Trading Corporation); Dr Peter Wardley (University of the West of England, Bristol); David Willetts, MP.

Some of the ideas in this study were presented to the annual conferences of the Political Studies Association held at York in April 1995 and at Glasgow in 1996; the Economics and Business Historical Society held at the University of Colorado at Boulder, USA, in April 1995; the Economic History Society at Lancaster in March 1996 and the first conference on Policy Transfer held at the University of Birmingham in October 1996. Thanks for their comments go to all conference participants, especially Dr Andrew Denham (University of Nottingham), Dr David Dolowitz (University of Birmingham), Professor Andrew Gamble (University of Sheffield), Dr Mark Garnett, Professor David Marsh (University of Birmingham), Professor Colin Thain (University of Ulster), Dr Mark Wickham-Jones (University of Bristol) and Dr Steve Wilson (Alice Lloyd College, Kentucky). I also wish to thank the economic historians at the University of Leeds for their helpful criticisms during a 'Lunch-time Workshop' in November 1995.

I am grateful to the library staff at the following universities who have helped me search for references: Bath; Bristol; Colorado at Boulder; Kent; Leeds; West of England; and to HM Treasury for providing the press releases.

Deep thanks need to be expressed to Professor Derek Aldcroft who began supervising this as a Ph.D. thesis at the University of Leicester and who agreed to carry on the task at Manchester Metropolitan University. Professors Derek Leslie, Malcolm Sawyer, Steven Tolliday and George Zis have also provided comments and references.

It is family and friends who are ignored when the words have to be written, and I wish to thank my parents and my brothers for their patience with my erratic behaviour over the last few years. Concomitantly, I must offer apologies to my friend Kim, who was frequently neglected during the writing of this book. I wish to thank her for the help she gave in cataloguing all the photocopied articles and newspaper cuttings.

Finally, thanks must go to Steve Dunn who provided invaluable help with the indexing.

Michael Oliver
University of Leeds

Abbreviations

CCC	Competition and Credit Control
CPS	Centre for Policy Studies
CSO	Central Statistical Office
DCE	Domestic Credit Expansion
ECU	European Currency Unit
EMS	European Monetary System
EMU	European Monetary Union
ERM	Exchange-Rate Mechanism
FEER	Fundamental Equilibrium Exchange Rate
G6	Group of Six
GDP	Gross Domestic Product
Gooies	Group of outside independent economists
IEA	Institute of Economic Affairs
IFS	Institute for Fiscal Studies
IMF	International Monetary Fund
ISIC	International Standard Industrial Classification
LBS	London Business School
MBC	Monetary Base Control
MTFS	Medium-Term Financial Strategy
NAIRU	Non-Accelerating Inflation Rate of Unemployment
NIESR	National Institute of Economic and Social Research
OECD	Organization for Economic Co-operation and Development
OPEC	Organization of Petroleum Exporting Countries
PBC	Political Business Cycle
PPP	Purchasing Power Parity
PSBR	Public Sector Borrowing Requirement
RPI	Retail Price Index

For my family, Kim and Harvey

Introduction

While the bulk of the literature on the economic record of the last 25 years has focused on macro and micro performance indicators (Allsopp, Jenkinson and Morris, 1991; Britton, 1991; Johnson 1991a), there have only been a few accounts by economic historians and historians on the origins and diffusion of the new economic strategy within the Conservative Party (Burk and Cairncross, 1992; Cockett, 1995). Some of these accounts are unsatisfactory because they automatically assume that economic policy changed course somewhere in the mid-1970s and that since this date policy has been rigidly fixed on a monetarist, free-market autopilot. In many respects, the work of the political scientists has been more instructive about the changes in policy during the last 20 years than that produced by the historian, although even here there has been a tendency to downplay some of the shifts in macroeconomic policy during the course of the 1980s (Gamble, 1994; Hall, 1992).

The basic facts are as follows. In 1979, a Conservative government was elected with a firm commitment to implement monetarist economic policies. During the early 1980s, policy inconsistencies arose which initially weakened the credibility of the monetarist experiment. Later, the differences in policy objectives between the Bank of England, chancellor, prime minister and Treasury fatally undermined the government's economic strategy. By the end of the 1980s, this resulted in a return to the traditional 'boom and slump' cycle which the Conservative government had promised to avoid when it entered office in 1979. Following its dissatisfaction with 'national monetarism' (Goodhart, 1989, p. 311), the Conservative government entered the exchange-rate mechanism (ERM) in October 1990 to give greater credibility to UK economic policy. Entry into the ERM (dubbed by some as a period of 'exchange rate monetarism') was brought to an abrupt halt in 1992 and left the authorities with an even greater credibility problem. Since leaving the ERM, the government has attempted to restore credibility by installing a new monetary framework.

This study wishes to focus on an area where there has been little work done, namely why the government abandoned its monetarist economic policy in the 1980s. The current literature in this area has been mainly polemical in nature, written by economists (Congdon, 1992a; Keegan, 1989; Smith, 1987, 1992), and there is scope for a more historical assessment of macroeconomic policy changes since 1979. Underlying this book is a deceptively simple question: what did the government learn from monetarism?

The literature on lesson-drawing in the social sciences is still at a formative stage of development and, as Chapter One will discuss in more detail, until recently there has been little consideration given by political scientists to this subject and an even greater reluctance to use historical case studies to support their conclusions. At the first annual conference on Policy Transfer at the University of Birmingham in October 1996, it became clear that political scientists were beginning to accept the limitations of learning studies that were not supported by historical data. In short, as this study will argue, if social scientists wish to discuss the concept of lesson-drawing it is essential that they consider historical data so that they can develop and further research in this area. Consequently, the aim of this investigation – to explain and account for the disintegration of the monetarist framework in the United Kingdom since 1979 through a 'social learning' model – will be supported by a combination of historical and economic analysis. The bulk of the chapters in this volume are intended to set out a narrative of events from which conclusions will be drawn in the final chapter.

The difficulty with writing a study so close to recent events is that it could be argued that the subject-matter discussed here really needs a thirty- to fifty-year gestation period to allow time for events to be properly digested. However, as this is a study of contemporary economic policy, which will utilize a political science model, it shifts the locus of the debate away from the more traditional accounts of the post-1979 period which have been offered so far by economic historians (Cairncross, 1992; Glyn and Booth, 1996; Pollard, 1992). Nevertheless, there are three caveats which need to be sounded to the reader from the outset.

First, the model employed to examine policy changes since 1979 is taken from the political sciences. Yet this model is not the sole property of the political scientist, in much the same way that history is not the exclusive preserve of the economic historian. As Pontusson (1995, p. 120) has argued, 'political scientists must (should) either seek to explain economic outcomes or incorporate economic variables into their explanation of policy outcomes'.

Secondly, the bulk of the analysis is centred on the developments in monetary policy (in particular, the downgrading of money targets) and exchange-rate policy (in particular, the elevation of exchange-rate targets) since 1979. Fiscal policy is discussed in this volume, but there are no explicit discussions on public expenditure planning and control or budgetary and taxation policy. Moreover, despite the fact that some would argue that the real 'counter-revolution' post-1979 occurred at the micro level, there are only passing references to microeconomic policy.

Finally, although the *sine qua non* for a piece of economic history research is that it 'must employ the conceptual instruments, the analytical categories and the type of logic forged by economic theory' (Cipolla, 1991, p. 7), this does not eliminate the possibility that a partisan tone may creep into the text on occasion. This author recognizes that there is a fine line to be drawn between contemporary and historical analysis but, given the extent of controversy still surrounding the monetarist experiment in the United Kingdom, it would be impossible to eliminate all traces of bias about the post-1979 period.

CHAPTER ONE

Social learning and policy transfer

> Historians have to be always on the look-out for indications that
> they need to modify or overhaul their initial model. ... The aim of
> research is not to twist facts to prove a theory, but rather to adapt
> the theory to provide a better account of the facts.
>
> (Cipolla, 1991, p. 17)

Over the past 20 years, the historian of contemporary economic policy-
making has increasingly had to share his research agenda with the
economist, the political scientist and the sociologist (cf. Britton, 1991;
Hall, 1982; Runciman, 1993). In many ways this is to be welcomed, as
it has opened up opportunities for more collaborative research projects
between these disciplines – which some economic and social historians
have long argued for (Wright, 1986).

Given that contemporary theorists of the state have begun to en-
croach on the preserve of the economic historian, it could be argued
that contemporary economic history (at least of economic policy-making) has been displaced by another social science discipline. However,
recent work by British political scientists on policy transfer and American political scientists on policy learning has demonstrated that there
are new and exciting lines of research which require the combined
attention of economic and social historians and political scientists. But
what is policy transfer and policy learning, and how can they be applied
to monetarism in the United Kingdom?

Policy transfer and economic policy shifts

According to a survey on the literature by Dolowitz and Marsh (1996a,
p. 344):

> Policy transfer, emulation and lesson-drawing all refer to a process
> in which knowledge about policies, administrative arrangements,
> institutions etc. in one time and/or place is used in the development
> of policies, administrative arrangements and institutions in another
> time and/or place.

They do not use the terms policy transfer and lesson-drawing inter-
changeably, unlike Rose (1993) who refers to the overall process by
which policy or institutions are transferred as lesson-drawing. Although
Dolowitz and Marsh initially played down the differences in terminol-

ogy in their review article, more recently they have begun to shift from this view. As the discussion at the first annual Policy Transfer Conference made clear, although policy transfer and lesson-drawing are not mutually exclusive terms, they do refer to different processes (Oliver, 1996a).

Table 1.1 presents a model of policy transfer. The first column ('Why transfer?') is divided into three, showing how the literature has categorized transfer studies. This tripartite division should not be seen as rigid. For example, Polsby (1984) has suggested that elections might force candidates to search for new solutions to existing problems, but this could be due to cyclical events at home (voluntary transfer) or because candidates are realizing that until they adopt new policies they will continue to fall behind economically and socially (perceptual transfer). Indeed, as will be seen, the introduction of monetarist policies by the UK government in the mid-1970s could combine all three explanations. There were problems with the existing Keynesian paradigm which led to voluntary transfer; the IMF required that the UK should set monetary targets, which was coercive transfer; finally, the international consensus (especially in the United States) began to shift to a more monetarist mode of thinking in the 1970s, which was coercive transfer.

However, it is far too simplistic to assume that the seven columns in Table 1.1 could account for the adoption and subsequent shifts in macroeconomic policy from the 1970s. Can it account for how the state, interest groups and other actors initiated shifts in policy? How does it address whether some of these agents and actors were more influential at shaping policy than others? More fundamentally, once policy has been transferred, can the existing literature explain how policy changes course and how lessons are drawn? The remainder of this section will briefly examine the three existing arguments in the political science literature which address *why* economic policies change course. The last argument will extend the discussion so that the wider questions raised above can begin to be considered throughout the remainder of the chapter.

The first explanation argues that macroeconomic policy is determined by the type of political party in government. The basis for this explanation follows the work of Hibbs (1977, 1982), who claimed to have found a link between 'party stripe' and economic outcomes in a study of 12 OECD countries during the 1960s. In short, he found that countries with higher inflation and lower unemployment rates were associated with 'left' parties while countries with lower inflation and higher unemployment were governed by 'right' parties. Similarly, work by Cowart (1978a, 1978b) in the field of monetary and fiscal policy

Table 1.1　A model of policy transfer

Why transfer?			Who transfers?	What transferred?
Voluntary	Coercive	Perceptual		
Problems/ dissatisfaction	Direct government imposition	Perceptions of falling behind	Elected officials	Policies
Cyclical events	Supra-national institutions	International consensus	Bureaucrats	Institutional
Political conflict	Inter-governmental organizations		Administrators	Ideology
Legitimate conclusions already reached	Trans-national corporations		Entrepreneurs	Ideas
			Political parties	Negative lessons
			Pressure groups	What not transferred
			Think-tanks	
			International organizations	

Source:　Dolowitz and Marsh (1996b)

From where?			Degrees of transfer	Restrictions/ facilitators	How demonstrated?
Past	Other political systems				
	Within-a-nation	Cross-national			
Internal	Regional/ state/local government	Governments	Copying	Policy complexity	Media
Global	Other bureaucratic agencies	Individuals	Emulation	Past policies	Reports (commissioned/ uncommissioned)
	Other groups or actors	Groups	Mixtures	Structural/ institutional	Conferences
		Institutions	Inspiration	Feasibility (ideology/ cultural proximity/ technology/ economic/ bureaucratic)	Meetings/ visits
				Language	Statements (written/ oral)
				Past relations	

and Castles (1982) in public expenditure concurred with Hibbs's analysis.

The problem with this analysis, as Alt and Chrystal (1983, p. 116) have noted, is that the shift from Keynesianism to monetarism in both the United States and the United Kingdom in the 1970s happened during a time when there was a 'left' party in government. Moreover, Schmidt (1982) has challenged the empirical validity of Hibbs's work and could find little support for the link between party incumbency and the trade-off between unemployment and inflation for the 1970s.

The second explanation, the PBC, argues that governments shift macroeconomic policy according to the date of the next election. In the run-up to an election, governments will follow a reflationary ('Keynesian') policy, but after being re-elected they will adopt a deflationary ('monetarist') approach. The work of Nordhaus (1975) and Tufte (1978) is the most prominent in this field, although both analysts disagree on what governments want to deliver to voters. Nordhaus argues that the aim of a pre-election expansion is specifically to achieve a full level of employment, while for Tufte, governments aim to produce a fall in unemployment and a rise in real disposable income.

Critics have pointed out that this approach also suffers from empirical limitations (Alt and Chrystal, 1983, p. 125; Whiteley, 1986, p. 82), leading one academic (Lewin, 1991, p. 63) to conclude that 'research of the 1970s and 1980s gives only very weak support to the theory of political business cycles if, indeed, one can speak of support at all'. The PBC theory also presupposes that politicians assume that voters have short memories and no expectations, so that 'voters are expected to make their choice at the ballot-box on the basis of what has happened to them over the last few months before the election' (Hood, 1994, p. 65). This assumption, that the electorate do not learn from the actions of politicians, is tenuous as Nordhaus (1989, p. 4) has recognized. Moreover, although the PBC is more capable of explaining 'why "left" governments as well as "right" ones should sometimes adopt "monetarist" macroeconomic policies' (Hood, 1994, p. 67) than the political incumbency approach, both explanations tend to suffer from taking too narrow a perspective. As Thompson (1994, p. 28) has argued:

> ... both accounts are too heavily focused on the ultimate ends of policy, particularly unemployment and inflation. As a result, they have little to say about governments' interests in relation to the means by which those ends are reached ... macro-economic policy concerns choices about means. Once this is accepted, it becomes a highly dubious proposition to suggest, for example, that ministers seek to accommodate voters' preferences on whether inflation should be controlled by monetary or fiscal policy.

The third explanation in the literature examines the way in which institutional structures shape macroeconomic policy. Over the last two decades, political scientists have offered alternative theories on how public policy is formulated (Caporaso and Levine, 1992; Krasner, 1984; Steinmo, Thelen and Longstreth, 1992; Wilensky and Turner, 1987). It is possible to bifurcate these analyses of the state into two: on the one hand there is an approach which has been labelled state-centric, while the other approach is identified as state-structural (Hall, 1993, p. 276).

Those who argue from a state-centric point of view (Krasner, 1978; Nordlinger, 1981; Sacks, 1980) tend to emphasize the autonomy of the state from interest groups, political parties and outside actors in the policy-making process. The last 25 years have seen an enormous growth in this literature, influenced by the work of Hugh Heclo (1974). In a pioneering study which examined social policy in Britain and Sweden, Heclo argued that the policy-making process could not be satisfactorily explained by the electoral process, by interest groups or by socio-economic developments: 'Forced to chose one group among all the separate political factors as most consistently important ... the bureaucracies of Britain and Sweden loom predominant in the policies studied' (Heclo, 1974, p. 301).

The opposite to this view is the state-structural approach (see Katzenstein, 1978, 1985; Skocpol and Ikenberry, 1983; Weir and Skocpol, 1985) which is 'less concerned with the relative autonomy of state institutions than with the effects of different decision-making styles in terms of degrees of corporatism' (Hood, 1994, p. 69). As Krasner (1984, p. 223) has noted, from the late 1950s until the mid-1970s, 'political scientists wrote about government, political development, interest groups, voting, legislative behaviour, leadership and bureaucratic politics, almost everything but "the state"'.

While the terms 'state-structural' and 'state-centric' are unfamiliar in the lexicon of the economic historian, some of the ideas which are central to these arguments have been hotly debated among economic historians in a wider context, such as the role of interest groups and institutions (North, 1984; North and Thomas, 1973; Olson, 1982). Moreover, common to both the economic historian and the political scientist is lesson-drawing. As Heclo (1974, pp. 305–6) acknowledges:

> Politics finds its sources not only in power but also in uncertainty – men collectively wondering what to do. ... Governments not only 'power' ... they also puzzle. Policy-making is a form of collective puzzlement on society's behalf. ... Much political interaction has constituted a process of social learning through policy.

As will be discussed below, social learning draws on both the state-centric and state-structural approaches. Originally deployed by those working in cybernetics, organization theory and psychology (Argyris and Schön, 1978; Bandura, 1977a, 1977b; Steinbrunner, 1974), social learning was discussed by Etheredge in his two accounts (1981, 1985) of governmental learning. Yet until recently, social learning was presented in the social science literature in a sketchy form in contrast to the model developed in organization theory and cybernetics (see Ellison and Fudenberg, 1993).

Thus although the published research among political theorists was moving the concept of social learning towards a mainstream tool for social scientists, a full-blown model had not been developed or applied satisfactorily to a specific empirical setting and the debate was in need of a fresh stimulus. The breakthrough came in two stages and from the same source.

The social learning model

The first breakthrough came when Peter Hall (1990) contributed a chapter to a book which examined the role of social scientists, policy-makers and the state. In this chapter, Hall (1990, p. 9) labelled 'the overarching framework of ideas that structures policy-making ... a policy paradigm'. With explicit references to the work of Thomas Kuhn (1970), Hall argued that Kuhn's analysis had a considerable validity within the social science sphere. Hall gave a new twist to the 'growth of knowledge' theory and takes the debate further than Dow (1985) or Mehta (1977), if only because he stresses the sociological and political issues associated with policy paradigms, rather than just the pure economics of paradigms.

Secondly, and more importantly, social learning was discussed at length in Hall's (1993) seminal article in *Comparative Politics*. In this article, Hall transported social learning from a social psychology theory to a social science model. He did so by doing four things.

Firstly, he was able to show how contemporary theorists of the state had moved tantalizingly close to forming a model of social learning by identifying three central features from the state-centralists and state-structuralists. First, policy at time-1 is affected by policy at time-0: in other words, policy-makers respond to either past successes or failures in policy and conduct future policy with regard to policy legacies (Sacks, 1980; Weir and Skocpol, 1985). Second, those who are determining policy are experts within their fields. Heclo's (1974, p. 308) model of Swedish and British bureaucracies demotes the influence of the politician and promotes the role of the specialist in detailed areas of policy-making. Third, social learning emphasized that governments act independently from societal pressure, to the extent that many interest groups and political parties play a very small part in developing policy (Heclo, 1974, p. 318; Sacks, 1980, p. 356).

Secondly, Hall provided the first explicit definition of social learning for the social sciences in which social learning is 'a deliberate attempt to adjust the goals or techniques of policy in response to past experience and new information. Learning is indicated when policy changes as the result of such a process' (Hall, 1993, p. 278).

Thirdly, Hall stated that policy-making should be seen as a process that usually involves three central variables: goals that direct policy in a certain area; the policy instruments used to attain those goals; and the precise settings of these instruments.

Fourthly, if these goals, instruments or instrument settings are altered, then there are four 'orders of change' which follow. First-order change occurs when the levels of the basic instruments of policy are altered. Second-order change is denoted when the instruments of policy as well as their settings are altered in response to past experience. Both first-order and second-order changes keep the existing policy paradigm, despite occasional modifications in the instruments. When the instrument settings, instruments and the goals behind policy shift, this process is known as third-order change. There is a final order of change, which Hall demotes to a bare footnote reference. In a fourth-order change, 'policy-makers learn how to learn' (Hall, 1993, p. 293).

In toto, the combined weight of these four factors can be said to have significantly enhanced our understanding of social learning. Hall has (for the moment) bridged the gap between the state-centric and state-structural theories and has provided a sound working definition of social learning. As Hall (1993, p. 276) remarks positively, 'social learning is on the verge of becoming a key element in contemporary theories of the state and of policy-making more generally', and it might also be added that it now plays a crucial role in the learning debate.

Problems with Hall's model

While this author believes that Hall has done much to take the debate forward, attention should be drawn to the fact that his account of social learning is not entirely convincing. In particular, his conceptualization of the model and the application of it to economic history post-1979 is rather unsatisfactory. Hall's analysis suffers due to word constraints, so it does not fully develop some of the more interesting arguments at length and is silent on others. In particular, there are four major deficiencies with his work which will be considered in subsequent chapters.

First, Hall concentrates more comprehensively on the development of economic policy in the 1970s than the 1980s, and by neglecting developments in policy throughout the 1980s (particularly after 1985) the scope of his thesis is limited. It is misleading and inaccurate to describe policy as 'monetarist' throughout the 1980s. During that decade, the British government shifted from an economic policy with firm monetary rules towards a pragmatic policy based along traditional Keynesian lines.

Figure 1.1 traces the evolution of macroeconomic policy since 1945. The pre-1979 days do have an important part to play in the story, and these are discussed in Chapters Two and Three. However, the time-scale examined here is concerned more with the 1980s and early 1990s than the 1970s. In Figure 1.1, the post-1979 period has been divided into five phases. During each phase, there were important changes made to the initial macroeconomic model, either because economic events forced changes to be made or because the government wished to experiment with new policy instruments.

Developments during each of the five phases can be quickly summarized. During phase 1 (1979–83), the government's monetarist economic experiment faced two difficulties. First, the chosen monetary aggregate (£M3) wandered outside its target band. This gave the impression that monetary policy was loose when in fact it was very tight, and merely encouraged a continuation of tight policies. Second, the domestic economy underwent a period of rapid contraction which was exacerbated by the tight monetary regime. A debate opened in policy-making circles as to whether the government should adopt a different monetary target or abandon monetarism altogether.

In phase 2 (1983–86), the government began to get bogged down with the sterling issue and money technicalities. Those economic advisers who had been supporting the government began to argue for membership of the exchange-rate mechanism (ERM) as a means of stabilizing currency fluctuations and for controlling inflation. There were also widespread arguments beginning to appear in the monetarist camp over which money aggregates to target. Chancellor Lawson was left with the problem of having to choose between conflicting advice from the experts. From 1985, the money targets were finally abandoned and policy became more pragmatic.

In phase 3 (1986–90), macroeconomic policies returned to a traditional 'stop-go' pattern. Conflicts in policy and personality became widespread including the disagreements between Thatcher, Lawson and Walters over whether the UK should join the ERM. There was also a failure on the part of the Treasury to predict the boom of the late-1980s.

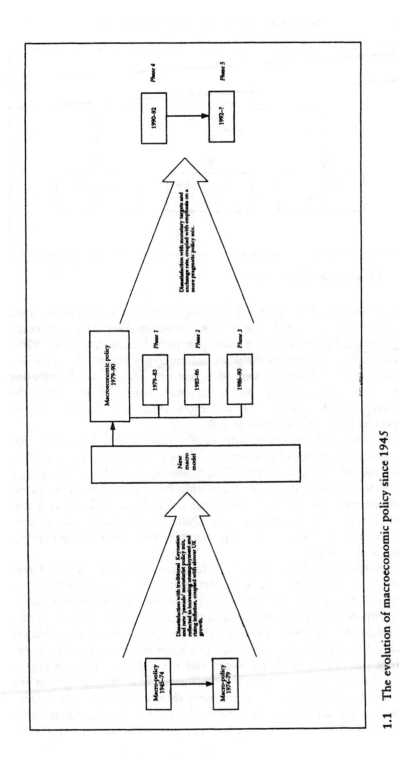

1.1 The evolution of macroeconomic policy since 1945

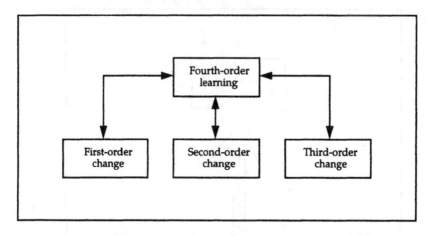

1.2   The social learning model

In phases 4 (1990–92) and 5 (1992–present), the government joined
and then left the ERM. Since 1990, policy-makers have not really
demonstrated that they have learnt the right lessons from the 1980s,
particularly in relation to the power of monetary policy. The abandonment of the ERM commitment after just two years was a humiliating
exercise in policy-making, and a case can clearly be made that the
recovery the UK economy has undergone since 1993 has come about
largely by chance rather than design.

The second shortcoming with Hall's work is that he argues that
changes in the setting of instruments do not automatically lead to policy
and paradigm changes. It is possible, however, to use the social learning
model to identify a dynamic relationship between instruments, instrument settings and policy changes since 1979. Figure 1.2 shows a dia-
gram of the social learning model. Quite clearly, Figure 1.2 is more
applicable to a range of learning examples and captures the bare essence of the model.

Throughout the 1980s, there were frequent first-order changes. However, the seemingly routine first-order changes (instrument settings) in
economic policy during the early 1980s were part of a wider dissatisfaction with the policy instruments, and this led to the adoption of alternative instruments. Between 1981 and 1985 there were several second-order
changes: the introduction of M0, the greater emphasis put on the exchange rate by Chancellor Lawson and the ending of overfunding in
1985. In other words, this study will argue that the changes in the
instrument settings and the instruments themselves (first- and second-
order change) led by 1981 to the abandonment of the strict monetarist
framework. Moreover, this was followed post-1985 by the adoption of

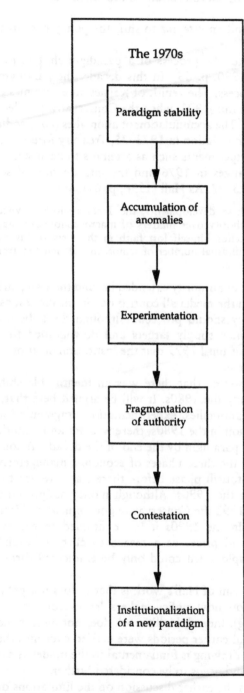

1.3 The 1970s' paradigm shift

a pragmatic policy and an *attempt* to shift the policy paradigm (third-order change).

Figure 1.3 illustrates the process of a paradigm shift in the 1970s, derived from Hall (1990, p. 68). In this decade, the paradigm shifted under a six-stage process. The zenith of Keynesian economics occurred between mid-1971 to mid-1973, when the Conservatives under Edward Heath were in power. The accumulation of anomalies (commodity prices rises in 1972–73, high inflation in 1973–75, Treasury forecasting errors in 1974–75) led to experiments such as attempts to keep sterling down on the foreign exchanges in 1976 and the introduction of severe incomes policies in 1975–77. As Hall (1990, p. 69) notes:

> In the face of these developments, the Treasury lost its virtual monopoly of authority over matters of macroeconomic management. The chancellor himself lost faith in the view of his own officials, and an unusual number of senior officials left the Treasury shortly thereafter.

This fragmentation of authority extended beyond the state, and 'think-tanks', City firms and the media all contributed in the contest as to how macroeconomic policy should proceed. Although the Labour government introduced money supply targets and downgraded the role of fiscal policy, it was not until 1979 that the institutionalization of a new paradigm was complete.

It is not clear, however, that there was an identifiable shift in the policy paradigm during the 1980s. It will be argued here that, despite the accumulation of anomalies, experimentation, fragmentation of authority and contestation in the 1980s, there was not an institutionalization of a wholly new paradigm by the end of the decade. As our earlier discussion suggested, the three phases of economic management in the 1980s led to a brief fourth phase before there was a return to greater paradigm stability in the 1990s. Although money supply targets had been abandoned, by 1992 the Conservative government had introduced an inflation target. In the 1990s it has continued to eschew direct controls on wages and prices as a means to curb inflation and to emphasize that unemployment could only be eradicated through supply-side measures.

A third major criticism of Hall's work is that it does not provide any detailed exposition on how policy-makers learn from their actions (fourth-order learning). Indeed, Hall's work does not discuss the extent to which the lessons of earlier periods were carried over into the 1980s and 1990s. As lesson-drawing is fundamental to the model, it cannot be dismissed so readily and needs to be considered further.

This also highlights the earlier discussion on the limitations of policy transfer as a tool to account for policy changes. While there might be a consensus beginning to emerge 'that policy-learning, leading to potential policy transfer, is an important enterprise' (Wolman, 1992, p. 28), there is still an ominous silence in the literature on what role social learning plays in the lesson-drawing process. While Rose (1993, p. 157) did not consider social learning, he ended his study by claiming that 'the critical issues of lesson-drawing are not whether we can learn anything elsewhere, but when, where and how we learn'. It is the contention of this book that, because of its dynamic composition, social learning gives political scientists a framework to address the 'when, where and how' of lesson-drawing, in marked contrast to traditional learning models which merely tend to stress 'who learns what from whom'.

Finally, Hall (1993, pp. 276–7) raises four research questions which he only partially answers in his article:

> How should we understand the relationship between ideas and policy-making? How do the ideas behind policy change course? Is the process of social learning relatively incremental, as organization theory might lead us to expect, or marked by upheaval and the kind of 'punctuated equilibrium' that often applies more generally to political change? Are bureaucrats the principal actors in social learning, or do politicians and societal organizations also play a role?

While it is impossible for Hall to consider these questions at length, this chapter has already touched on some of these issues and will return to them in Chapter Seven.

Social learning is a relatively new concept, but one which social scientists should be encouraged to use to complement rather than replace policy transfer. In so far as social learning can bridge the gap between the state-centric and state-structural arguments, it provides state theorists with an attractive new model. By seeking to test and reconceptualize Hall's model, this study avoids the dense and technical explanations behind the economic variables and provides an accessible account on what has determined macroeconomic policy shifts since 1979.

CHAPTER TWO

A failure of Keynesianism?

[T]he common-sense conclusion is that Britain and other Western countries had full employment for a quarter of a century after the war because their governments were committed to full employment, and knew how to secure it; and they knew how to secure it because Keynes had told them how.

(Stewart, 1986, p. 146)

In recent years, the academic literature on Keynesianism has swelled considerably. Very loosely, it is possible to group this literature into three strands. First, there has been a debate among economic historians as to when the Treasury adopted Keynes's ideas (Booth, 1983; Rollings, 1988; Tomlinson, 1984). Second, there has been a discussion on how 'Keynesian' the policies were that governments implemented post-1945 (Congdon, 1998; Peden, 1988; Schott, 1982; Tomlinson, 1981a, 1981b). Third, the question has been raised (and challenged) as to whether 'Keynesian' economic policies really did create full employment (Matthews, 1968; Stafford, 1970).

While each of these areas is a fascinating topic for the economic historian to consider, these debates have a limited use in a chapter which is concerned with addressing a separate issue: the rejection of Keynesianism by policy-makers. The demise of Keynesianism is a historical process which can utilize the above explanations, yet it is also possible to account for its demise by invoking the social learning model, as Hall (1993) has demonstrated.

The aim of this and the next chapter is to provide a synthesis of the Keynesian and monetarist arguments and to explain why Keynesian economic policies were rejected in favour of monetarism. This chapter will concentrate on the Keynesian era, leaving a discussion on the ascendancy of monetarism until Chapter Three.

The structure of the rest of the chapter is as follows. The first section will discuss Keynesian economics, the policy framework which successive Conservative and Labour governments used and the performance of the British economy from 1945 down to 1979. The evolution of monetary and exchange-rate policy between 1945 and 1979 will then be reviewed. Finally, British economic policy post-1945 will be assessed from a broader perspective.

Economic policy and performance: 1945–79

As Snowdon, Vane and Wynarczyk (1994, p. 11) have recently noted:

> at the theoretical level Keynesian economics created schizophrenia
> in the way economics was taught, with courses in microeconomics
> typically concentrating on issues relating to allocation, production
> and distribution (questions of efficiency and equity) and courses in
> macroeconomics focusing on problems associated with the level
> and the long-term trend of aggregate output and employment, and
> the rate of inflation (questions of growth and stability).

Bearing this in mind, perhaps it is a little harsh to assert that Keynesianism
failed when it is unclear what aspects of economic policy Keynes would
have agreed with post-1945. Cairncross (1992, pp. 7–8) has noted that
on the one hand 'Keynes himself would have had serious reservations
about demand management', and on the other 'the very idea of managing demand was profoundly Keynesian'. To try to extricate Keynes's
ideas from those of his followers would be a lengthy undertaking and
outside the remit of this study, but in what follows we trace the evolution of the Keynesian framework and then examine British economic
performance between 1945 and 1979.

The main thrust of Keynesianism can be found in Keynes's (1936)
tome, *The General Theory of Employment, Interest and Money* (hereaf-
ter abbreviated to *General Theory*), and which can be explained without recourse to IS–LM diagrams or national income equations. In it,
Keynes argued that the economy has no automatic, self-correcting mechanism which can eliminate unemployment. In direct contrast to the classical economists (who argued that unemployment could be eliminated
entirely by the market and without government intervention) Keynes
was concerned that an economy could be caught in a situation of
underemployment equilibrium, with low levels of economic activity as a
consequence (Keynes, 1936, p. 249).

When Keynes was writing his *General Theory* in the 1930s, the so-
called 'Treasury view' held sway. Expressed simply by Churchill (*Parliamentary Debates*, 15 April 1929, vol. 227, col. 54):

> the orthodox Treasury doctrine which has steadfastly held that,
> whatever might be the political or social advantages, very little
> additional employment and no permanent additional employment
> can in fact and as a general rule be created by State borrowing and
> State expenditure.

According to this view, if the government borrowed to finance public
works, funds would be denied to private industry, with any rise in
employment created by government-backed public work schemes
matched by a fall in private employment.

The 'Treasury view' was not the only objection to the *General Theory*. Roger Middleton (1985, Ch. 8) has discussed the other fears raised by the critics, including how public works would be implemented and the loss of confidence which would be engendered in the financial markets following a budget deficit. Yet if the 1930s were not ripe for the advent of Keynesian economics, by the 1950s it was more readily accepted into mainstream policy-making (Dow, 1964). Three things stand out in particular, which *in toto*, added weight to the Keynesian case.

First, the Second World War had seen government intervention on a far greater scale than before and had altered the relationship between the state and the people (Hancock and Gowing, 1949, p. 541). Second, national accounting methods had progressed remarkably through the 1940s and, with the formation of the Economic Section and CSO, led to a greater awareness of economic difficulties and shortcomings (Cairncross, 1985, Ch. 2). Third, the White Paper *Employment Policy* (Ministry of Reconstruction, 1944, p. 2) stated that the government accepted 'the maintenance of a high and stable level of employment after the war' which was a definite snub to the classical economists. Although the final draft of the White Paper did not specify a particular level of unemployment as being the full employment figure, throughout the post-war period, 3 per cent of the population unemployed was taken as a fully employed economy. It was argued that any figure lower than that could lead to higher inflation if workers sought pay rises which employers would have to concede if labour was scarce.

Peden (1988, p. 16) has drawn attention to the fact that fiscal policy was 'barely mentioned' in the *General Theory* of 1936, but turned up four years later in *How to Pay for the War*, where Keynes (1940) suggested how the 'inflationary gap' could be calculated. By the 1950s 'the centre-piece of policy ... was demand management, and on this both parties accepted the central place of fiscal policy' (Tomlinson, 1990, p. 257). The role of monetary policy was not absolutely clear; it was used as a supplementary tool of demand management to 'back up' fiscal policy, and as a means of protecting the exchange rate through high interest rates in the recurrent balance of payments crises throughout the period. Although the Conservatives revived the use of monetary policy after 1951 (Dow, 1964, pp. 66–70), both the Conservatives and Labour 'spoke the language of Keynesianism. But we spoke it with different accents and with differing emphasis' (Butler, 1971, p. 160).

Recent work has cast considerable doubt as to whether the UK really ever had a Keynesian revolution. Conducting a series of statistical tests for three time-periods (1948–94, 1948–74 and 1975–94), Congdon (1998) has shown that the level of economic activity was not a significant influence on the change in the cyclically adjusted budget position. He does concede however, that:

> Of course, the demonstration that statistically there never was a Keynesian revolution does not rule out the possibility that, from time to time, key decision-makers and their advisers did alter fiscal policy in a Keynesian manner. ... The absence of a Keynesian revolution in fact does not exclude the possibility that there was a Keynesian revolution in intention.

Indeed, this does not vitiate the view of Longstreth (1983) who labelled the period from 1947 until 1960 as 'pure and simple Keynesianism', although he is careful to differentiate the use of demand management between the Conservative and Labour Parties. According to Longstreth (1983, p. 13): 'Conservative policy embraced a rather different set of priorities reflecting a rather tenuous attachment to the Keynesian programme. Chief among these was the revival of an international role for sterling and an ultimately convertible currency.'

We shall deal with the sterling issue at greater length in the next two sections, but it is interesting to note that, by the end of the 1950s, the conflict between macroeconomic objectives was already apparent. Equally, by this date the international growth divergence from the 1950s had put pressure on policy-makers to find new solutions for Britain's economic ills. To accompany the existing macroeconomic instruments, both Conservative and Labour governments introduced agencies to tackle the growth issue, including the setting-up of the National Economic Development Council in 1962 and the Department of Economic Affairs in 1964. In addition to these, both political parties tried to implement microeconomic policies which would harness the work of the above bodies (Kirby, 1991).

Unfortunately, the National Plan drawn up by the Department of Economic Affairs was a failure. In part this was because it was 'no more than the promulgation of hastily conceived and wildly ambitious targets for growth that bore little relation to the actual trajectory of industrial sectors' (Hall, 1986, p. 88), but also because

> many students [had become] finally convinced that the government had abandoned its growth and employment objectives and would be prepared to deflate to the extent necessary to maintain the exchange rate. Thus the National Plan was written off by many people two months before it was published.
> (Brittan, 1969, p. 199)

Meanwhile, policy-makers had turned their attention to two further areas of concern: the growth in public expenditure and wage inflation. The Plowden Report (HM Treasury, 1961) had argued that there should be a shift away from the counter-cyclical public works policy as set out in the 1944 Employment White Paper. Yet public expenditure continued to grow: from about a third of GDP in 1961 to 40.2 per cent in 1967/68 (Pliatzky, 1982, p. 213). Controlling prices and incomes between 1964 and 1970 became something of a bugbear for the Labour Party: voluntarism was abandoned in favour of legislation, which led to increasing hostility between the government, TUC and industry (Panitch, 1976).

With internal factors beginning to work against the British economy, the situation was hardly more fortuitous externally. By the late 1960s, the fixed exchange rate was placed under pressure as the balance of payments in the USA moved into deficit. This combined to weaken the dollar and provide other advanced countries with additional dollar reserves, which stoked up inflationary pressures.

Until the end of the 1960s, the maintenance of full employment and low inflation was successful. However, from the late 1960s the rise in inflation took place against the background of a rise in unemployment in the UK. The upsurge in wage inflation between the late 1960s and early 1970s led those of a monetarist persuasion (Ward and Zis, 1974; Zis, 1975) to argue that the wage explosion and labour unrest was a response to the demand and monetary conditions in Britain and the United States. This analysis was in contrast to economists, who gave more weight to the supply-side origins of the wage explosion (Soskice, 1978).

If anything, the period between 1971 and 1973 was the high-water mark of Keynesian economics. The promises made by Edward Heath during the 1970 election – that, if elected, the Conservatives would cut taxes, reform industrial relations and reduce state intervention – appeared to repudiate past policies (Gamble, 1980; Holmes, 1982). The reality was less sanguine, and the 'Barber boom', coupled with industrial conflict, effectively ended Heath's premiership. Although a former Treasury minister to Heath later claimed that he had nothing to recant over this period (Higgins, 1992), another former minister in the Heath government has written that 'The Heath government showed, in particular, that socialist policies pursued by Tory politicians are if anything even more disastrous than socialist policies pursued by Labour politicians' (Thatcher, 1995, p. 196).

Some authors have also recently sought to reassess the 1974–79 period in a favourable light (Artis and Cobham, 1991; Artis, Cobham and Wickham-Jones, 1992). Although the revisionist view of Artis et al. is to be welcomed, few would deny that the performance of the British economy was particularly poor during this period or that the Labour Party's shift from traditional macroeconomic objectives marked a break with the past (Oliver, 1998). Although the Labour Party introduced monetary targets, they did not elevate monetarism to such a high degree of pulchritude as did the post-1979 Thatcher government (Thain, 1985). James Callaghan's address to the 1976 Labour Party conference was a clear expression of how economic priorities had changed from those enshrined in the 1944 White Paper on employment policy, when he announced that:

> The cosy world we were told would go on forever, where full employment would be guaranteed by a stroke of the chancellor's pen, cutting taxes, deficit spending, that cosy world is gone. ... We used to think that you could spend your way out of a recession, and increase employment by cutting taxes and boosting Government spending. I tell you in all candour that that option no longer exists, and that in so far as it ever did exist, it only worked on each occasion since the war by injecting a bigger dose of inflation into the economy, followed by a higher level of unemployment as the next step.
>
> (Labour Party, 1976, p. 188)[1]

But this did not imply that macroeconomic policy was going to be deflationary during a major recession (Thain, 1985, p. 44), that incomes policies were going to be abandoned (Mosley, 1984, p. 129), or that money supply targets would become the kernel of policy (Wass, 1978). The Treasury and the Bank of England remained divided on the issue of monetarism (Laidler, 1989b), and Chancellor Healey's own views were best expressed in later years when he admitted that he was an unbelieving monetarist who viewed the Thatcher government's attempts at 'punk' or 'sado-monetarism' with disdain (Healey, 1989, p. 491).

Having accounted (albeit briefly) for some of the economic policies, we turn to examine the macroeconomic performance of the period. Since unemployment, inflation, the balance of payments and economic growth have been mentioned in the preceding discussion, the remainder of this section will concentrate on these aggregates.

Over the following pages, a series of tables and figures places the performance of the British economy in an international context. Tables 2.1 and 2.2 are more long run in nature and contain perhaps the most depressing set of statistics presented here. While the UK experienced its highest-ever growth in output per worker between 1951 and 1973 (Table 2.1), the more salient feature is that this period also witnessed the largest gap between Britain and the fastest-growing countries (Table 2.4). Although the growth record of the United States was more akin to the British economy (Tables 2.1, 2.3, 2.4), Table 2.2 illustrates the superiority of American productivity for most of the twentieth century. Japan's economic strength emerged to dominate the post-war period down to 1973 (Table 2.1), although there were signs of convergence with other nations by the end of the 1970s (Table 2.4).

Table 2.1   Growth rates of real output per worker employed, 1899–
1979 (% p.a.)

	1899– 1913	1913– 1924	1924– 1937	1937– 1951	1951– 1964	1964– 1973	1973– 1979
USA	1.3	1.7	1.4	2.3	2.5	1.6	–0.2
Japan	1.8	3.2	2.7	–1.3	7.6	8.4	2.9
France	1.6	0.8	1.4	1.7	4.3	4.6	2.8
Germany	1.5	–0.9	3.0	1.0	5.1	4.4	2.9
UK	0.5	0.3	1.0	1.0	2.3	2.6	1.2

Source: Matthews et al. (1982, p. 31)

Table 2.2   Real GDP per hour worked, 1870–1979 (UK = 100 in
each year)

	1870	1913	1938	1950	1960	1973	1979
USA	97	135	154	185	188	156	150
Japan	17	23	35	24	33	62	70
France	48	60	82	70	84	105	114
Germany	50	65	73	54	84	100	113

Source: Crafts (1991, p. 263)

Table 2.3   Rate of growth of productivity (real values added per
employee) in manufacturing, 1960–79 (%)

1960–68		1968–73		1973–79	
USA	3.2	USA	3.8	USA	0.9
Japan	9.0	Japan	10.4	Japan	5.0
France	6.8	France	5.8	France	3.9
Germany	4.7	Germany	4.5	Germany	3.1
UK	3.4	UK	3.8	UK	0.6

Source: Meen (1988, p. xxvi)

Table 2.3 gives a hint of the major sectoral change which the UK
experienced after 1945 – the sharp fall in her share of world manufacturing output. This has led some to conclude that this had repercussions
for the UK's balance of payments equilibrium on current account

Table 2.4   Annual growth rate, per capita GDP, 1960–79 (%)

1960–68		1968–73		1973–79	
USA	3.1	USA	1.8	USA	1.5
Japan	9.3	Japan	6.8	Japan	2.5
France	4.2	France	5.0	France	2.6
Germany	3.2	Germany	4.0	Germany	2.5
UK	2.4	UK	2.9	UK	1.5

Source: Meen (1988, p. xxiii)

Table 2.5   International comparison of unemployment rates, 1950–80 (%)

	1950	1955	1960	1965	1970	1975	1980
USA	5.3	4.4	5.5	4.5	4.8	8.3	7.0
Japan	1.8	2.4	1.7	1.2	1.1	1.9	2.0
France	n.a.	n.a.	n.a.	1.7	2.4	4.1	6.3
Germany	10.2	4.3	1.0	0.5	0.8	1.6	3.1
UK	2.9	1.9	2.9	2.5	3.1	3.9	7.4

Source: Broadberry (1994, p. 201)

(Figure 2.1), which became 'increasingly incompatible with the maintenance of full employment and a reasonably strong growth performance
relative to other countries' (McCombie and Thirlwall, 1994, p. xviii).
The UK's unemployment performance in the 1950s and 1960s was
better than during the 1970s (Table 2.5), although on the basis of this
table the upward trend was particularly marked by 1980. Similarly, the
upward inflationary trend from the 1960s (Table 2.6, Figure 2.2) shows
an intractable problem for policy-makers which the Thatcher government was determined to address.

Monetary and exchange-rate policy: 1945–79

As was suggested in the previous section, from the mid-1940s until the
1970s, British economic policy was characterized by a fixed exchange
rate, restricted international capital mobility and orthodox Keynesian
economic management. One theoretical model which neatly married
Keynesian demand management to economic policy within the Bretton

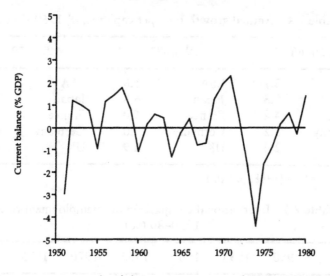

2.1 Current account surplus/deficit as a percentage of GDP, 1950–80

Source: Central Statistical Office (1994)

Woods environment was the approach to the balance of payments developed by Fleming (1962) and Mundell (1963). The Fleming–Mundell analysis of the early 1960s and the investigation by the Radcliffe Committee (HM Treasury, 1959) into the operation of UK monetary policy were extremely influential on policy-makers (Laidler, 1989b). The practical suggestions of both the model and the Radcliffe Committee were that monetary policy should be responsible for the external balance while fiscal policy should be assigned the task of maintaining domestic balance.

The realities of demand management (or 'fine-tuning') were not as smooth in practice, and led to the infamous 'stop-go' cycles of the

Table 2.6 International comparisons of inflation, 1950–81 (%)

1950–64		1965–73		1974–81	
USA	2.2	USA	4.3	USA	8.4
Japan	4.2	Japan	6.2	Japan	7.0
France	6.0	France	5.0	France	11.0
Germany	3.2	Germany	4.5	Germany	4.7
UK	4.0	UK	5.9	UK	16.0

Source: Crafts and Woodward (1991, p. 6)

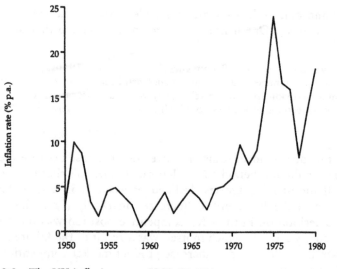

2.2 The UK inflation rate, 1950–80 (%)

Source: Central Statistical Office (1994)

1950s and 1960s (a more detailed discussion on 'stop-go' is given in the next section). For much of the period, demand was crudely encouraged by fiscal stimulation (e.g. 1953, 1955, 1959, 1963), and the subsequent overheating was solved by a tightening of monetary policy (e.g. 1951, 1957, 1961, 1964, 1967) to cure the deficit on the balance of payments.

One of the practical problems with the fixed exchange rate was that it was difficult to identify whether a deficit was either structural or merely short term in nature on the current and capital accounts of the balance of payments. The Fleming–Mundell model tended to ignore the interaction between the current and capital accounts and, as such, it was essentially short run in outlook. This merely reinforced the inadequacies of short-term economic management, with the destabilizing 'stop-go' cycles. There is irony to be found here in that the deflation associated with trying to solve the balance of payments crises of the 1950s and 1960s ultimately did not rid the British economy of such cycles but, in fact, weakened the balance of payments further, thus necessitating further doses of 'stop-go' medicine. This product of harsh treatment was continued until November 1967, when what had long been avoided was eventually implemented – a devaluation of sterling.

When the UK had last devalued in 1949, it had been encouraged to do so by the United States which recognized that this was a one-off adjustment to post-war conditions. Indeed, Britain did not act alone and the entire sterling area (except Pakistan), Western Europe (except

Switzerland) and non-sterling countries outside Europe devalued more or less simultaneously. One historian has recently suggested that after devaluation:

> Sterling was the emblem of Britain's world status in the 1950s. To its adherents, it represented not simply successful economic recovery from a victorious but immensely costly war, but restoration to a position of economic leadership which had been surrendered in 1931.
>
> (Alford, 1996, p. 242)

However, this does tend to somewhat overstate the case because the 1949 devaluation did not herald a New Jerusalem. Britain's share in the exports of all industrial countries declined between 1953 and 1959 while the share of the EC countries increased markedly (Lamfalussy, 1963). This deterioration in the UK's competitive position was due to slower productivity growth, which in itself was a result of the failure to reform industrial relations and to increase product market competition (Bean and Crafts, 1996).

From the mid-1960s, sterling was increasingly put under pressure as the current account steadily deteriorated. After taking office in October 1964, the Labour government decided that it would not devalue. It is difficult to weigh up whether this decision was influenced more by economic analysis or political expediency. For domestic political reasons, Wilson did not want his party to be known as the devaluation party (following the devaluations of 1931 and 1949). At a wider level, such an action would have shocked international opinion and displeased America, as confidence in the dollar would inevitably have been shaken. The economic rationale also appeared sound: poor British export performance was a reflection of non-price competitiveness rather than a price disparity, so any short-term relief could be applied through mild deflation. Consequently, the subject of devaluation became known as 'the unmentionable' (Brandon, 1966, pp. 40–44).

The unmentionable did not disappear, as three sterling crises in as many years were inflicted upon the British economy. In much the same way as Chancellor Lamont in the early 1990s, James Callaghan invested much time and effort ruling out a realignment of sterling in this period as he sought in vain for alternative and less painful methods of adjustment. Recently, Callaghan has suggested that his opposition to devaluation was partly based on moral reasons, but he also realized that, with such a young team of ministers in government, the credibility of the party would have been lost quite quickly if he had realigned the currency (Cairncross and Cairncross, 1992, pp. 97–8). With the British economy in a stagnant state, the drain on reserves continuing throughout 1967 and with poor prospects for the balance of payments, the decision to devalue on 18 November was more or less inevitable.

The outcome of the devaluation has been examined in detail by several authors (Worswick, 1971; Artus, 1975) who suggest that, allowing for the initial J-curve effect, the final outcome was successful for the current account deficit.[2] Such a conclusion suggests that Britain should devalue whenever there is a problem with the balance of payments. This would be wrong on at least two counts. First, the 1967 devaluation was assisted by short-term money illusion in the labour market. This slowly disappeared after devaluation, and the competitive advantage of devaluation was reduced by price inflation. Secondly, as monetarist (and non-monetarist) economists recognize, the fall in the exchange rate could generate higher inflation, thereby offsetting the impact of devaluation.

A caveat needs to be sounded concerning the theoretical claim of the Fleming–Mundell model that monetary policy is ineffective with a fixed exchange rate. Up to the mid-1960s, monetary policy was being used in much the same way as in the 1950s to meet the periodic balance of payments crises. Following the 1967 devaluation, the new chancellor (Roy Jenkins) introduced a DCE target with the aid of the IMF in 1969–70. This marked a new direction for monetary policy.

According to the Bank of England (1969, p. 363): 'Put briefly, DCE may be viewed as the total arrived at after adjusting the increase in the money supply to take account of any change in money balances directly caused by an external surplus or deficit.' DCE is thus an effective indication of how expansionary monetary policy can be in an open economy with a fixed exchange rate. If a country was experiencing a drain on its foreign reserves then, by adopting a DCE target, it could force a deflationary adjustment (i.e. restrict the money supply) and achieve external balance. The practical use of DCE in a British context was highly effective at restoring the balance of payments by 1969, although some authors have argued that it was more to do with the tighter monetary conditions leading to a capital inflow (Goodhart, 1984, p. 72). Although DCE targets were dropped after 1970–71 and only taken up again in late 1976, the authorities were pleased with their success at using monetary aggregates as intermediate target variables. As James (1995, p. 191) has suggested, DCE targets were the 'beginning of an intellectual conversion, but not yet of a political turning'.

Further developments in monetary policy were initiated in 1971. CCC (Bank of England, 1971) was designed to encourage competition among the clearing banks for new business while ending the existing distortions in the financial system which had favoured the development

of secondary banking. Qualitative and quantitative controls were abandoned, the new system of control extended a reserve asset ratio to all
banks, and the power to call for special deposits was retained. The
spirit of CCC reflected a preference for indirect rather than direct
government control, and a belief in market forces. As such, it was a
decisive shift away from the restrained attitude towards competition in
the money markets which had existed since the 1930s (Artis and Lewis,
1991, p. 12).

The floating of the pound in 1972 had implications for the conduct
of economic policy in general and for monetary policy in particular. In
the floating era of the 1970s, there were two economic models which
grew in prominence: the monetary approach to the balance of payments
and Dornbusch's 'overshooting' model.

The monetary approach to the balance of payments, developed from
the late 1950s, concurred with the Keynesian conclusion about the
impact of monetary policy in the open economy, but showed that an
excessive increase in the money supply would lead to a depreciation in
the exchange rate and leave the UK economy with a higher price level
(Johnson, 1972; Polak, 1957). The crucial difference between the monetarist and the Fleming–Mundell models is that the former argued that
a monetary expansion affects prices rather than output in the long run.[3]
This argument attracted considerable interest when inflation rose in the
six-year period after the 1967 devaluation, much as the monetarist
model had predicted.

The Dornbusch (1976) overshooting model of exchange-rate determination was a hybrid of the Fleming–Mundell model and the monetary
approach. It is Keynesian in some of its short-run features (emphasizing
price stickiness), and monetarist in the long run (the goods market
reaches equilibrium at full-employment output). The model attempted
to explain the large fluctuations in exchange rates since the advent of
floating rates by suggesting that exchange rates in the short run can
overshoot their long-run equilibrium. This explanation was later used
by Buiter and Miller (1981) to account for the appreciation of sterling
in 1980 and 1981.

Given this background, a series of investigations by the Bank of
England in the early 1970s had been examining both the Keynesian and
monetarist arguments. The Bank estimated money demand equations
for M1 and old M3, which were seen as sufficiently reliable for policy
purposes (Table 2.7 lists the abbreviated definitions of the money supply which are referred to in this study). As the Bank of England (1978,
p. 32) acknowledged in a paper on the conduct of monetary policy in
this period, 'importance was now attached to the monetary aggregates;
their rate of growth was to be controlled by the market instrument of

Table 2.7   Abbreviated definitions of the money supply

Narrow aggregates ('narrow' money)

M0	Notes and coins in circulation with the public plus banks' till money (vault cash) and bankers' balances with the Bank of England.
NIBM1	Notes and coins in circulation with the public plus non-interest-bearing current accounts.
M1	NIBM1 plus interest-bearing current accounts and sight deposits.

Broad aggregates ('broad' money)

Old M2	Notes and coins in circulation with the public plus net deposits of clearing banks (unofficial name). Published data stopped in 1969.
Old M3	Notes and coins in circulation with the public plus deposits of all banks (both deposits and current accounts). Renamed M3c in May 1987.
£M3	Notes and coins in circulation with the public plus sterling deposits of all banks (i.e. old M3 omitting foreign currency deposits). Renamed M3 in May 1987.
Adjusted M3	£M3 plus commercial bills in issue (acceptances) excluding holdings by banks and by the Bank of England (an unofficial series). Published data stopped September 1980.
PSL1	£M3 plus private-sector holdings of bills (official series). Renamed M4 in May 1987.
PSL2	PSL1 plus building society deposits. Renamed M5 in May 1987.
M4	£M3 plus net building society deposits.
M5	M4 plus bills and other money market instruments.

Note: Although M0 is sometimes referred to as the 'wide monetary base' it none the less constitutes a form of narrow money and should not be confused with the 'broader' definitions given here.

Source: Derived from Pepper (1993, Appendices 1–2, p. 56).

interest rates'. This did not make the Bank of England 'monetarist' at this stage, but moved the locus of debate decisively away from the views of the Radcliffe Committee.

However, with CCC and the freeing of the pound, two big constraints on monetary policy had been abolished within a very short time, and these were reinforced by the relaxation of controls on commercial rents and property development. The combination of falling interest rates in 1971–72 with an expanding bank and property market, led to a boom in house and property prices (the 'Barber boom') and an emerging current account deficit. Notwithstanding the imposition of quantitative restrictions on the banking system via the Supplementary Special Deposit Scheme (the 'corset') in December 1973, the rise in world commodity prices in the same year and the quadrupling of oil prices in 1973–74 added to the upward trend in inflation.

Although inflation had peaked by 1975, the authorities were concerned by three developments: the growth of the PSBR and how it was funded (it was around 10 per cent of money GDP by 1976, with more importance being attached to funding from outside the banking system[4]); the fall of sterling on the foreign exchanges; and the high rate of inflation. By December 1976, the IMF had agreed to help overcome the UK's worsening financial difficulties on condition that monetary targets were reintroduced and adhered to.

Clearly, monetary targets were not introduced by the Labour Party as a *deus ex machina* and, as Fforde (1983, p. 204) notes, after 1976 policy was 'monetarily constrained Keynesianism'. Yet in one important respect there was a change: the strong upward rise of sterling during 1977 marked a further turning point for policy and gave succour to the monetarist debate. It is important to consider the conflict which arose between monetary targets and the exchange rate during 1977 in the context of what was to happen in the late 1980s.

In his *Tract on Monetary Reform*, first published in 1923, Keynes argued that the exchange rate

> cannot be stable unless both internal and external price levels remain stable. If, therefore, the external price level lies outside our control, we must submit either to our own internal price level or to our exchange being pulled about by external influences. *If the external price level is unstable we cannot keep both our own price level and our exchanges stable. And we are compelled to choose.*
>
> (Keynes, 1923, pp. 125–6; emphasis added)

Such a dilemma became very apparent for the authorities in 1977. As the exchange rate strengthened over the first half of the year, so the Bank intervened in the foreign exchange market to check the appreciation of sterling. The result was faster growth in the money supply than officials had planned (16 per cent out-turn against a target range of 9–13 per cent in the 1977/78 financial year), which breached the strict requirements of the IMF programme. The choice between holding sterling at a competitive level and following the monetary targets was a difficult one and, while the authorities responded to the call from the monetarists and stopped the intervention for fear of higher inflation, some accounts of this episode have suggested the policy predicament was intense within government (Congdon, 1987, p. 56).

Healey later argued that, in rejecting the advice given by the permanent secretary at the Treasury that intervention should continue on the foreign exchanges, his action was the correct one to take (Healey, 1989, p. 435). As Riddell (1983, pp. 59–60) notes, Healey's monetarism 'was the response of a clever and flexible man to the breakdown of the post-war consensus on economic management and to external pressure'. Perhaps, in this instance, it was irrelevant that Healey did not accept the monetarist arguments, for he behaved like a monetarist. However, the different response by Chancellor Lawson (a self confessed monetarist) some ten years later to a similar situation is rather more puzzling, and will be examined in detail in Chapter Six.

The problem in perspective

If the discussions in the first two sections have implied that Britain's growth failure was an indictment of Keynesian economic policy, this would be an oversimplistic and incorrect conclusion. Many books and articles have examined the 'growth issue' and have apportioned blame *inter alia* on microeconomic issues such as special interest groups (Olson, 1982), trade unions (Batstone, 1988), or education and training (Aldcroft, 1992) rather than focus exclusively on macroeconomic explanations.

However, despite many of the valid and important arguments about the failings of microeconomic policy since 1945, debates about the growth failure can enter the proverbial 'chicken and egg' quandary. Even when measures were introduced to improve productivity, educational opportunity and union reform, Britain's growth rate failed to overtake her overseas competitors. This leads to two considerations: were the microeconomic policies designed by policy-makers flawed, or was the greater handicap macroeconomic policy?

Recently, this has become the locus for debate. Crafts and Woodward (1991) suggest that there are two separate schools of thought on Britain's economic situation: 'Thatcherites' and 'centrists'. They define 'Thatcherites' as those who share the views of the Conservative Party under Margaret Thatcher, while the 'centrists' are towards the centre-left of the political spectrum.

The Thatcherites argue that the single most important cause of Britain's post-war decline was the *nature* and *extent* of economic policy. They believe that policy was misdirected in two ways. First, there was little or no recognition that the most effective way to correct market failures was to use market solutions. Second, post-war policy was growth-reducing. The Thatcherites argue that because post-war governments clearly stated that they aimed to manage the economy to obtain full employment, stable prices, growth and so on, this overshadowed the state with bureaucracies.

The centrists have not been so critical about the direction of post-war policy and point to far fewer failures in the Keynesian era, but they do not reject the Thatcherite argument completely. For example, they would agree that striving for a post-war consensus between unions, employees, management and government was bound to cause some efficiency and growth to be lost. Yet the centrists place much less emphasis on the market as a solution, citing Britain's supply-side weaknesses such as poor industrial relations, inadequate education and training and low levels of civil research and development which need government intervention. Secondly, they argue that it is not clear to what extent policy failures were a result of unfortunate policy errors. For example, there was bound to be some unprofitable and poorly performing nationalized industries because Whitehall was inexperienced in their operation.

Yet the centrists would agree that in some areas they made mistakes. They would be critical of post-war government investment policies for not recognizing that high growth tends to generate its own investment. More fundamentally, they would argue that Britain's management and labour force remained relatively uneducated.

For the Thatcherites, the key to the golden age was stability in financial policy at home and abroad. Right up to the mid-1960s, financial policy in the USA was restrained and was stable. Without any supply-side shocks, world rates of inflation were low. Hence the Thatcherites believe that deterioration was inevitable in the late 1960s and throughout the 1970s as devaluation, the money explosion of the early 1970s and the expansionary policies of the Johnson administration and the Vietnam War filtered through the world's financial markets.

The centrists do not deny that the relative prosperity of the golden age was a result of the absence of external economic shocks of the USA's restrained financial policy. But although a centrist would confirm that demand management may not have been wholly successful (due to policy errors resulting from bad data, etc.), he would not say Keynesianism was defunct. In contrast, the crux of the Thatcherite argument is that poor financial discipline via Keynesian fine-tuning disrupted Britain's growth rate after 1945. In the Thatcherite account, greater weight is attached to the 'stop-go' cycle as an explanation. The 'stop-go' cycle was mentioned in the previous section and a further discussion is relevant here.

Perhaps the best historical textbook account of 'stop-go' is given by Pollard (1982). To précis his explanation, let us take the cycle from its 'go' stage. If the government wanted to increase demand in the economy it would cut taxes and would also loosen interest rates, allowing firms and consumers easier and cheaper access to credit. Having obtained the money, consumers would turn to British businesses to supply goods. As long as British businesses could supply the orders there would not be a problem, but before long, spare capacity within firms to meet these orders would have been used up (firms would have used up spare capacity due to poor existing investment levels) and particular bottlenecks would develop.

The bottlenecks would be met by imports but, because firms' order books were full and delivery dates would be lengthening, Britain found that she would be importing more than she was exporting and a balance of payments deficit would result. While a temporary deficit might be paid for out of Bank of England reserves, after a while the foreign exchanges would became jittery. Then a run on the pound would develop. If the deficit was particularly high, then there would be a fear of devaluation.

By now, the Bank of England and the Treasury would shout 'stop' and the whole 'go' process would be reversed. Interest rates would be tightened to curb credit and purchasing power and the government would cut its spending. Eventually the 'stop' would work: output would have declined, imports would have fallen, the balance of payments would right itself and a spare capacity gap would emerge once more as firms found themselves lacking orders. The economy was ripe for another bout of 'go'.

Some authors have questioned to what extent stop-go policies have contributed to low growth (Thain, 1984), and Tomlinson (1990, p. 259) has even remarked that the criticisms made of stop-go have been 'much ado about nothing'. Perhaps during the long boom after the Second World War, it is possible to agree that 'stop-go' would have had a less damaging impact against the background of 'super-growth'. Yet from the early 1970s, when 'super-slump' displaced the earlier favourable conditions, the effect of the cycle, coupled with the other disturbances, added to the economic malaise. Table 2.8 tells quite an interesting story: in the post-1973 cycle, there was a below-average-trend rate of growth, above-average inflation and below-average productivity improvement.

The 'stop-go' cycle suggests that the balance of payments can act as a constraint when a country imports more than it exports and consequently has to pay for its imports (Thirlwall, 1979). If Britain exported fewer goods and services and at the same time imported more goods

Table 2.8   Cycle features (peak to peak), 1955–79 (% per annum)

	1955–60	1960–64	1964–69	1969–73	1973–79
Growth	2.6	3.2	2.4	2.7	1.0
Inflation	3.5	3.1	3.4	9.3	16.2
Productivity	2.9	2.3	2.7	2.5	0.8

Source: Martin (1990, p. 85)

and services, then ultimately she would not be able to pay her import bill. Other countries would stop supplying Britain with goods and she would not be able to service her debts. Obviously the ultimate logic, whereby the British people could lead a life of leisure, importing whatever was required without exporting anything in return, could never arise as other countries would cease overseas lending (Coutts et al., 1990). Thus the threat of this constraint on growth meant that policymakers had to keep a watchful eye on the balance of payments.

The 'stop-go' explanation also seems to combine the other reasons for slower growth in the UK: inflationary pressure, shortages of goods, exchange rate crises and full employment. While all these factors are interlinked, a major stimulant to the process was monetary policy. The increase in consumption of consumer durables (washing machines, furniture, refrigerators) was stimulated by lower interest rates; the eventual excess demand then leads to shortages and price increases in shops; the fall in the value of the pound leads to spiralling import costs for producers which feeds through into higher prices, and so on. To rephrase Keynes (1913), bankers can be held accountable for the alternations of boom and depression.

Coats's (1981b, p. 387) fascinating survey on the rise of specialist economists in Britain quotes from a Bank of England article which admits that, until 1960, the Bank appears to have been 'positively averse to economics'. Coats (1981b, p. 388) also notes that until the 1970s, the Treasury was 'seriously undersupplied with monetary expertise'. Eltis (1976) is even more scathing, and has suggested that policymakers have never really understood how monetary policy works in Britain. His argument is that Keynesian fine-tuners of the post-war years misunderstood Keynes's simplified explanation of how portfolioholders could hold their wealth in only two assets: money and bonds. This led to the belief that money influences the price of bonds and nothing else – exactly the opposite of what happens in the real world. For example, if government action doubles the prices of houses, building land and commodity prices, it is bound to affect the inflation rate.

Eltis also argues that the evidence given to the Radcliffe Committee by Harrod, Kahn and Kaldor (Britain's three prominent Keynesians) on interest rates, was tied to a rigid and inappropriate Keynesian theory. In his memorandum to the Committee, Harrod (1960, p. 114) stated that 'If the quantity of money available were restored to a more normal relation to the money value of the national income, the long-term rate of interest would come down to 3 per cent quite naturally, without any fuss or bother.' Yet as Eltis (1976, p. 17) observes:

> Roy Harrod's thinking was clearly still locked into the simple two-asset Keynes model of 1936, where extra money cannot raise the rate of interest. In the real world, Lord Barber raised the money supply vastly faster than the national income, and the rate of interest did not fall to 3 per cent. It rose towards 17 per cent, and the increase in the money supply was partly responsible for this.

For Eltis, and later for Congdon (1992b), who took up a similar theme of Keynesian abuse, the most worrying aspect of this misunderstanding has been that prime ministers, chancellors, cabinet secretaries, senior trade unionists, academics et al., have 'been taught these theories of money and interest which are contradicted by many of the observed facts' (Eltis, 1976, p. 13). The implications of such a situation, where the wrong lessons are being learnt by policy-makers, could mean that unless and until the conventional Keynesian wisdom was disproved, the UK economy would be condemned to repeat cycle after cycle.

In 1968, Matthews posed this question:

> When the question is asked, *why* have we had full employment since the war? most people tend to reply, without thinking very much, that it is because we have had a full-employment policy – we have had the Keynesian revolution. Now supposing this were the right answer, it would be a remarkable thing. It would mean that the most important single feature of the post-war British economy has been due to an advance in economic theory. It would be a most striking vindication of Keynes's celebrated dictum about the ultimate primacy of abstract thought in the world of affairs.
>
> (Matthews, 1968, pp. 555–6)[5]

Angus Maddison (1991, p. 168) has noted that 'success in the golden age was due in considerable measure to enlightened policy', but he noted that international economic performance had been aided by increased liberalization of international trade, a backlog of growth possibilities following the end of the Second World War and favourable circumstances that produced low inflation. Furthermore, several authors have suggested that fiscal policy in Britain was a destabilizing influence between 1945 and 1973 (Dow, 1964; Price, 1978); while a study by the OECD found that, in six out of seven countries which it examined, fiscal policy stabilized output growth with the exception of the UK (Hansen and Snyder, 1969). As Mosley (1984, p. 106) has noted, during this period public investment was cut or postponed when there was a balance of payments crisis but it was seldom used as a 'deliberate measure to relieve unemployment'.

By the early 1970s, Keynesian economic policy had evolved quite considerably from what was initially intended and, although this chapter has suggested that it is unfair to blame Keynes for all that went wrong after 1945, it is not an unreasonable criticism to suggest that some aspects of Keynesian demand management were unfavourable to steady economic growth. Keynes wrote the *General Theory* to rescue capitalism from demise during the inter-war years, but the legacy of Keynesianism by the 1970s was stagflation (Cairncross and Cairncross, 1992), which paradoxically, threatened to destroy many capitalist economies.

There are two final observations which should be made. First, while Keynes had legitimized government intervention in the economy for successive post-war governments, there were signs that by the 1970s some saw widespread state withdrawal as the *sine qua non* of economic rejuvenation. Yet just because economic policy and performance had been erratic after 1945, it did not follow that the only option was for a government to revert to the pre-war 'Treasury view'.

Second, Keynes's predilection with the short run and not the long run unfortunately seemed particularly attractive to post-war economic policy-makers. As we have seen, even before the end of the golden age, not all were convinced that the Keynesian revolution had been beneficial to the British economy. The next chapter discusses how the Keynesian consensus was challenged by the monetarists and the New Right.

Notes

1. Callaghan had infuriated some members of his party nine years earlier when he had argued in the House of Commons that trying to keep low levels of unemployment was erroneous. 'We must have a somewhat larger margin of unused capacity than we used to try to keep. That is the truth of the matter' (James, 1995, pp. 188–9).
2. Following a devaluation, the current account is likely to deteriorate before it improves as earnings from exports will be sluggish while more will have to be paid for imports. This so-called *J*-curve effect is a consequence of unfavourable short-run price elasticities for exports and imports.
3. This conclusion had been reached by Friedman 20 years earlier (Friedman, 1953), who had also outlined the merits of a *de jure* floating exchange-rate regime. Interestingly, the Keynesian James Meade had also made a case for floating rates in 1955 (Meade, 1955).

4. *Funding* is where the authorities offset the impact on the broad money supply of the PSBR and the underlying change in the foreign exchange reserves by selling government debt to the UK private sector (excluding banks and building societies) and to the overseas sector.
5. Matthews later retreated from this scepticism about policy's contribution to full employment in the UK (Matthews, Feinstein and Odling-Smee, 1982, p. 313).

CHAPTER THREE

Towards a new economic policy: the 1970s

> Something must make at least a few scientists feel that the new proposal is on the right track, and sometimes it is only personal and inarticulate aesthetic considerations that can do that. Men have been converted by them when most of the articulable technical arguments have pointed the other way.
>
> (Kuhn, 1970, p. 158)

While the previous chapter made it clear that by May 1979 the control of inflation was the top priority of the Thatcher administration, little was said about *how* this shift occurred. It is a relatively easy task to describe the characteristics of particular policies a government wishes to follow, in contrast to having to account for how new economic ideas are spread by individuals through to policy specialists and on to politicians who then have to be voted into office via the democratic process. This is a fascinating aspect of our story, and this chapter takes the analysis one stage further and explains the importance that several prominent British economists, financial journalists and politicians began to give to a new economic policy in the 1970s.

As a prelude to a discussion on post-1979 developments, it will be necessary to provide some basic but non-technical theory. This will be included in the first section. For a new economic strategy to be implemented in the UK it was clear that a shift in political thinking would be a prerequisite for economic change. The political dimensions are also examined in this chapter, along with the support given to monetarism by the media. The final section outlines the economic instruments the Thatcher administration intended to use.

Healey (1993) has suggested that the changes the Thatcher government promised Britain as a cure for her economic ills should not be underestimated. How radical the changes were begin to become apparent in this chapter. How long they lasted will form the remainder of this study.

The counter-revolution

The purpose of this section is to examine some of the developments which arose from the challenges to Keynesianism. What stands out, taking a broad sweep from the 1950s, is the rise of monetarism, the growth of expectations analysis and a greater emphasis given to the supply side of the economy.

At this stage, two caveats need to be sounded as to how the debate is presented in this section. First, much has been written on the re-emergence of classical economic thought in the United States from the 1950s and the rise of the expectations school in the 1970s, so it would be unproductive to provide a blow-by-blow narrative of developments from this date. Second, the term 'monetarism' has been widely used throughout the literature and has embraced a variety of definitions. We must be very careful to identify precisely what the monetarist arguments are before we begin to examine the disagreements which arose between the monetarists during the 1980s.

What is being attempted in this section is a synthesis of the alternative arguments to orthodox Keynesian economic management. For our purposes, the term 'counter-revolution' will more than suffice as a general description of these and other developments, and can be placed into three subsections.

Monetarism

When Friedman revised the classical quantity theory of money (Friedman, 1956), he emphasized that there was a stable functional relationship between the demand for real balances and a limited number of variables. For Friedman, if the demand for money is stable then velocity will also be stable, changing in a predictable manner if any of the limited number of variables in the demand for money function should change. In short, 'the conclusion is that substantial changes in prices or nominal income are almost invariably the result of changes in the nominal supply of money' (Friedman, 1968a, p. 434).

Friedman implied that, as the demand for money was a stable function of the level of output, the demand for money did not respond very much to changes in the interest rate. Indeed, Friedman (1959) claimed that the demand for money was inelastic with respect to the interest rate, an assertion he later withdrew (Friedman, 1966) after Laidler (1966) showed that he had used a faulty statistical method to reach his conclusions. Thus the main monetarist contention, that *'inflation is always and everywhere a monetary phenomenon* in the sense that it can be produced only by a more rapid increase in the quantity of money than in output' (Friedman, 1970b, p. 24) and that the demand for money was a stable function of a limited number of variables, is an empirical issue.

Yet ever since Brunner (1968) coined the term 'monetarism', several authors have sought to present a series of common ingredients which define monetarism (Burton, 1982; Laidler, 1981a; Mayer, 1975; Vane and Thompson, 1979).[1] According to Peter Jay (1993), such studies are misguided because:

> All that monetarism ever said was that there was a relationship subject to a substantial time lag of up to two years between the amount of money in circulation and changes in the price level. I think that it was true then and is true now, and is true in all conceivable societies, whether you are a Fascist, Eskimo or Hottentot. It has nothing whatsoever to do with any political philosophy, it is simply a scientific law, or proposed scientific law, and it is like all other scientific laws – it is either true or not.

Friedman's initial work was followed by a detailed empirical investigation of the demand for money in the United States between 1869 and 1957 (Friedman and Schwartz, 1963), which claimed that the demand for money function was indeed stable and that faster rates of growth in the money supply between these dates had led to changes in prices and output levels.

Friedman's critics raised two fundamental questions over his analysis. First, how did faster rates of money growth lead to higher output and prices? Second, how was the faster rate of money growth divided between higher output and rising prices?

The first question can be dealt with by reference to the 'transmission mechanism'. Monetarists have suggested that when money balances are increased, people will try to return to their old balance levels and spend their excess money holdings on a range of goods and assets, thereby increasing prices and output (Laidler, 1977). As Friedman acknowledged:

> The difference between us and the Keynesians is less in the nature of the process than in the range of assets considered. The Keynesians tend to concentrate on a narrow range of marketable assets and recorded interest rates. We insist that a far wider range of assets and interest rates must be taken into account – such assets as durable and semi-durable consumer goods, structures and real property. As a result we regard the market rates stressed by the Keynesians as only a small part of the total spectrum of rates that are relevant.
>
> (Friedman, 1971, p. 27)

Thus, in the traditional Keynesian world, an increase in the money supply will encourage people to buy bonds, which drives down the rate of interest and stimulates investment and leads to a greater output. Whereas monetarists believe that changes in the money supply will directly affect expenditure, Keynesians 'regard a change in the interest rate as the means whereby people are induced to hold a larger or smaller quantity of money' (Friedman, 1972, p. 944). Given the myriad of long- and short-term interest rates and the problem of measuring real interest rates under inflationary conditions, monetarists argue that attention should be given to the money stock in preference to interest rates.

This raises the issue of the monetary growth rule. This 'rule' has been somewhat problematical for the monetarists. Many monetarists have fluctuated between the positive and negative arguments for stable money-supply growth. As Mayer notes, 'if it were shown conclusively that discretionary policy can stabilize the economy, then probably most monetarists would reject the monetary growth rule' (Mayer, 1975, p. 302).

But the issue of a monetary growth rule cannot be so readily dismissed. Friedman's ambivalence towards such a rule is problematical. In an IEA pamphlet, he wrote of the monetary growth rule: 'It will not produce perfect stability; it will not produce heaven on earth; but it can make an important contribution to a stable economic society' (Friedman, 1970b, p. 28).

Given a serious inflationary disturbance, can the monetarists offer a solution other than suggesting that steady money-supply growth will result in stable prices in the long run? The monetarists may be able to set out the conditions for monetary equilibrium, but they 'appear to have nothing relevant to say about appropriate policies in disequilibrium or about the passage from disequilibrium to equilibrium' (Congdon, 1978, p. 19).

This is coupled to the second criticism levelled at monetarism, about how a faster rate of money growth is divided between higher output and rising prices. Friedman once stated that this area was the 'missing equation' of monetarist theory (Friedman, 1970a, pp. 221–2).[2] This failure by Friedman to provide a clear analytical response to this problem even led Johnson (1971, p. 12) to comment that the monetarist counter-revolution would 'peter out' because:

> I believe the Keynesians are right in their view that inflation is a far less serious social problem than mass unemployment. ... [T]he second reason is that monetarism is seriously inadequate as an approach to monetary theory, judged by prevailing standards of academic economics, and in the course of repairing its intellectual fences and achieving full scientific respectability it will have to compromise irretrievably with its Keynesian opposition.

Consequently, by the end of the 1960s monetarism needed to address directly the second criticism. It did so with the development of the adaptive expectations hypothesis, which carried monetarism forward into the 1970s, while providing a firm rebuttal to Keynesians who had been sharpening their attacks on the 'missing equation'. We can examine this development in two stages: first, the 'natural rate hypothesis', and second, the rise of 'expectations', both of which are discussed below.

The 'natural rate hypothesis' stemmed from Friedman's 1967 presidential address to the American Economic Association (Friedman, 1968b). In this address, Friedman argued that the level of unemployment in the long run was dependent on the real wage rate (as opposed to the nominal wage rate). To reduce unemployment in the long run, the level of real wages had to be altered without recourse to an expansionary monetary or fiscal policy. Friedman argued that the factors which determined real wage rigidity lay in the hands of individuals and institutions, and that government could help the unemployed only by making the opportunity costs of unemployment less pleasurable or by removing structural rigidities in the labour market.

This was the direct antithesis of Keynesianism. Friedman's theory suggested that unemployment was a 'voluntary' act of workers who 'priced themselves out of work' by refusing to accept lower real wages. It also implied that the economy would automatically move towards a 'natural rate' of unemployment since, given the rigidities in the labour market (trade unions, unemployment benefits, etc.), output was fixed in the long term by non-monetary factors. If the rate of growth in the money supply did change, then this would be reflected in higher prices rather than greater output. Moreover, while the monetarists had been arguing that fiscal policy was impotent at influencing aggregate demand, they could now suggest that monetary policy was little better and affected inflation rather than output.

The role of expectations

The natural rate hypothesis on its own could not completely convince the critics of the validity of the monetarist argument. When Friedman extended his natural rate argument and combined it with the Phillips curve, it formed the 'missing equation' which the monetarists could now use to relate output and price responses to a change in the quantity of money (Friedman, 1975). We shall refer to this development as the 'adaptive expectations' Phillips curve, to distinguish it from the 'new classical' school modifications which will also be discussed.

A brief summary of the monetarist argument is as follows. Suppose that the government is unhappy with the existing level of unemployment in the economy. It recognizes that, while unemployment will fall if it expands aggregate demand, the trade-off will be a higher rate of inflation (the Phillips curve). It will be recalled that the monetarists believe that employees target real and not nominal wage increases and that the labour market is mostly in equilibrium. Consequently, the monetarists warn that if the government expands demand and more employees enter the labour market in the belief that real wages have risen, then they will be suffering from 'money illusion'. Employers recognize that prices will rise, and seek to hire more staff because they see that real wages are going to fall. In the short term, employment expands as inflation rises. As workers do not suffer from permanent money illusion, they will recognize that the initial wage gains are a temporary phenomenon and will withdraw from the labour market, returning to the ranks of the unemployed. As Casson (1983, pp. 250–51) notes, 'Once the real wage has been fixed, expansionist fiscal and monetary policies will be purely inflationary: "crowding out" in the product market will be complete, and the employment multiplier will be zero.'

Thus in the monetarist world, any trade-off between employment and inflation exists only in the short run. In the long run, the Phillips curve is assumed to be vertical in which no trade-offs are possible. Attempts by government to reduce the level of unemployment below the natural rate will lead to rising inflation coupled with higher unemployment!

Expectations are the crucial element in the process, for two reasons. As workers cannot suffer from permanent money illusion, employment is sustained above the natural level only if inflation accelerates to keep employees' expectations about the rate of inflation consistently below the actual rate. Secondly, inflation decelerates when unemployment is above the natural rate. This can be explained by the workers gradually adapting their expectations of inflation to the actual rate.

The adaptive expectations theory is in marked contrast to the rational expectations theory, formed from the 'new classical' school (Sargent and Wallace, 1976). In the rational expectations model, changes in output and employment from their natural levels are the result of so-called 'random shocks', which are mainly unanticipated changes in the money supply. In contrast, the adaptive expectations explanation emphasizes past rates of inflation as the sole determinant of future rates. The rational expectations school argues that, until the variable being predicted is stable over a period of time, expectations formed of it will be habitually wrong. The rational expectations school stresses that individuals assess all available information, including government policy and forecasts of future inflation rates.

This would imply that the impact of attempts by government to pump-prime the economy and reduce unemployment would be transitory. Individuals would witness the inflationary impact of such a policy, and whenever future government expansions were announced, they would adjust their behaviour accordingly. In short, individuals form their own expectations rationally and do not make systematic mistakes.

In the unrealistic rational expectations model, there is no lag in expectations and markets clear virtually instantaneously. With reference to the Phillips curve, they predict that any change in aggregate monetary demand will be reflected purely in terms of changes in prices and that real aggregate demand will remain the same. Because of this, the rational expectations school argues that the Phillips curve is vertical in the short run, as well as the long run. This is in contrast to the adaptive expectations school, which argues that the Phillips curve is vertical *only* in the long run.

Although we have only covered the basic technical complexities of the expectations theorists, it is the practical policy suggestions resulting from these two schools which will be of real interest to us. These will be covered in later chapters, although we shall dwell briefly on the differences of opinion between the two later in this chapter, when we examine the investigation into monetary policy by the Treasury and Civil Service Committee in the early 1980s.

The supply side

The final component of the counter-revolution was the growth of supply-side economics. While the arguments from the monetarists and the 'new classical' school were formed out of academic rigour and were a product of the American universities, the supply-siders originated from a different stable and pursued their objectives with different means. According to Herbert Stein, an economics professor at the University of Virginia who first used the term 'supply side', such men wanted to make a 'splash' politically. For another economics commentator, who worked for the *Wall Street Journal*, 'Milton Friedman and his monetarist colleagues ... managed to merchandise their particular prescriptions with considerable skill. The promoters of monetarism, however, rate as rank amateurs compared to the promoters of supply-side economics' (Malabre, 1994, p. 175).

The men behind the supply-side arguments were journalists with a limited training in economics who had become disillusioned with Keynesian economics in the United States. As such, a job in journalism during the 1970s was not a handicap when it came to promoting new economic ideas. Indeed, those like Jude Wanniski, who joined the *Wall Street Journal* in the early 1970s, recognized that the public perception of professional and academic economists was at a low ebb and sought to capitalize on this. Wanniski used his writing powers so that supply-side economics and the *Wall Street Journal* became synonymous and inseparable.

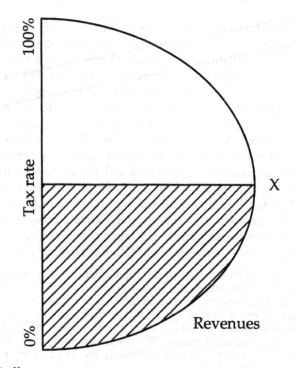

3.1 The Laffer curve

Yet as we shall see in the case of the *Financial Times* and *The Times* in Britain, the 1970s were a time when journalists and academics could benefit from each other. In the United States, Wanniski turned to the 'radical fringe' of academia to gain support for his arguments, with two of the most notable proponents being Arthur Laffer and Robert Mundell (Dornbusch and Fischer, 1984, p. 573). Behind this new approach were two arguments: first, that if the government reduced taxes people would work harder and tax revenues would rise and not fall; second, that tax cuts would increase the growth rate of output and reduce inflation. Laffer was also armed with a deceptively simple tool to demonstrate the validity of these arguments (Figure 3.1).

At a zero tax rate, no revenues will be collected. On the other hand, a tax rate of 100 per cent will also yield no revenue as no one will bother to work. The peak of the curve occurs at point X, and at this tax rate, the most revenue can be collected. Although the curve in Figure 3.1 is symmetrical, X does not necessarily correspond to a 50 per cent tax rate (it could represent 40 per cent, 70 per cent or even 90 per cent). For Laffer, the crucial problem was that in America during the 1970s, tax rates had moved above X and were penalising work incentives. By cutting taxes,

incentives would return, production would increase and the budget deficit would decrease. Higher production and a shrinking budget deficit
would then ease inflationary pressures. Laffer argued that when the
Kennedy administration had adopted such an approach in the early
1960s, this had positive effects on the American economy.[3]

From the mid-1970s, Wanniski had contacts with several Republican
politicians who expressed support for the tax-cutting arguments of the
Wall Street Journal. As campaigning for the 1980 presidential election
began, the *Journal* drew on a wider pool of economic talent to promote
its tax-cutting messages. Not all agreed with the arguments of Wanniski
and Laffer, but the effect of Milton Friedman, Herbert Stein, Walter
Heller and Arthur Schlesinger all writing in America's leading 'journal
of ideas' (Parsons, 1989, p. 161) impressed Ronald Reagan, the leading
Republican contender for president. Reagan promised that if elected, he
would lower tax rates. According to Malabre (1994, p. 187):

> to ensure that Reagan stayed the supply-side course after his ar-
> rival at the White House, Kemp [a Congressman] and his supply-
> side friends carried out what Wanniski has described as 'guerrilla
> warfare.' When a Reagan speech suggested, for example, that his
> administration was perhaps cooling to the supply-side push for
> lower taxes, Wanniski recalls, 'We would call Kemp and scream,
> Deviation! Deviation! Deviation! And he would call people and
> scream, Deviation! Deviation!'

The basic arguments of supply-side economics were also augmented
by politicians in the Reagan camp to make them appear compatible
with monetarism. Some went as far as to suggest that monetarism and
supply-side economics were mutually dependent. This approach was
taken by Manuel Johnson, an assistant secretary for economic policy in
the United States Treasury during Reagan's first term of office. Johnson's
(1982) contribution to an edited collection of essays on supply-side
economics is politically adroit, written to counter the criticisms that
there were significant inconsistencies between the two theories and, by
implication, government policy. There were others who argued the
more realistic (and, as it turned out, more accurate) scenario that it was
impossible to have heavy tax cuts *and* run burgeoning budget deficits
(Orzechowski, 1982).

In office, the Reagan government combined the worst of all possible
worlds: they ignored the deficit and cut taxes. Michael Evans's (1983)
account of this makes depressing reading, even though it was written at
an early stage in the Reagan years. The effects of 'Reaganomics' were
predictable even then to the majority of economists who had never been
convinced of the Wanniski–Laffer arguments, far less in the ability of
the Reagan administration to control the deficit.

The problem for both the American monetarists and the supply-siders was that their two experiments unravelled quite rapidly in the early 1980s. Added to which, the monetarists and supply-siders fell out in public, and the supply-siders admitted that there were policy differences within the Reagan administration (Stockman, 1986, p. 8). Indeed, the irony was that, rather than burying Keynes under monetarist and supply-side rhetoric, the American press ultimately revived the fortunes of Keynesianism (Canterbery, 1987).

The new right

Three institutions in particular were crucial in the dissemination of the counter-revolution in the UK. Indeed, parallels have been made in the literature to this process and the flow of ideas following the inventions during the Industrial Revolution (Hall, 1992). While it might be difficult for some critics to talk about the Industrial Revolution and monetarism in the same breath, there was a crucial part played by the trinity of politicians, the City and the media. It should be recalled from Chapter One that the social learning model in particular stresses that the move from one paradigm to another is assisted by a debate taking place outside as well as inside the state. In this respect, the ideas that were being discussed in private among prominent Tories in the mid-1970s were also being expressed openly in the leader columns of the *Financial Times* and *The Times*. Not only does the period from 1975 until Margaret Thatcher came to power in 1979 provide a classic example of how policy-making can be conducted on different stages at several levels, but it also showed that the electorate by 1979 did have two clear choices over economic policy and ideology.[4]

The Conservatives in opposition

Between 1965 and 1975, when Edward Heath was leader of the Conservatives, the general consensus on economic policy within the party was basically Keynesian. For some members of the Tory Party this became an issue, as a variety of new economic problems arose which met with little success by the application of old doctrines.[5] It was only when the Conservatives were forced into opposition in February 1974 that splits began to appear in this consensus.

It was Sir Keith Joseph's conversion to monetarism in April of 1974 which was to become the lodestar for the Conservatives in the following years. Joseph's empathy towards the writings of Friedman is explained in his 1977 pamphlet for the CPS (Joseph, 1977). From the intense reading which he did on liberal economics between 1974 and 1979, Joseph compiled reading lists which he insisted on giving to civil servants upon his arrival at the Department of Industry in 1979 (Stephenson, 1980). Out of this conversion came one of the most important political speeches of the 1970s, given to an audience at Preston on 5 September 1974. In it, Joseph noted that:

> Fine-tuning, quarterly budgets, short-term adjustments have not worked and will not work. ... What I am saying is that it is the methods that successive governments have used to reduce registered unemployment – namely expanding aggregate demand by deficit financing – which has created inflation, and without really helping the unemployed either. ... What we have to do ... is to set a level of domestic demand sufficient for that level of full employment that can be sustained without inflationary pressures. ... This would entail additional unemployment but failure to take these steps would lead to worse unemployment later.
>
> (*The Times*, 1974a)[6]

In common with the supply-siders, Joseph's analysis of the situation was expressed in a clear and concise form which could even be understood by those without an economics degree. This was the deceptively simple, almost painless side of monetarism. However, it would be quite wrong to suggest that Joseph's view was shared by the majority in the Conservative Party. Edward Heath was anti-monetarist in his views and he was supported in this antipathy by most of the Shadow Cabinet (Walker, 1987). Bearing this in mind, it seems surprising that Heath granted Joseph permission for the setting up of the CPS in 1974.

Recent research has examined the nature and impact of such think-tanks in contemporary Britain and has questioned the influence of the CPS and IEA on the policy-making process. It is difficult to agree with the analysis offered by Denham and Garnett (1996) who, after failing to produce any qualitative or quantitative evidence, conclude that think-tanks have had a limited impact on policy formulation. As this author has argued elsewhere, this cannot be the case (Oliver, 1996b). The CPS's work was an integral part of getting the message across to a wider spectrum of people, and it gave Joseph an outlet outside the House of Commons for his views.

When asked by Anthony Seldon in an interview for the journal *Contemporary Record* about the idea behind the CPS, he said: 'I did it to try to persuade myself and then, heaven help us, the party and the country, that the German social market philosophy was the right one for the Conservatives to adopt' (Joseph, 1987, p. 29). But it did not give Joseph a solid power base which he needed to build upon, and it was only the fortuitous circumstances of a leadership contest in February 1975 which began the long process of turning the Conservative Party towards Friedman's prescriptions for the 'British Disease'.

The leadership election should not be seen as a referendum on monetarism, and nor can Mrs Thatcher's surprising win indicate that she had a ground swell of support in the party for her 'conviction' views (cf. Wickham-Jones, 1997). Moreover, any Tories who thought that the Thatcher–Joseph interest in monetarism was merely a fad were going to be disappointed, given Mrs Thatcher's longevity in high office and her continuing penchant for Friedmanism! The groundwork had been done by Joseph, but it was now up to Mrs Thatcher to carry the party in the direction in which its leader wished to go. It was here that she faced an uphill task.[7]

From an early stage, Margaret Thatcher spelt out her beliefs in speeches to the party and wider audiences, both at home and abroad. In one of her first major speeches as party leader entitled 'Let the Children Grow Tall' (Thatcher, 1989, p. 1, *et seq.*) given to the Institute of Socio-Economic Studies in New York on 15 September 1975, Margaret Thatcher addressed some of the issues which were direct from the Joseph–Thatcher stable. She touched on at least one of the United States supply-side arguments, and echoed Joseph's earlier claim that 'monetarism is not enough':

> a progressive redistributive tax system such as ours has much worse effects on the *executive or professional with a high salary* ... you are ... all familiar with the arguments about the dulling of personal incentives which this causes. We have that problem. And we have many others as well.
> (Thatcher, 1989, pp. 8–9; emphasis in original)

Her distaste for inflation had a common appeal:

> Savers and retired people have already suffered severely from the costs of accelerating inflation, which they have done nothing to cause. Why should they make yet further sacrifices to induce those who have already gained so much at their expense to desist for a while?
> (Thatcher, 1989, p.10)

In focusing on the public versus private arguments and the role of the state, Mrs Thatcher noted:

> At the end of the day, a public spending bill which exceeds the taxable capacity of the economy sucks away money which should be spent on investment in industry or private housing. ... I conclude, therefore, that the persistent expansion of the role of the State and the relentless pursuit of equality has caused, and is causing, damage to our economy in a variety of ways. It is not the sole cause of what some have termed the 'British sickness', but it is a major one.
> (Thatcher, 1989, pp. 11–12)

These three extracts from her speech, underpinned by a kudos for individualism at the social and economic level, became the Thatcher hallmark. It is interesting to note that this speech was taking back many of the ideas from whence they came. Nor was this audience alienated by their visitor's suggestion that America should 'spare a few moments to learn from our recent experience. ... And to reaffirm, before it is too late, those true values which both our countries traditionally have shared' (Thatcher, 1989, p. 16–17).

Nor did the Conservative Party Conference in 1975 react badly to the free enterprise approach, and actually endorsed the Thatcher message with 'rolling breakers of cheers, shouts and foot-stamping' (*The Times*, 1975). Slowly and steadily, Keith Joseph's conversion, born from conversations with Alfred Sherman, Alan Walters and Peter Bauer, took hold of the Conservative Party through Mrs Thatcher's leadership. Indeed, by 1979, the Conservative manifesto emphasized 'sound money' and trade union reform above all other priorities, confirming the influence Mrs Thatcher had exerted on her party in a short space of time (Craig, 1990, p. 268).

The role of the media and City institutions

The role played by the financial press during the 1970s in introducing, explaining and criticizing the monetarist arguments should not be underestimated. From *The Economist* (which claims that its readership controls over half the world's GDP) to the broadsheets and tabloids, the popular media could claim to have ready access to a larger percentage of people than either Joseph or Thatcher could hope to reach through the CPS.

But, by its very nature, the power which the press possesses can be a double-edged sword. The history of the media's involvement with monetarism is a fickle one and, unlike their more scholarly counterparts in academia, the popular press is always in search of a 'sound bite'. Something novel always excites attention and, even though academic journals had been publishing articles on monetarism for a considerable time, the press seized upon monetarism as the 'new idea' after Friedman's 1967 presidential address to the American Economic Association. Consequently, while the new ideas coming across the Atlantic seemed fresh and were welcomed by the British press, there was the possibility that journalists would promise much from Friedman's theories and then lose interest or be unable to explain events if the outcome did not turn out as planned.

There were no grand illusions in the minds of the two top economic commentators, Samuel Brittan and Peter Jay. Their articles on the monetarist arguments in the *Financial Times* and *The Times*, respectively, were detailed, analytical and realistic. Their contribution to the debate was also important because their 'conversion' was done at a highly public level (through articles in their newspapers) and because the two were respected for their sound economic training.[8] It was acknowledged that if these two commentators agreed that something was wrong and they had found a solution to Britain's economic ills, then there must be something in the monetarist arguments.[9] Concomitantly, Samuel Brittan's later derision of monetarist policies in the *Financial Times* from the mid-1980s was an equally powerful indictment of policy failure and a new weapon used to support ERM entry.

The Times (1968a) was the first newspaper in the UK to publish monetary statistics on 24 September 1968, and this was followed by a leader on 15 October entitled 'Understanding the role of the money supply' (*The Times*, 1968b). These initial stirrings soon became more widespread and by the mid-1970s there were leading articles in the *Financial Times* and *The Times* echoing the sentiments expressed by Joseph in his Preston speech. Under the editorship of Lord Rees-Mogg, *The Times* in particular became noted for the hundreds of column inches dedicated to the views of the New Right, while the views of the Keynesians were consigned to the less influential 'Letters' column.

It was not only these newspapers which adopted a monetarist stance: The *Daily Telegraph* and the *Banker* sided with the arguments of the monetarists, and even the *Guardian* and the *Observer* were forced to make room for the new economics. *The Economist* was slow to take up the monetarist case, given the clear indications by even the Labour chancellor that the Keynesian consensus had broken down. But as Parsons has written since:

> What is ... most interesting was not the slowness of *The Economist* in finally coming round to accepting free market ideas so much as the rapidity with which the rest of the financial popular press took up with 'monetarism' and the 'big government' argument.
> (Parsons, 1989, p. 193)

No doubt this was part of a self-reinforcing process, as Hall (1982) has suggested, and it became increasingly difficult for any journalist to get an economic story published that did not contain monetarist references.

As suggested earlier, the enthusiasm of the press diminished from the early 1980s: not least as *The Times* changed editors, Peter Jay left and Samuel Brittan began to focus attention on 'exchange-rate' monetarism (see Chapter Five). Perhaps the public was also becoming bored with the constant monetarist rhetoric, which did not seem quite so revolutionary in the midst of the worst recession since the early 1930s. Brittan (1982, p. 16) had even given a warning that the public would soon become 'hopelessly confused between (a) issues on which every citizen has a right to be informed, (b) questions of general economic theory, and (c) highly technical questions best left to a few banking specialists.'

As Hall (1982, pp. 471–92) has noted in his extended account of the progress of monetarism in the UK, most commentators have not accounted for the shift of power which took place in the late 1970s towards the financial markets in the City of London (see Oliver, 1998). After the transformations in the gilt market following CCC, brokerage houses began to employ young economists to provide more accurate analyses of the markets and of the economy. Many of these new recruits were monetarists who 'were more likely than their elders to rebel against traditional Keynesian doctrine' (Hall, 1982, p. 477). Coupled with this, the market-place for economic ideas was widened by the appearance of City circulars. These were weekly or monthly publications, written by senior economists who provided comments for their clients on the size of the PSBR and the rate of growth of the money supply. In the words of Gordon Pepper, whose *Monetary Bulletin* for W. Greenwell and Company was a pioneering circular, 'I have been drifting reluctantly, but almost continuously, further and further away from the Keynesian approach towards the monetarist approach for the sole reason that the latter appears to produce the better results in practice' (Pepper, 1977, p. 7).

As the circulars became steadily more monetarist, their comments and analyses were picked up by *The Times* and reported to a wider audience. Pepper's influence was such that he began to tutor Margaret Thatcher in monetary economics when she was leader of the opposition (Lawson, 1992a, p. 80). In short, the entire process of the monetarist infiltration was one of self-perpetuation from the think-tanks, through the media and the politicians. Once the process had become established, it was inevitable that economic policy would change as a result.

The new macro model

Having described the 'counter-revolution', the final section of this chapter will outline the economic model the post-1979 Conservative administration intended to implement.

As will become apparent throughout this study, the methods, aims and objectives of the Thatcher government were highly controversial. One of the most controversial issues was the debate over how the money supply could be controlled. This debate has often been highly technical, with a variety of economic opinion on how the government could control the money supply. The simple monetarist elucidation of the 1960s and 1970s has produced more rigorous technical explanations of money supply control during the last 15 years. The disputes which have arisen from this form an important part of the story on policy fragmentation in the 1980s.

While the debate over monetary control shifted to ever higher levels of technical complexity in the 1970s, many of the supporters of monetarism claimed that the practical returns from monetarism required a longer gestation period than many critics' models could theoretically demonstrate. Furthermore, the techniques of monetary control introduced in 1976 had, by the mid-1980s, undergone several stages of metamorphism.

The medium-term financial strategy

The medium-term financial strategy (MTFS), introduced in 1980, was the central framework for the government's macroeconomic policy. References to the MTFS within the *Financial Statement and Budget Report* gave the best possible 'official' guide on the government's policy. Due to the importance given to the MTFS and its exposition of government policy, this section of the statement was keenly scrutinized by economic commentators after its publication on Budget day to see whether the government had altered instruments and policy targets. The story of the downgrading of the MTFS is taken up later in the book, but we need to consider here why the MTFS was introduced and what led to its prominence in the government's macroeconomic strategy.

The question of who suggested such an approach to economic policy is not clear. Alan Walters has suggested that:

> In 1975–76, for example, Britain witnessed the development of monetary targets and the eschewing of finely tuned fiscality. The medium-term financial strategy of the government of Mrs Thatcher was a lineal descendant of these brave measures of Mr Healey.
>
> (Walters, 1986, p. 10)

By 1978, Nigel Lawson, was arguing for 'a long-term stabilization programme to defeat inflation, recreate business confidence and provide a favourable climate for economic growth' (Lawson, 1978). He later claimed, with typical modesty, that the MTFS was his invention, while acknowledging that several economists had 'suggested something similar' (Lawson, 1992a, p. 69).

One such economist was Tim Congdon, who had reported on the activities of the House of Commons Expenditure Committee in 1974 and 1975 for *The Times*. Congdon had seen via the Expenditure Committees that the way fiscal policy operated in practice was far removed from the textbook descriptions, and became convinced that fine-tuning was 'an illusion' (Congdon, 1992a, p. 37). Both Lawson and Congdon also acknowledge an important source of inspiration in their discussions with Terry Burns and Alan Budd at the LBS in the late 1970s; Budd and Burns were also advocating policy decision-making within the confines of a medium-term framework in LBS publications (Budd and Burns, 1977).

By the late 1970s, then, there were economists working alone or in groups who had suggested a new policy framework for the UK. We can perhaps suggest that Congdon's first-hand experience of crude Keynesian inadequacies had led him to advocate alternative polices; Burns and Budd had given greater academic cohesion to these policies, and Nigel Lawson's political dexterity could sell the new MTFS to the Conservative Party. The perceived failings of Keynesian economic policy coupled with the ideas of three economists and one politician were crucial to the success of the MTFS, while the elevation of Burns to be the government's chief economic adviser in 1980 was important to take the message into the Treasury. By 1980 the MTFS had five main features (Burns, 1988).

First, that macroeconomic policy should be conducted within a medium-term perspective. Clearly, this represented a shift from how economic policy was visualized in the 1960s and 1970s, and a response to the criticisms of macro models and policy as seen by the Ball Committee on Policy Optimization (1978). The thinking behind the MTFS also represents what Allsopp called the 'three Cs': credibility, consistency and continuity (Allsopp, 1985, p. 2). This is echoed by Peter Middleton (1989, p. 49) who later wrote that the MTFS was important for three reasons:

> policy [was given] a sense of purpose which can be presented with simplicity, coherence and clarity. Second, it implies the intention to eschew measures which might bring short-term benefits but with long-term costs. Third, the medium-term dimension to policy itself adds greatly to market credibility and the chances of success.

Nigel Lawson was aware that economic progress under the MTFS banner would be slow and that political events could encourage deviations from the outlined measures. The bulk of this study investigates at what stage the 'three Cs' were frustrated in the 1980s.

Second, there was an identifiable shift from a real to a nominal framework within the MTFS. In simple terms, what separated the medium-term financial strategy from Wilson's National Plan and Heath's industrial regeneration plans was:

that it is confined to charting a course for those variables – notably the quantity of money – which are and must be within the power of governments to control. By contrast, governments cannot create economic growth. All the instruments which were supposed to do this have succeeded only in damaging the economy and have ulti-mately broken in the hands of the governments that sought to use them.

(Lawson, 1980a, p. 16)

The purpose of this framework was to reduce nominal (or money) GDP until it was consistent with stable prices and real GDP. But the emphasis on nominal GDP was not made explicit in 1980 (indeed, during the first year of the MTFS Chancellor Howe and his colleagues believed that they could control the stock or supply of money), and it was only in stages throughout the 1980s that official sources indicated that this had been an objective of policy. To use the word 'objective' might be misleading: Westaway and Wren-Lewis (1993, p. 233) have argued that as nominal GDP was eventually given more attention than £M3, this implies that nominal GDP became an intermediate target. While Burns (1988, p. 430) stresses that figures for nominal GDP should not be seen as 'precise targets', his discussion is vague over whether nominal GDP is an indicator, intermediate target or final ob-jective of policy. Such vagaries later became a hallmark of the MTFS and lessened its consistency.

As hinted earlier, the shift from real to nominal variables and the emphasis on a declining money GDP was accompanied by a more active use of monetary policy. This is the third trait to note, in particular the elevation of interest rates over direct controls as the main instrument of monetary policy.[10] The authorities were determined to announce a tar-get aggregate for the money supply (in 1980, £M3) and would raise interest rates if monetary growth appeared excessive. Higher interest rates would then effect the exchange rate, liquidity, the cost of credit and expectations, so that spending and ultimately the demand for money would be curbed. The definition of the money supply target in the 1980 *Financial Statement and Budget Report* added the proviso that 'the way in which the money supply is defined for target purposes may need to be adjusted from time to time as circumstances change' (HM Treasury, 1980, p. 16) as a footnote to Table 5. This innocuous footnote led to a major source of disagreement among the monetarists and threatened the credibility of the monetarist experiment at its very inception.

The fourth feature was that the shift from real to nominal variables was also accompanied by greater emphasis on controlling the public sector borrowing requirement (PSBR). The authorities intended to use fiscal policy as a means of influencing interest rates for a given money target: by reducing the PSBR as a percentage of GDP, the money supply would not grow so quickly, and interest rates could be kept low. The PSBR was thus an important link between monetary and fiscal policy. However, it should be spelt out that while fiscal policy was not seen as a short-term policy instrument, there would be 'a "stepped" PSBR profile, with the PSBR not changing much as a proportion of GDP in recession years, but falling fairly sharply in non-recession years' (Lawson, 1980b, p. 4).

The final feature was that macroeconomic policy alone could not improve the growth rate and 'at the same time, the Government will continue to pursue policies to strengthen the supply side of the economy, by tax and other incentives and by improving the working of the market mechanism' (HM Treasury, 1980, p. 16). As Brittan (1982) has argued, if nominal GDP is directed towards a target path and is consistent with declining prices and steady real GDP growth, then an improved supply-side performance should give a better split between inflation and output.

The state of the debate by 1980

The new macroeconomic strategy placed the control of inflation above the commitment to full employment. Central to the MTFS was the emphasis given to controlling the growth of the money supply. Yet while the monetarists agreed that the money supply needed to be controlled, it was unclear among some of them why that emphasis was placed on broad money (£M3) and not narrow money (M1). This will be a theme to which we shall return later. The MTFS had also stressed the need for controlling the PSBR so that the money supply would not grow so quickly, but a very important question remained. What was the *precise* role of fiscal policy?

If we consider these two areas, among others, we are able to outline the state the macroeconomic debate had reached by the early 1980s. This is a particularly useful exercise, as it highlights the contrasting views on the monetarist arguments held by economists, while suggesting where the monetarists parted company during the 1980s. Moreover, this subsection also allows us the opportunity of providing a comparison between British and American monetarism.

Concurrent to the publication of the MTFS in March 1980, the government's newly formed Treasury and Civil Service Committee was investigating the debate surrounding monetary control. As one former Chairman later acknowledged (Higgins, 1992), the Treasury and Civil Service Committee provided almost instant economic history throughout the 1980s, in that they documented economic opinions from government ministers in a more comprehensive way than before 1979. The report *Monetary Control* (Treasury and Civil Service Committee, 1980c) was an especially pertinent document, given the challenge to the post-war economic consensus which was being offered by the Thatcher government. The evidence (both written and oral) taken during the course of the investigations from the distinguished panel of economists, government advisers and politicians laid out clearly the stage the economic debate had reached by the early 1980s.

The Treasury and Civil Service Committee sent out 35 questions to 32 individual institutions and academic witnesses on 24 April 1980, and received 29 replies. The majority of these were published in July (Treasury and Civil Service Committee, 1980a) and November 1980 (Treasury and Civil Service Committee, 1980b), with oral evidence taken by the committee published in February 1981 (Treasury and Civil Service Committee, 1981). The questionnaire sent out was structured to address the theory, evidence and priority of government policy. During the course of the investigation, the committee identified four prominent schools of thought: 'gradualists', anti-monetarists, 'new classical', and 'pragmatists'. Let us consider briefly what each school had to say about the role of monetary policy.

The committee took evidence from two prominent 'gradualists': David Laidler and Milton Friedman. According to Laidler (1981b, p. 158), a 'Gradualist monetary policy involves reducing the rate of growth of the money supply in the expectation that this will reduce the inflation rate', and that:

> The case for gradualism rests on the proposition that, ultimately, the main burden of adjustment will be borne by the price level. I stress the word ultimately, because in my view, the brunt of the impact of monetary policy falls not upon the price level at all, but rather upon interest rates and real income (and therefore employment). Only later do effects on the price level begin to come though. It is this belief above all which leads me to advocate a slow, rather than a rapid, reduction in the monetary expansion rate as the correct response to a deeply embedded inflation, and which sets my view apart from the so called 'new classical' economists.

For Laidler in particular, it would be folly to pursue a rapid reduction in monetary growth, precisely because inflation expectations are slow to respond. A sharp monetary contraction would lead to a pronounced recession, with high unemployment. Far better, argued the gradualists, to adopt a 'steady as she goes' monetary policy, with Friedman even predicting that a 'modest' reduction in output and employment would be a side-effect of reducing inflation to single figures.

As for the important question on the 'transmission mechanism' of monetary policy, Friedman was dismissive that the exchange rate affected domestic prices:

Monetary policy actions affect asset portfolios in the first instance, spending decisions in the second, which translates into effects on output and then on prices. The changes in exchange rates are in turn a response to these effects of home policy and of similar policy abroad. This question is topsy-turvy. Floating exchange rates are necessary in order for monetary policy proper to be possible. They are a facilitating mechanism not a 'transmission mechanism'.

(Friedman, 1980, p. 61)

This view is in contrast to the evidence given to the committee by the 'pragmatic' James Tobin (perhaps the world's most distinguished Keynesian monetary economist):

The way monetary policy works, as I understand it ... is through the exchange rate and the workings of monetary policy here seem, at least in considerable part recently, to have produced a recession by appreciating the sterling exchange rate and reducing the competitiveness of Britain in foreign trade and producing a current account deficit as the high interest rates produced by the monetary policy bring in funds from overseas.

(Tobin, 1981, pp. 210–11)

It follows that the erosion of competitiveness will reduce exports and increase imports and induce a recession in output and employment. Ultimately, the recession will slow wage inflation. Because of this, the 'pragmatists' believed that attempts to combat inflation by money supply control alone would be unwise: the result would be high interest rates, high unemployment and low output, while the 'inertia' of inflation would mean that prices only come down slowly.

Both the anti-monetarist and 'new classical' schools are at the opposite ends of the economic spectrum, and adopt the most contrasting views to the two other schools. Flexible prices are assumed to be paramount within the new classical model of the UK, as outlined by Professor Patrick Minford. In written and oral evidence to the Treasury and Civil Service Committee, Minford indicated that the best way of ridding inflation from the economic system was to reduce the rate of growth of the money supply while announcing that this policy would be continued in the future. In reply to questions 20 and 21 from the committee, Minford argued that the Thatcher government would lose credibility and its battle against inflation if it undertook a 'U-turn' in policy (Minford, 1981, p. 28).

Lord Kaldor, the 'anti-monetarist' *par excellence*, was every bit in favour of such a 'U-turn'. In his view there was no basis at all for the central economic policy of the Thatcher government. Prices do not respond flexibly to market conditions, and efforts to control the money aggregate (£M3) are misplaced, argued Kaldor. It is the flow of income, the general price level and the level of interest rates that generate the demand for money. Given that prices and wages are 'sticky downwards' in the Kaldorian model, it will require large fluctuations in interest rates to generate any significant changes to the money stock, with severe consequences for real output (Kaldor, 1980).

There were also disagreements among the two pro-monetarist groups which were mentioned earlier, and which ought to be considered further. The *Memoranda on Monetary Policy* was a cosmopolitan document, which sought evidence from America, Germany, France, Canada and Switzerland. Although the Treasury and Civil Service Committee made the broad four-school classification, it did not dwell on the subtle but important differences between British and American monetarism. Essentially, for the UK, Congdon has suggested that British monetarism exhibited four features by 1979 (Congdon, 1987). As we consider each below in the light of evidence given in the report *Monetary Policy*, some of our themes in later chapters begin to take shape.

The first is that broad money was seen as the appropriate intermediate monetary target, with an emphasis on the control of bank credit. This is known as the 'credit counterparts approach' to the money supply. Without becoming too technical, the 'credit counterparts approach' differs from the 'money multiplier approach' adopted in the United States, which emphasizes control of 'high-powered money'.

The success of monetarism in the intellectual battle of the late 1970s owed a great deal to the excellent fits of theory with recent observation, that is to say, the growth of the money supply (£M3) preceding the rise in prices consistently by about two years (see Figure 3.2). That was crucial to the choice of a broad rather than a narrow money target in the UK.

However, Friedman (1980, p. 57) did not hide his disapproval of the existing methods of British monetary control when he responded to the Treasury and Civil Service Committee's questionnaire in 1980:

> I could hardly believe my eyes when I read, in the first paragraph of the summary chapter [of the Green paper on Monetary Control], 'the principal means of controlling the growth of the money supply must be fiscal policy – both public expenditure and tax policy – and interest rates'. Interpreted literally, this sentence is simply wrong. Only a Rip Van Winkle, who had not read any of the flood of literature during the past decade and more on the money supply process, could possibly have written that sentence.

But this reproach by Friedman is misplaced in the British context. First, central bank techniques in the United States have followed an 'open-market' policy while Britain followed a 'bank-rate policy' (Keynes, 1930, pp. 224–5). Second, in Britain, bank deposits are viewed as the counterpart to bank credit. Thus British monetarists will

concentrate their attention on variables believed to be relevant to
the behaviour of bank credit. By far the most important of these is
the short-term rate of interest, set by Bank of England operations
in the money market. The contrast with the American monetarist
position, with its concern over the quantity of reserves rather than
the price at which they are made available to the banking system, is
virtually total.

(Congdon, 1987, p. 44)

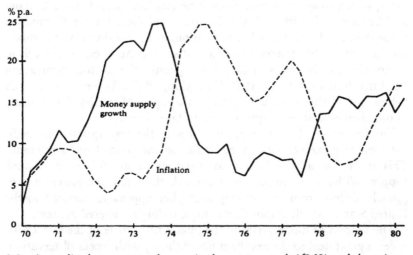

3.2   Annualized percentage changes in the money stock (£M3) and the price
level, 1970–80

Source: Beenstock (1980, p. 54)

The second distinguishing feature of British monetarism identified by
Congdon again attracts criticism from Friedman. The question was
raised at the beginning of this subsection of what precisely the role of
fiscal policy was within the government's strategy. It will be recalled
from our earlier discussion on the MTFS that the authorities intended
to use fiscal policy as a means of influencing interest rates for a given
money target: by reducing the PSBR as a percentage of GDP, the money
supply would not grow so quickly, and interest rates could be kept low.
This characteristic, where fiscal policy was to be made consistent with
monetary policy and lose its pre-1979 demand management status, led
Friedman to comment that 'there is no necessary relation between the
size of the PSBR and monetary growth'. Did this make the role of fiscal
policy redundant in the British MTFS?

Not necessarily. As Congdon points out, there is an institutional difference between the two countries in that the Federal Reserve is responsible
for monetary policy and the Treasury for fiscal policy in the United

States, while the two policies are more integrated in the United Kingdom. Concomitantly, given that the majority of transatlantic monetarists favour money base control, they find the substantive emphasis given to the PSBR within the British credit counterpart's approach as alien.

The third difference between British and American monetarism is over the role of trade unions. David Laidler (a British monetarist who emigrated to North America) accorded a more prominent role to trade unions in the inflationary process than American monetarists, when he formulated his 'gradualist' approach (Laidler, 1982, pp. 176–7). Patrick Minford's Liverpool model placed the unions centre stage in his explanation of distortions to the natural rate of unemployment (Minford, 1985a). But Friedman is ambivalent towards this issue. He maintains that they alter relative wages but not the absolute level of wages, and that 'what produced ... inflation is not trade unions, nor monopolistic employers, but what happens to the quantity of money' (Friedman, 1975, p. 33).

The final feature of British monetarism by the late 1970s was the avoidance of a specific exchange-rate objective. Friedman's evidence to the Treasury and Civil Service Committee in favour of a floating rather than fixed rate was supported by British monetarists after the 1977 dilemma. In that year Ball, Burns and Laury had suggested that 'our conclusion would be similar to that of the monetarists in that floating the rate provides an extra degree of freedom to pursue a rate of inflation in the long run different from that of our competitors' (Ball et al. 1977, p. 23).

By 1979, Mrs Thatcher's 'monetarist' administration believed firmly that broad money supply targets were the way forward for the British economy. Credibility had to be gained from the financial markets by sticking to policy rules. A high PSBR would not be tolerated and fiscal policy was going to lose the status of demand management. There would be no deviation from a money supply target, regardless of the exchange rate. Also, legislation would be introduced to end the power of the trade unions, which the Conservatives believed had adversely affected the natural rate of unemployment.

The way forward under the Conservatives was for a British strand of monetarism, combined with American supply-side economics, to end the 'British disease'. Taken together, these policies looked like turning the post-war consensus firmly on its head. But unfortunately for the government, several problems arose during the 1980s which, well before the end of the decade, had academics, politicians, Keynesians and monetarists questioning the wisdom of the entire economic strategy.

Notes

1. It is interesting to note that the mentor of monetarism, Milton Friedman, has had his ideas extended by his protégés, allowing for a degree of reinterpretation. As we saw in Chapter Two, much the same happened to Keynes's theories in the post-war period.
2. Twenty years on, it is still admitted by monetarists that, during a period of monetary disequilibrium, the connection between money and prices 'may be difficult to identify' (Congdon, 1989a, p. 70).
3. This view was challenged by Walter Heller (1982) who was an architect of the 1960s tax cuts and who claimed that the Kennedy reductions were an incentive to capital formation, which was entirely different from Laffer's arguments.
4. After Sir Keith Joseph's speech at Preston in September 1974, Denis Healey (*The Times*, 1974c) later said that: 'We can thank [Sir Keith] for making the election issue clear. The British people are asked to vote either for a slump and class conflict on an unprecedented scale or for national unity in the fight for full employment and social justice.'
5. Fisher (1973, p. 284) notes that Keith Joseph represented an economic extreme on the right within the shadow cabinet during the 1965–70 Wilson years, diametrically opposite ex-Chancellor Maudling, who had presided over the 1962–64 boom.
6. This speech was given front page coverage in *The Times* of 6 September 1974, and provoked a leading article on the same day entitled 'The Sharp Shock of Truth' (*The Times*, 1974b).
7. It would be wrong to suggest that it was just Mrs Thatcher and Keith Joseph who were attempting to convince the Conservative Party. Among the more prominent Conservative MPs who were either persuaded by the New Right arguments or who sought to displace older Conservative thinking, John Biffen, Geoffrey Howe and Nigel Lawson loom large (Gamble, 1994, Ch. 3).
8. Interviewed by the author, Samuel Brittan (1994) argued that his contribution to the debate was primarily intellectual, and not confined to merely publicizing the monetarist cause.
9. Although Peter Jay claimed in 1993 to this author that he was still a monetarist, he gradually became more sceptical about the general direction of economic policy post-1979. See Jay (1990).
10. As Pliatzky (1989, p. 126) notes, quantitative ceilings on bank lending, foreign exchange market intervention and funding policy are three further instruments of monetary policy. Quantitative controls were abolished in 1979; the government had publicly ruled out foreign exchange intervention, while funding policy was pursued for a short time in the 1980s. In short, 'for practical purposes, the weight of day-to-day monetary policy has rested heavily on interest rates'.

CHAPTER FOUR

False start and policy confusion: 1979–83

Credibility – whether at academic or street level – is essential to any theory on which effective policy is based.

(C. Johnson, 1991b, p. 2)

This chapter examines the first five years of the Thatcher administration and the frustrations which beset policy-makers from an early stage. The coverage on this period is not exhaustive and the concise account given here restricts itself to four sections, which, *in toto*, provides a mixed record of the early Thatcher years.

As events unfolded between 1979 and 1980, it became necessary that the government's economic strategy earned credibility rapidly, to prevent the monetarist experiment from unravelling. In the pursuit of sound finance, there were many unpalatable decisions which the authorities had to undertake. Some of the more important decisions are outlined in this chapter. It is important to remember that supporters of Friedman had argued that the gains from following a monetarist economic policy would be a gradual affair, in lumpy instalments (Burns, 1981). The first section outlines the initial problems the Conservatives faced with controlling the money supply during the 1980–81 recession. The test this placed on the government's credibility is discussed.

The 1981 Budget was an important political and economic watershed for the government and one which pushed the economic strategy into uncharted territory. This Budget is covered in the second section. This is followed by an exposition of what later became a major dilemma for policy-makers: monetary control or exchange-rate targets? Finally, the last section of this chapter notes the success that the government had in reducing inflation but examines why the authorities had a patchy success at meeting the monetary targets.

As Sir Leo Pliatzky (1989, p. 127) has observed, in the early 1980s the Thatcher government was on a very difficult and high learning curve. In this chapter we shall begin to discover what lessons they learnt during this period.

A British recession?

Arguably the closest Mrs Thatcher's government came to its professed belief in market forces was in the early 1980s, when traces of Friedman could be detected in many announcements from ministers. Indeed, it was during the first 24 months that the government earned itself a reputation as the toughest administration to govern post-war (if not twentieth-century) Britain.

It will be recalled from Figure 2.2 that, since the 1960s, the UK had experienced a protracted problem with inflation. Mrs Thatcher believed that previous governments had either ignored the rise in inflation, or had concluded that the costs of ridding inflation from the system would require a high sacrifice ratio[1] (Thatcher, 1995, pp. 567–8). The monetarist model, endorsed by Mrs Thatcher, suggested that as inflation had taken a long time to become established in the UK economic system, it was going to be a while before it was eliminated. The size of the sacrifice ratio would be determined by the speed with which individuals and institutions adjusted their expectations of future rates of inflation downwards, which in turn was connected to the credibility of the monetary authority. However, during the first 18 months of the government's first term, the ideological niceties of monetarism were quickly replaced by a political realism that permanent price stability would be an arduous struggle and not without some expensive side-effects.

The first problem was that the chosen broad monetary aggregate (£M3) wandered outside its target band. Emphasis had been placed on a broad aggregate partly due to the success of DCE (see Chapter Two) and partly because there appeared to be a 'triangular relationship' between the size of the PSBR, the growth of broad money and the level of interest rates. Also, £M3 appeared to be an excellent guide to the boom in 1973 and, according to Walters (1986, p. 118), 'the arguments in favour of adopting one broad £M3 target appeared quite cogent if not overwhelming'.

However, between 1980/81 and 1981/82, the Treasury had difficulty in attaining the £M3 target. What can explain this wayward performance?

In the early 1980s, the two most important factors causing £M3 to exceed its target band were the abolition of exchange controls in October 1979, followed by the removal of the 'corset' in June 1980. The latter was inevitable following the abolition of the former, and both now made it possible for banks and building societies to increase lending. The increases in lending to individuals (particularly for house purchases) were remarkable. For example, the year to November 1981 saw a surge in lending by over 70 per cent for residential mortgages; in money terms this represented advances of £3.5 billion a year. This reintermediation (where banks seek to channel funds to themselves and away from building societies and inter-company loans) inevitably had consequences for £M3, necessitating an upward revision in the monetary targets set in the Budgets of March 1982 and March 1983.

The second problem that occurred in the first 18 months was that the domestic economy underwent a period of rapid contraction. For the bulk of the country, this was a far more costly and meaningful affair than the government failing to attain its monetary targets. The question that provoked heated debate at the time and which still exerts an emotive response in some quarters was whether Mrs Thatcher's economic policies caused the recession between 1979 and 1981.

In his account of policy of this period, Walters (1986, p. 155) pauses to give a cautionary warning over the question of where the responsibility for the recession lies:

> Economic policy does not depend entirely or even primarily on economic principles and evidence. Political, social and psychological factors must play a considerable part in any successful policy. Yet all an economist can do is to examine critically the economic ideas which lie behind a particular policy; he will have only a sketchy idea of the other determinants of policy. Similarly, the assessment of a policy – such as that so loosely but evocatively described as Thatcherite – must be in terms of an *alternative feasible* policy.

For a study which is examining the development of economic policy in the 1980s, this quotation serves as a useful reminder that when we judge the contractionary effect or otherwise of monetary or fiscal policies in this period, we cannot simply weigh their impact in isolation to the political, social and psychological factors to which Walters refers. As for the 'alternative feasible policy' open to the government, it is clear that Walters has in mind counter-cyclical fiscal policy, along the traditional Keynesian lines. Yet it was this alternative policy above all else which the Thatcher government wished to avoid.

In July 1980, a leader in *The Times* (1980) entitled 'Intent, Friedman: Result, Hayek' noted that, although the Thatcher government had started out with a gradualist approach to reducing inflation, 'events and policies may be forcing it nearer to the sort of circumstances suggested by Professor Hayek'. The Hayekian approach advocated that it was necessary to eradicate inflation from the system, *at whatever cost in the short term*. By adopting this strategy, the difficulty for the government in the short term was succeeding with a political balancing act of appearing concerned about the debilitating effects of the recession, while in practice doing very little to mitigate its effects.

Professor James Tobin (1981, p. 208) remarked to the Treasury and Civil Service Committee in 1981 that:

> the UK has embarked upon a very interesting and, if I may so say, risky experiment in macroeconomic policy and monetary policy. This kind of experiment has been discussed a good bit in the United States and in the economics profession in general and it amounts to what is sometimes called a credible threat policy.

The origins of the 'credible threat policy' appear in the work of Fellner (1976, 1979, 1980), and were taken up by the 'new classical' economists in the 1980s who used it to explain why the Thatcher government initially failed to reduce inflation. For Matthews and Minford (1987, p. 62), the disinflation was severe and 'expectations were quite unprepared for it'. As Sargent (1993) notes, sudden changes in policy regime can be damaging if the policy regime has little credibility. In these new classical models, an important influence on credibility is the growth path of government debt. Although there was a tight monetary policy in the early 1980s, there were big fiscal deficits which were being financed by borrowing at high nominal interest rates. As Leslie (1993, p. 69) explains, 'consequently, agents formed the view that the deficits would be monetized some time in the future and this view led to high current inflation – despite the severe recession'. Concomitantly, given the unpopularity of the government, it was not clear who would win the next general election, and in short:

> This reinforced the expectation of future profligacy ... [and] the economy ended up with the worst of both worlds. There was a surprisingly strict monetary policy which caused the severe downturn. Because the whole policy regime lacked any credibility, it failed to control inflation promptly. It was not a failure of monetarism, rather a failure of the government to comprehend properly the logical consequences of its own poor reputation.
>
> (Leslie, 1993, pp. 69–70)

Table 4.1 profiles the recession. By the end of 1979, real GDP, exports, fixed investment and investment in stocks began a decline which lasted until at least the third quarter of 1981. Consumer expenditure held up throughout, as did government consumption. However, such figures do not put the recession into any historical context and hide the human cost of the recession. It was the deepest downturn in economic activity since the Second World War, and led some commentators to draw parallels with the inter-war years (Buiter and Miller, 1981). The scale of stock-shedding by firms was indeed unparalleled to earlier recessions. As firms attempted to stave off bankruptcy and came to realize that a counter-cyclical macroeconomic policy was not on the agenda, unemployment rose.

While we noted in Chapter Two that unemployment had been on a rising trend since 1973–74, the doubling of unemployment between the end of 1979 and mid-1981 was indeed dramatic by pre-1979 standards (manufacturing employment fell from seven million to six million). For a political party which had claimed in its 1979 election campaign that 'Labour wasn't working', these figures were not a good start to a period in government. Equally frustrating were the inflation figures which remained resolutely in double figures from the end of 1979, peaking at 22 per cent in May 1980 (RPI basis).

Could these appalling figures be blamed on government policy? Early investigations by Artis et al. (1984) did indeed blame policy for the state of the balance sheet during this period, even though a follow-up study by Artis and Bladen-Hovell (1987) placed slightly less weight on policy effects. As Chrystal (1984, p. 33) has argued, 'It is hard to look at what happened in Britain after 1979 and be comfortable with the story that policy changes made by the Thatcher government are entirely responsible.'

As far as policy is concerned, two critics have concluded that both fiscal and monetary policy were too tight between 1979 and 1981. On fiscal policy: 'By Keynesian principles of the determination of aggregate demand and output, the depth of the depression in the United Kingdom can be partly explained by the tight fiscal stance, induced by the MTFS' (Buiter and Miller, 1983, p. 327), and on monetary policy: 'The role played by restrictive monetary policy is central to our interpretation of the current depression' (Buiter and Miller, 1981, p. 342).

However, after examining the literature on the monetary and fiscal arguments, the evidence presented begins to take on the feel of 'where you stand depends on where you sit'. On balance, perhaps monetary policy could have been loosened (Buiter and Miller, 1981) as opposed to a tightening of fiscal policy (Forsyth, 1980). If we consider the effects of the stringent monetary policy, a further criticism that we can make is that the costs for sterling were excessive.

As (Dimsdale, 1991, p. 132) has noted, 'The degree of overvaluation of sterling in the second half of 1980 was unprecedented in the post-war period and well in excess of the overvaluation resulting from the return to the gold standard in 1925.' The 40 per cent increase in UK relative unit labour costs between 1978 and 1981, combined with the strengthening of the nominal exchange rate, did not help the position of British industry. Why did sterling appreciate so sharply in this period? There are two reasons commonly given for this.

The first is the so-called 'Dutch disease' effect (Forsyth and Kay, 1980; Chrystal, 1984). By 1980, Britain was a net exporter of oil, whereas only four years earlier she had been entirely dependent on

Table 4.1 Expenditure on the gross domestic product, 1973–83 (£ million, 1985 prices, seasonally adjusted)[1]

Year and quarter	GDP at factor cost (expenditure based)	Final expenditure on goods and services at market prices						
		Total	Consumer expenditure	General government consumption	Gross domestic fixed capital formation	Value of physical increase in stocks and work in progress[2]	Exports of goods and services	Imports of goods and services
1973	260 907	376 018	180 843	62 430	55 818	6 595	69 186	73 045
1974	256 994	374 264	178 216	63 598	55 465	2 980	74 257	73 801
1975	254 961	366 758	177 500	67 147	53 383	−3 402	72 144	68 901
1976	261 693	381 230	178 279	67 977	54 277	1 622	78 712	72 224
1977	268 410	385 714	177 483	66 855	53 307	3 416	84 128	73 344
1978	276 252	399 938	187 510	68 400	54 914	2 867	85 701	76 458
1979	283 955	414 725	195 664	69 776	56 450	3 328	88 924	83 814
1980	278 160	405 285	195 825	70 872	53 416	−3 371	88 726	80 781
1981	274 964	399 644	196 011	71 086	48 298	−3 200	88 064	78 522
1982	279 738	407 791	197 980	71 672	50 915	−1 821	88 798	82 348
1983	290 148	425 443	206 932	73 089	53 476	1 357	90 589	87 709

Table 4.1 continued

1979: 1	69 236	99 882	47 747	17 201	13 798	1 070	19 884	19 516
1979: 2	71 997	105 917	50 423	17 533	13 983	358	23 547	21 143
1979: 3	71 159	104 217	48 398	17 490	14 198	1 287	22 665	21 636
1979: 4	71 563	104 709	49 096	17 552	14 471	613	22 828	21 519
1980: 1	70 812	103 875	49 708	17 706	13 955	−711	23 219	21 817
1980: 2	70 018	101 568	48 576	17 563	13 447	−285	22 260	20 920
1980: 3	69 180	100 810	49 163	17 744	13 157	−882	21 688	19 244
1980: 4	68 150	99 032	48 378	17 859	12 857	−1 493	21 559	18 800
1981: 1	68 043	98 449	48 919	17 785	11 946	−1 398	21 395	18 014
1981: 2	68 516	99 034	49 053	17 792	12 121	−1 373	21 626	18 884
1981: 3	69 088	101 297	49 062	17 875	12 179	−287	22 589	21 143
1981: 4	69 317	100 864	48 977	17 634	12 052	−142	22 454	20 481

1 For years up to and including 1982, totals differ from the sum of the components because of the method used to rebase on 1985 prices.
2 Quarterly alignment adjustment included in this series.

Source: Central Statistical Office (1993, pp. 21, 26)

imported oil. Consequently, as the oil trade balance improved, the exchange rate appreciated and manufacturing exports contracted. While this account of sterling's appreciation is not rejected by all economists, there is a dispute as to whether this mono-causal explanation is adequate (Niehans, 1981; Buiter and Miller, 1981).

The alternative reason given by Buiter and Miller (based on the overshooting model of Dornbusch) is that monetary policy in Britain was too tight, which resulted in an excessive appreciation of sterling. This view was acknowledged by the Treasury and Civil Service Committee (1981) when they took evidence on the principal transmission mechanism of monetary policy in an economy with a floating exchange rate. Walters (1986) takes issue with the implications of the transmission mechanism of the appreciation of sterling via a decline in exports and increased import penetration. Following the analysis of Beenstock (1983, pp. 203–7), Walters notes that the current balance actually improved between 1979 and 1983, with the inverted *J*-curve effect failing to materialize. Indeed, as Foreman-Peck (1991, p. 177) observes, between 1980 and 1983 the current balance yielded positive balances of over £17 billion.

While the performance of UK exports continued to improve in the second half of the 1980s through to the early 1990s, recent research by Anderton (1996a) is less sanguine about the effects of sterling's overvaluation between 1979 and 1981. Using highly disaggregated bilateral trade flows data to the four-digit (ISIC) level, he has presented evidence suggesting that the temporary appreciation of sterling encouraged both UK consumers and producers to switch permanently from domestically produced goods to imports. Despite the slow-down in import penetration in the second half of the 1980s and the strong UK recovery in capital expenditure, it is clear that in virtually all of the sectors examined by Anderton (1996b) there is a lower level of UK investment relative to that of her competitors in 1990 compared with 1979.

Figure 4.1 shows that the recession was not confined solely to the United Kingdom. Although the fall in GDP between 1980 and 1981 was the sharpest in the UK, other European countries, and particularly America, experienced a further downturn in economic activity in 1982. The reason commonly given for this stresses the strength of the US dollar. As the dollar appreciated against other currencies, it caused two effects. First, oil prices rose (oil prices are determined by OPEC in dollars, so that a rise in the dollar against a particular currency raises the price of oil in that currency). Second, interest rates were raised by governments to prevent their currencies from depreciating, with deleterious affects on domestic economic activity. As Britain was self-sufficient in oil and had already tightened its monetary policy, the British

4.1 Industrial production for four European countries and the USA, 1978–84 (% p.a.)

Source: Aldcroft (1993a, p. 246)

economy was not as badly affected by the 1982 downturn as the United States, Europe or Japan.

The causes of the recession, coupled with the missed money targets, were seized upon by government critics (particularly the Keynesians) as evidence that theoretical monetarism was causing widespread damage to the British economy. Some monetarists went on to argue subsequently that £M3 was perhaps not the best measure of the money supply and that other monetary aggregates should be used.[2] As Laidler (1985) admitted, the growth of £M3 did give the impression that monetary policy was loose when in fact it was very tight and merely encouraged a continuation of tight policies (this is considered in more detail in the final section of this chapter).

The 1981 Budget: an exercise in restoring credibility

In her autobiography, Margaret Thatcher (1993, p. 129) recalls how she felt about the economy at the end of 1980:

> By the end of 1980 I began to feel that we risked forfeiting the public's confidence. Unpopularity I could live with. But loss of

confidence in our capacity to deliver our economic programme was
far more dangerous ... our credibility was at stake.

By early 1981, it was clear that the Thatcher experiment was not
going very well. The PSBR for 1980/81 was on course for exceeding its
target by about 1.75 per cent of GDP. On the monetary side of the
MTFS, £M3 was outside the target ranges by about 30 per cent. At the
time of the March 1981 Budget, the British economy had been in
recession for five successive quarters. Given this background, the cla-
mour for reflation was particularly evident among some economists,
notably (but by no means exclusively) the Keynesians.

If we accept that the government's firm resistance to reflate during
1979 and 1980 was the first real test of its commitment to pursue wider
goals by new means, then the Budget of 1981 was undoubtedly the next
step towards earning full policy credibility.

Broadly speaking, the origins of the 1981 Budget evolved from the
wish on behalf of the prime minister and chancellor to return the
economy to the MTFS path, envisaged at the time of the 1980 Budget.
The 1980 Budget had forecast a PSBR of £8.5 billion for the 1980/81
financial year – the out-turn was some £5 billion higher at around
£13.2 billion. By February 1981, the Treasury was estimating that the
PSBR for 1981/82 would be £14.5 billion.

Sir Geoffrey Howe suggested that if the government wanted to get the
PSBR down to around £10 billion, he would have to raise taxes by
some £4 billion (Howe, 1994, p. 203). There were differing suggestions
as to what should be done. Alan Walters, who had just been appointed
as economic adviser to the prime minister, argued for trenchant public
spending cuts with a rise in income tax: 'I would have preferred to have
a figure below £10 billion but at that late stage of the budget process
there were few alternatives left' (Walters, 1986, p. 87).

Yet, as Mrs Thatcher points out in her autobiography, the increase in
taxation would make it a 'political nightmare' (Thatcher, 1993, p. 135).
Sir Geoffrey Howe (1991, p. 98), in a speech to the Institute of Fiscal
Studies in 1991, concurs with this view: 'Mrs Thatcher reacted ... by
saying to us all that she had not been elected to put up taxes. Quite
right too!' Instead of agreeing to a rise in income tax which was being
proposed by Alan Walters, Howe consulted Arthur Cockfield who suggested that a large part of the reduction could be met by freezing
personal allowances. This decision, coupled with rises in excise taxes,
and a once-and-for-all tax on banks' current accounts at 2.5 per cent,
implied a severe tightening of fiscal policy (see Table 4.2).

Margaret Thatcher's account of her own role in the decision process
is far more involved than either Howe's (1991) or Lawson's (1992a).
According to Lawson, Mrs Thatcher was effectively sold the idea of

Table 4.2   The 1981 Budget (figures are on an indexed basis)

	£ billion
Estimated PSBR outcome, 1980/81*	13.5
Expected PSBR, 1981/82 before Budget measures	14.5
Effect of Budget measures:	
Non-indexation of income tax allowances and thresholds −1.9	
Increase in excise duties above indexation −1.2	
Oil tax increase and other −1.2	
Expenditure changes +0.3	
Total impact of Budget	−4.0
Forecast PSBR, 1981/82	10.5
Actual outcome	8.6

*   Final outcome £12.5 billion.

Source: Lawson (1992a, p. 96)

higher taxation, in return for a (two percentage points) reduction in the minimum lending rate. It was basically Walters who had advised the prime minister that monetary policy was too tight and fiscal policy too loose. However, the £M3 target was not being achieved, so did the reduction in interest rates signify that monetary policy would play a less significant role in the MTFS? We take up this issue in the next section.

The reaction to the Budget in political and economic circles was mixed. The so-called 'wets' in the cabinet were incensed at the contents. Writing 11 years after it was presented to a hostile House of Commons, Ian Gilmour (1992, p. 36) recalls that it was 'astonishingly perverse and bound to lead to prolonged and astronomic unemployment'. Gilmour (Lord Privy Seal), along with two other cabinet colleagues, Peter Walker (Agriculture Secretary) and Jim Prior (Employment Secretary), even considered resigning before the Budget, but decided against such a course of action, which could have damaged sterling and the economy (Walker, 1991, p. 159).

In later years, the so-called 'drys' that were to enter cabinet after the 1981 Budget, gave the decisions surrounding the Budget folklore status. Norman Tebbit (1988, p. 180) recalls that:

> Gradually it was becoming clear that she was a Prime Minister unlike any since Churchill. ... Geoffrey Howe's brave anti-infla-

tionary budget of 1981 caused a good deal of dissent within the Cabinet with several ministers openly trying to duck their collective responsibility.

Nicholas Ridley (1992, p. 168) who was a minister in the Foreign Office in March 1981, later wrote that:

> The Prime Minister is said to have hesitated much before agreeing to the famous 1981 Budget. ... It did seem pretty draconian to any outsider, including me. But I had great faith in the efficacy of a monetarist solution to the problem of inflation... . I judged the 1981 Budget to be necessary.

While some in the Conservative Party threatened to rebel unless specific fiscal proposals were watered down, the bulk of the changes appeared to attract little dissent, which is surprising considering the challenges made to traditional policy-making within the 1981 Budget.

For the opposition, Peter Shore MP (*Parliamentary Debates*, 11 March 1981, vol. 1000, col. 919) concluded that:

> I do not give a fig for the Chancellor's monetary and PSBR targets. I welcome his failure to achieve them because success in such targeting would have caused still greater ruin to British industry. ... I devoutly hope, for his own sake but still more for the sake of the country, that this is the last Budget that the Chancellor and the wayward mistress of No. 10 will present.

The most public display of shock was the letter signed by 364 economists which was sent to *The Times* on 30 March 1981. The signatories declared:

> (a) There is no basis in economic theory or supporting evidence for the Government's belief that by deflating demand they will bring inflation permanently under control and thereby induce an automatic recovery in output and employment;
> (b) present policies will deepen the depression, erode the industrial base of our economy and threaten its social and political stability;
> (c) there are alternative policies;
> (d) the time has come to reject monetarist policies and consider urgently which alternative offers the best hope of sustained economic recovery.
>
> (*The Times*, 1981)

If the Government was trying to attract credibility, this letter with signatories by five former chief economic advisers could have come as a severe setback. Yet it was precisely because those who had signed came from such entrenched Keynesian backgrounds that gave succour to the government's cause. The government would have been surprised if the Budget had led to anything other than outright condemnation! Moreover, the credibility effect of the 1981 Budget was actually reinforced as the economy showed some signs of recovery in the second quarter of the year.

Which monetary aggregates?

It is important to discuss the monetary base control (MBC) debate, and its upshot, which flared up initially in the period between 1979 and 1980, when £M3 was particularly aberrant. Some of the most influential economic advisers to Mrs Thatcher (including Professors Griffiths, Pepper and Walters), along with Friedman himself, believed that control of the money supply should stem from the monetary base. As such, these economists are sometimes referred to as 'narrow monetarists', as they urge targeting of narrow monetary aggregates.

In America, monetarists focused on the monetary base because they believed it to be the best indicator of future changes in the money stock. As Chapter Three noted, much of Friedman's (1980) evidence to the Treasury and Civil Service Committee, following the publication of the official Green Paper *Monetary Control* (Bank of England and HM Treasury, 1980), contained scathing comments and incredulous disbelief about how money supply control could proceed outside such a framework. The sharp divisions between those who believed in M0 and those who believed in broad money were to intensify as the 1980s unfolded, and are discussed in Chapter Five. The inconsistency between M0 and £M3 as monetary barometers did not help the government's case and caused monetarism to suffer a serious setback. In an interview with the author, Walters (1992) noted that he wished that the authorities had focused on the narrow aggregates in 1979.

Broad monetarist economists did, however, question the relevance of MBC to the British banking system (Congdon, 1987, p. 47), while the Bank of England (1979) expressed reservations about the use of this method in the UK, as it feared that any wild oscillations in interest rates would be detrimental to the UK economy. However, for the bulk of the monetarists, the decision that MBC would not be introduced in the UK was a clear sign that 'Thatcher's policies [were] being "sabotaged" by the bureaucracy', and rejected by the 'Bank of England as unworkable on the basis of what it regarded as good economic arguments, deeply rooted in the ... Keynesian tradition' (Laidler, 1989b, p. 1154). According to Mrs Thatcher's account (1993, p. 133), she supported such a move with Alan Walters, but was not supported by the Treasury.

On reflection, it is slightly surprising that the majority of the monetarists were denied what they considered to be the fundamental instrument of controlling the money supply by a hostile Treasury and diffident

Bank of England. If inflation did not come down, then the MBC supporters could claim that it was because a proper monetarist experiment
had not been tried, and could then apportion blame to the Treasury.

Following on from the Green Paper, the authorities prepared a series
of discussion papers, culminating in new arrangements from 5 August
1981 (Bank of England, 1980, 1981a, 1981b). The minimum lending
rate was suspended, and instead the authorities gave market forces a
greater role in the determination of interest rates.[3] The reserve asset
ratio and the cash ratio were abolished, and all banks were required to
hold half of one per cent of eligible liabilities at the Bank of England.
However, the Bank did continue to intervene in short-term smoothing
operations via funding procedures.

At the same time as the debate about MBC, the CPS suggested that
Professor Alan Walters should prepare a report on the appropriateness
of £M3, following the contradictory messages of this monetary aggregate for policy. However, Walters instead chose the politically independent Jürg Niehans of Bern University, who in due course published a
report on the alleged overvaluation of sterling (Niehans, 1981).

Niehans showed that, due to actual tightness of monetary policy,
sterling had appreciated sharply, and suggested that there should be
more active exchange-rate targeting. This idea was not entertained by
Walters (1992), who vigorously opposed such targets, yet it confirmed
to him that £M3 was, in his own words, 'not the right wagon to ride'.
He also recognized that the report would rankle within certain parts of
the government as politicians had put their faith in £M3, and the
Niehans investigation could undermine the validity of the government's
economic strategy.

Indeed, the financial secretary at the Treasury, Nigel Lawson, was
nonplussed at the outcome of Niehans's report and told the Zürich
Society of Economists that:

> the strong exchange rate, high interest rates, the tight corporate
> liquidity position and decelerating inflation – would appear to
> confirm the message of the narrow money figures: namely, that
> monetary policy has indeed been tight. Unfortunately, it is not
> quite as simple as that. For the purpose of setting the annual target
> for monetary growth ... we have ... chosen broad money as the
> most useful guide.
>
> (Lawson, 1981, p. 11)

Lawson also remained firm in his belief that the government did not have
a policy for the exchange rate, which should be left to the market. For Dr
Otmar Emminger, former president of the West German Bündesbank,
this smacked of perversity. Dr Emminger's evidence to the Treasury Committee called for a simple solution – a looser monetary policy (Emminger,

1983, p. 245). However, by adopting an easier monetary policy to lower the nominal exchange rate, this might have resulted in higher inflation and a deterioration in the real exchange rate, and the authorities did not want a return to the policy dilemmas of the 1970s.[4]

The questionnaire on monetary policy (Treasury and Civil Service Committee 1980a, p. 2) placed the essence of the monetary targets versus exchange-rate debate into a very straightforward question: 'Can the exchange rate be controlled without undesirable loss of control over the appropriate monetary target?' In the 1981 Mais Lecture, Sir Geoffrey Howe's answer was part Keynes and part Friedman: 'You cannot have it both ways and also hold the exchange rate at a particular level. If any inconsistency emerges, the monetary targets have to come first' (Howe, 1981, p. 12).

Walters still claims that, from autumn 1981 to spring 1983, exchange-rate policy was not pro-active, even though it appeared that the authorities were following some form of target. When asked about this recently he said:

> I won't say for a moment that the exchange rate did not influence government policy when it so clearly did, but the proof of the pudding is really that the exchange rate fell from February 1981 (against the dollar), through to 1983. The exchange rate was fairly useful for indicating undue laxity in monetary policy.
>
> (Walters, 1992)

Yet Keegan (1989, pp. 106–7 *et seq.*) clearly illustrates two periods when an interventionist policy was being followed. The first was between autumn 1981 and summer 1982 (when the 'floating' Lawson was at the Department of Energy), and the second was between autumn 1982 and spring 1983. Interest rates were cut in the earlier period, despite the fact that £M3 was outside its target range for the 1981/82 financial year. However, a political motive may have played a far larger role in this pragmatic tilt than was acknowledged by the government at the time (or subsequently), as unemployment continued to rise and British industry struggled to regain pre-1979 output levels. In the second period, rises in interest rates reversed the previous falls. These rises should have stemmed any fall in sterling, but failed to do so, and the authorities were mindful not to increase interest rates as the election loomed. Indeed, in order to appeal to voters, monetary policy was relaxed between March and April 1983. Treasury officials, however, wanted to see exchange-rate stability and the best means of obtaining such a goal, in their opinion, was to maintain an implicit target for the pound.

Although the possibility of joining the ERM had been discussed in the first year of the Thatcher administration, it had not been considered enthusiastically by either the chancellor or the first lord of the treasury. It was only Nigel Lawson (as financial secretary) who, on 15 June 1981, attempted to raise the issue with Howe (Lawson, 1992a, p. 111). In a later memorandum, Lawson claimed that:

> [We are] receiving increasing evidence of the weakness of £M3 as a reliable proxy for underlying monetary conditions, without any greater confidence being able to be attached to any of the other monetary aggregates. This clearly strengthens the case for moving over to an exchange-rate discipline.
>
> (Lawson, 1992a, p. 112)

While Howe was first unconvinced by Lawson's argument, Thompson (1996, pp. 25–6) offers evidence that by autumn 1981, the chancellor was becoming seriously interested in ERM entry. According to a non-attributable interview from a Treasury insider, Thompson has even suggested that in January 1982 the UK was only ten days away from joining the ERM. If this is true, it lends weight to Keegan's earlier argument. Indeed, the Budget of 1982 marked an important change in emphasis on the exchange rate, with a statement in the *Financial Statement and Budget Report* (HM Treasury, 1982, p. 14) that:

> The exchange rate is a route through which changes in the money supply affect inflation. It can also be an important influence on financial conditions. External or domestic developments that change the relationship between the domestic money supply and exchange rate may therefore disturb the link between money and prices, at least for a time ... they are a reason why the Government considers it appropriate to look at the exchange rate in monitoring domestic monetary conditions and in taking decisions about policy.

Fforde (1983, p. 208) also offers a fascinating view from inside the Bank of England on the discussions over sterling and the monetary aggregates during this period. He noted that:

> it is clear that we pay close attention to the exchange rate when taking policy decisions, in particular it was clear last autumn ... that a further depreciation of sterling would have been most unwelcome to the UK authorities ... although the behavioural characteristics of the exchange rate, as an intermediate target, can be as tiresome as those of a monetary aggregate, its political economy is much superior.

There was also a change in emphasis by Lawson on the rules versus discretion issue in 1982, which seemed to signify a more pragmatic approach to monetary targets. Thus: 'If, on the other hand, the discretion is being exercised by those whose commitment to the policy, and to the overriding need to maintain financial discipline, is beyond doubt, then there is no cause for such misgivings' (Lawson, 1982, p. 5).

Perhaps it is unsurprising that the 1982 Budget also brought into play two new monetary targets for M1 and PSL2 (private sector liquidity, second definition). This certainly did not square with the single-track monetarism of the late 1970s and early 1980s. If their introduction was the official acknowledgement that £M3 could not tell the full monetary story, then policy-makers were walking on the fence between abandoning the monetarist strategy on the one hand, and keeping some elements as a token gesture to the monetarist supporters on the other. Such 'pragmatic monetarism', as this new strategy was called in the literature (Smith, 1987), was the first stage in the dismantling of an experiment which was finally brought to a close in 1985.

Inflation control and overfunding

This section will discuss in more detail how the monetary aggregates were regulated between 1979 and 1983. As indicated in the previous section, the government began to select different target variables from an early stage in the history of the MTFS. Did this mean that £M3 was redundant in the strategy once it had achieved some success? Moreover, given the fall in inflation from 1980, was the monetarist experiment vindicated?

Unfortunately, these questions do not have straightforward answers. As we have seen throughout this chapter, there was something of a shift from such bold statements as 'the control of the money supply will over a period of years reduce the rate of inflation' (HM Treasury, 1980, p. 16), made at the start of the monetarist experiment. Additionally, the authorities became disillusioned with attempting to keep the growth of £M3 within the target ranges, and this led to the introduction of other monetary targets. Moreover, the authorities made greater use of a technique known as overfunding in the early 1980s to achieve the money supply targets, and this had begun to attract criticism by the mid-1980s. The intention of this section is to consider some of these points in more detail.

In his autobiography, Lawson (1992a, p. 72) recalls that before the 1980 Budget, he was asked by a group of senior Treasury officials to forecast what inflation would be over the medium term:

> Never one to resist a challenge, I scribbled down an illustrative path, culminating in 5 per cent in the final year (1983/84). Inflation at the time of our discussion stood at virtually 20 per cent. With the exception of Terry Burns, they all thought I had taken leave of my senses. ... In fact, inflation turned out to be slightly below 5 per cent in 1983/84.

Considering that inflation fell from 22 per cent in May 1980 (measured on the RPI basis) to 4 per cent in April 1983, it would seem to confirm that the government's economic strategy was on track, and that Lawson's reputation as an economic forecaster was assured.

Given the preceding debate in the last section over the initial set-backs to the monetarist experiment, the fall in inflation was excellent news for the monetarists. While admitting that 'from an historical perspective the cost of controlling inflation has been appalling', Congdon (1982a, p. 14), writing at the time of the Falklands conflict in May 1982, noted:

> By chance the timing of the landing in San Carlos Bay coincided almost exactly with that of the announcement of the April retail price index. It showed a 9.4 per cent rise in the previous 12 months. The Government has achieved one of its symbolically most important objectives – single-figure inflation. Over the two years to the general election the rate of price increases is likely to decelerate further.

However, there were a number of economists who questioned whether the fall in inflation from 1980 was due to the monetarist policy. In particular, Beckerman (1985), Beckerman and Jenkinson (1986) and Rowlatt (1987) all claimed that the slow-down in inflation could be explained by the fall in world commodity prices. A more recent attempt to account for price inflation between 1971 and 1992 concluded that world inflation and import prices had a significant role to play, but emphasized that it 'neither confirms nor contradicts a monetarist analysis of the inflationary process' (Soteri and Westaway, 1993, p. 86).[5]

Although it is not the intention of this study to test the empiricism of the monetarist arguments via econometrics, nor to dwell upon the nexus between the rate of growth of the money supply and the rate of change in prices, we should note that there is no available evidence to support the view that officials abandoned the monetarist strategy because they thought that the answer to controlling inflation was to be found in worldwide price falls. In fact, quite the opposite view was taken by Lawson in a speech which he gave to the Lombard Association in 1986. Speaking some six months after he had effectively abandoned the monetarist experiment, Lawson argued that lower inflation had resulted entirely from the government's economic strategy, and that it was 'not at all the fortuitous gift of some global fairy godmother' (Lawson, 1986, p. 15).[6] The ending of the monetarist experiment was due to other factors which will be discussed at length in Chapter Five.

According to Christopher Johnson (1991a, p. 69), the question of why inflation fell faster in the UK than other industrial countries in the early 1980s and then rose before every other country in the latter part of the decade had 'everything to do with British policy'. He notes that the main success of the MTFS was on the fiscal side, and that the 'MTFS was weakened by its shaky foundations in monetary theory' (C. Johnson, 1991a, p. 74). But how did the MTFS marry together fiscal and monetary policy and why did monetary policy undermine the MTFS?

To consider these questions, we need to examine two things in more detail. Firstly, the credit counterpart approach to the money supply which we mentioned in Chapter Three. Secondly, how the monetary targets were selected. By exploring these two areas we can begin to account for why Nigel Lawson later dismantled the monetarist strategy.

When targets were first adopted for broad money in 1976, the monetary authorities sought to control this aggregate by combining fiscal policy, interest rates and funding policy. In short, the authorities approached the question of monetary control from 1976 in terms of the credit counterparts to M3. In the credit counterpart approach, the change in £M3 equals the public sector borrowing requirement *minus* net purchases of public sector debt by the non-bank private sector, *plus* the change in bank lending to the private sector, *less* any increase in external and foreign currency finance, *less* increases in the banks' net non-deposit liabilities (Bank of England, 1984b). Even though this is strictly an accounting identity, how the PSBR is financed has three implications for the growth of broad money.

First, 'full funding' is said to occur if the PSBR is equal to sales of public sector debt to the private sector and overseas plus any external flows to the public sector. Second, 'overfunding' is where the authorities sell more government debt than is needed to fund the PSBR. Finally, 'underfunding' is where the authorities sell less government debt than is needed to fund the PSBR. Figure 4.2 shows how the PSBR was funded in the UK from 1970 to 1988.

We also need to note that there is a 'narrow' and 'wide' definition of funding. Until 1984/85, the narrow definition was used to assess the funding position. This excluded the external financing element from any assessment of whether the PSBR was over- or underfunded. The wide definition (used when discussing full funding in the preceding paragraph) includes external finance of the public sector. Following the announcement by Chancellor Lawson in his October 1985 Mansion House speech, the broad definition was used from the year 1985/86.

We now need to consider how the funding rule was applied for the period between 1979 and 1983. Due to the thirty-year rule and the Official Secrets Acts, complete sets of forecasts for the counterparts of £M3 are not yet available. However, Cobham (1989a) has constructed data sets which, despite their speculative nature, shed some light on the assumptions behind the £M3 targets.

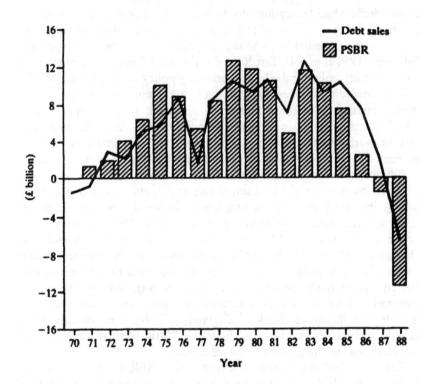

4.2   Funding the PSBR, 1970–88 (£ billion)

Source: Artis and Lewis (1991, p. 186)

Table 4.3 provides a summary selection of relevant data for the years 1978/79 to 1983/84, drawn from Cobham (1989a) and Temperton (1991). Column (1) gives the £M3 target ranges, while column (2) gives the out-turn over the target period. Columns (3) and (4) assess to what extent the monetary targets were reasonable (that is, consistent with the authorities' economic and velocity forecasts) and feasible (that is, consistent with their counterpart forecasts which have been estimated by Cobham). Finally, columns (5) and (6) indicate whether the PSBR was fully funded, overfunded or underfunded during the period under discussion. This is only a summary of a more detailed breakdown of how the PSBR was financed by the private and overseas sectors between 1978/79 and 1983/84, but it will suffice for our purposes.

Between 1978/79 and 1980/81, the PSBR was either under- or fully funded on both the narrow and broad definitions. For each of these years, Cobham has suggested that the choice of monetary targets was indeed feasible in relation to the authorities' expectations for the counter-

Table 4.3   £M3 targets and other indicators, 1978/79–1983/84 (%)

Year	£M3 target range (1)	Out-turn over target period (2)	Choice of money targets		Over (–), under (+) or full (F) funding of PSBR	
			Reasonable (3)	Feasible (4)	Narrow definition (5)	Broad definition (6)
1978/79	8–12	10.5	Yes	Yes	+	F
1979/80	7–11	9.6	No	Yes	+	+
1980/81	7–11	19.1	No	Yes	+	+
1981/82	6–10	13.7	Yes	Yes	–	–
1982/83	8–12	11.1	No	Yes	+	–
1983/84	7–11	9.5	Yes	Yes	–	–

Notes:
(1)   Targets (at annual rates) for April 1978 to April 1979; June 1979 to April 1980; February 1980 to April 1981, and similarly for remaining years.
(2)   As given in *Bank of England Quarterly Bulletin, Financial Statistics*, various issues.
(3) & (4)   See text for details and explanation.
(5) & (6)   Derived from Temperton (1991).

Sources: Adapted from Cobham (1989a, pp. 48–52) and Temperton (1991, p. 66)

parts. However, the targets were unreasonable on three out of six occasions, given the forecasts of velocity growth in each year. For example, money GDP was expected to grow 3 per cent faster in 1979/80 than 1978/79, but the target range was only 1 percentage point lower than the previous year. £M3 grew within the target ranges during 1978/79 and 1979/80. There was no conflict between the exchange rate and domestic monetary policy in 1978/79, while in 1979/80 the target was achieved by the disintermediation associated with the corset. The 7–11 per cent target range was retained in the year 1980/81, even though the money GDP forecast was only one-quarter of one per cent lower than the previous year. As noted earlier, the chancellor was aware of post-corset reintermediation in this year, but the authorities decided not to tighten monetary conditions further.

From 1981/82 to 1983/84, full funding was replaced by overfunding on both narrow and wide definitions (except 1982/83 on the narrow definition). Whether the authorities intended to overfund for each of these years is a moot point: the discussion and figures presented by

Cobham (1989a, pp. 46–7) suggest that, on the basis of the credit counterparts, the authorities intended to fund fully the PSBR. However, it is more likely that due to the private sector's demand for credit, overfunding became increasingly necessary during this period (Bank of England, 1984b, p. 488).

We can now return to the broader question of how useful the monetary targets were at curbing inflation. It was argued by some that money targets would help influence inflation expectations (Lawson 1980b),[7] and the governor of the Bank of England in the 1978 Mais Lecture gave the official justification for introducing money targets. Indeed, the governor argued that monetary targets should be used for several reasons, including 'The main role ... for monetary targets is to provide the framework of stability within which other policy objectives can be more easily achieved' (Bank of England, 1978, p. 34).

Yet on the basis of Table 4.3, neither purpose would appear to be served particularly well by the money targets adopted between 1978/79 and 1983/84. For instance, it is not clear why such tight target ranges were chosen for 1979/80 or 1980/81 when they did not relate to the growth of money GDP and £M3 in the previous period or the money GDP forecast for the target period. This leads Cobham (1989a, p. 53) to note:

> it seems highly unlikely that the authorities had any serious intention of affecting inflation expectations, while the lack of relationship between the money GDP forecasts and the targets implies that the targets were a potential source of instability rather than stability.

Indeed, while the targets were hit four times out of a possible six, the frequent revisions to the target ranges at the time of each Budget did not engender confidence in the ability of the authorities to manage money.[8]

This chapter has shown that developments during the 1979–83 period fit in with first-order change as exemplified by Hall (1993). For example, there were adjustments to the settings of basic instruments every year, which arose because officials were unhappy with the results of earlier targets and because shocks to the economy required changes to be made. Secondly, while Margaret Thatcher took her role as first lord of the treasury very seriously, there was never any real attempt by her to jettison the technical advice given by her officials and to conduct macroeconomic policy on entirely her own terms. Indeed, from an early stage she was surrounded by specialists including Professors Griffiths and Walters, whom she admired for their monetarist viewpoints. Consequently, while the prime minister and chancellor had a powerful influence over the direction of policy, they could not solely conduct the monetarist experiment without the technical support of their advisers.

At the beginning of the last section, two questions were posed: was £M3 redundant in the strategy once it had achieved some success, and was the monetarist experiment vindicated? It is clear that the developments in policy after 1983 indicated that the monetarist experiment was not exonerated. Indeed, the evolution of policy between 1983 and 1986 suggested that the authorities regarded any success in policy during 1979–83 as strictly limited. Yet in some respects, it is too simplistic to say that 'monetarism' was abandoned following the false start and confusion in policy of the early 1980s. Even if policy-makers were unsettled by their monetarist experiences, Fforde (1983, p. 207) has noted:

> it would scarcely have been possible to mount and carry through, over several years and without resort to direct controls of all kinds, so determined a counter-inflationary strategy if it had not been for the initial 'political economy' of the firm monetary target.

In so far as assessing whether £M3 was the best aggregate for the task of monetary targeting, we shall have more to say on this in later chapters.

Notes

1. The *sacrifice ratio* is the amount of lost output that an economy experiences in order to reduce inflation.
2. The failure to hit the money targets could also have been due to Goodhart's Law. This 'law' states that, whenever the authorities attempt to control an indicator, its behaviour is distorted, and the efforts to use it are frustrated.
3. Since this date, the MLR has only been used twice: once during the January 1985 mini-sterling crisis; and second when sterling left the ERM in September 1992.
4. For an argument along these lines, see Maynard (1988, p. 63).
5. Soteri and Westaway (1993, p. 93) admit that 'the rate of inflation over the last five years [1988–92] has tended to be higher than can be explained' by their calculations. Perhaps the monetarist argument – that a looser monetary policy from 1987 caused the price rises of the late 1980s – has some validity. We shall return to this point in Chapter Six.
6. This reference is rather poignant when we consider Lawson's increasing concern for global price movements between 1985 and 1987 and his belief that he could stabilize currencies.
7. Sir Geoffrey Howe (1982, pp. 18–19) giving evidence to a Treasury and Civil Service Committee on the 1982 Budget, adopted a more cautionary stance in 1982: 'I think that it may have been unduly optimistic to imagine that the [monetary target] was likely to be in the forefront of the minds of actual pay bargainers ... it is the actuality of falling inflation, and the

expectation of further falls in inflation, that transmits itself into the minds of pay bargainers.'

8. In a lecture to the IFS in 1991, Sir Geoffrey Howe (1991, p. 97) recalls that he was presented with a chart when he left the Treasury in 1983. On it was a record of how the money aggregates had been within their target bands during 1982/83, 'countersigned by Peter Middleton, Terry Burns, Eddie George and Alan Walters'. Apart from this note of self-congratulation, Howe admits that he became agnostic with monetary targets.

CHAPTER FIVE

From monetarism to pragmatism: 1983–86

> It is in this context – namely, the central role of the exchange rate –
> that macroeconomic policy under the Conservatives must be judged.
> (Maynard, 1993, p. 65)

Between 1983 and 1986, the government's enthusiasm for the monetarist model quickly vanished. As we saw in the previous chapter, this had
begun during the first 18 months after the 1979 General Election, and
by the start of their second term in 1983 the pace towards pragmatism
quickened further. Whereas the experiment between 1979 to 1981 occurred against the backdrop of recession, the first stages of financial
liberalization and political attrition, both the economic and political
environment from 1983 to 1986 was far more favourable for a continuation of the monetarist experiment. Inflation continued to fall, economic growth recovered, and the Conservatives were re-elected in 1983
with a bigger majority (144 seats as opposed to 44 in 1979). The only
bleak spot was the rise in unemployment which was unabated throughout the 1979–86 period.

Why did the Conservative government abandon its economic strategy
in this latter period, when it had passed through the severe turbulence
of the early 1980s with only minor casualties?

With hindsight, there were two big problems for the monetarist strategy throughout the 1980s. The first we touched upon earlier, namely
the problems associated with trying to control money as restrictions on
money lending were being lifted from 1979. This first phase of financial
liberalization was followed by a series of measures throughout the
1980s which made it far easier for the public to obtain credit than at
any other time in British history.

The second problem with the monetarist strategy concerned the
exchange rate. This study argues firmly that the conflicts which arose
over exchange-rate management should be seen as central to any
account of the decline in British monetarism. Given a choice over
pursuing money supply targets or tracking the exchange rate, the
former option was vigorously defended by Chancellor Howe in 1981,
as was noted in Chapter Four. Yet as this chapter makes clear, following the exchange-rate crisis of January 1985, the latter option was
favoured when, under a new chancellor, 'benign neglect [of the ex-

change rate] is not an option' (*Parliamentary Debates*, 19 March 1985, vol. 75, col. 785).

This chapter expands on some of these initial thoughts, and will suggest that the rise in unemployment, the problems with the exchange rate and the dissatisfaction with existing monetary aggregates led to the abandonment of the monetarist strategy.

The unsuccessful policy: unemployment

Between 1983 and 1986, one of the Thatcher government's biggest problems was the inexorable rise in unemployment. It could be argued that this was a bigger problem between 1979 and 1981, with the recession and labour-shedding in Britain's manufacturing base. Perhaps it was easier in the earlier period for ministers to exculpate themselves from the steep rise in unemployment and to blame the recession as the cause. In this section, we explain how government ministers defended their attitude and policies towards unemployment between 1983 and 1986 when growth replaced recession. It will become apparent that the government attempted to defuse criticism of its approach to unemployment on two broad fronts: by providing more training places and by arguing that inflation control would eventually lead to employment creation.

The general trend of unemployment for five OECD countries over the last 20 years is shown in Figure 5.1. It will be recalled from Table 2.5 that the UK's unemployment trend was upwards by 1970. Between 1970 and 1979 unemployment roughly doubled in the UK and then *more than doubled* between 1979 and 1982. From 1982 it rose more slowly, stabilizing in 1985/86 at 11.2 per cent, before returning to its 1980 level by 1990. Yet far from promising government action along traditional Keynesian lines, Nigel Lawson (1984a, p. 2) in his 1984 Mais Lecture declared that the objective of macroeconomic policy was to conquer inflation: 'And it is the creation of conditions conducive to growth and employment, and not the suppression of price rises, which is or should be the objective of microeconomic policy.' The considerable amount of public comment which this lecture achieved might seem surprising, given the practical demonstration by the Thatcher government of such a credo from a very early stage. But it attracted such interest for two reasons.

First, it was a restatement of the government's approach to the conduct of economic policy. Why this should have been necessary is interesting. Perhaps Nigel Lawson wanted to make clear that he was as committed a 'monetarist' as his predecessor. Alternatively, perhaps the

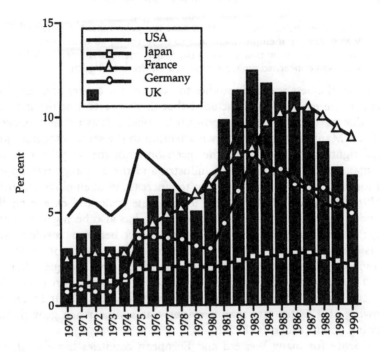

5.1 Unemployment for five OECD countries, 1970–90 (%)

Source: Layard, Nickell and Jackman (1994, pp. 134–6)

chancellor wished to make it clear that, in spite of the recovery, the government did not propose any 'job-creation' measures on traditional Keynesian lines. Ironically, Lawson's monetarism was not as zealous as his predecessor's, and became considerably less so within six months.

The second reason was that this speech turned the post-war consensus once and for all on its head. At the time, there were many who accused the government of standing idly by and watching unemployment rise to levels not seen since the early 1930s. There were even those who argued that the Thatcher government was the sole cause of the sharp rise in unemployment. Yet even the sternest critics of the Thatcher government later realised that 'The policies pursued by them did not aim deliberately to create mass unemployment (they believed such mass unemployment to be politically fatal) but the issue was now seen in a new light' (Tomlinson, 1994, p. 261). Writing at the time, Beckerman (1985, p. 2) noted that:

> Anecdotal evidence about individual firms, plus the stark fact that inflation was slowing down, plus the view that mass unemployment must surely smash the power of labour and induce the 'breath

of realism' in the labour market that the government maintained
was necessary if employment was to be restored, all made it easier
to accept the view that as far as the wage–unemployment relationship was concerned we were now in a different ball game.

One of the best academic studies to examine the causes of unemployment in the early 1980s concluded that three-quarters of the increase
was due to the Thatcher government's policies (Layard and Nickell,
1985a). Many writers have drawn attention to the severe monetary and
fiscal tightening of 1979–81, the recession from the oil price rise, the
'de-manning' of manufacturing industry and the exchange-rate appreciation, all of which contributed to the increase in unemployment from
1979[1] (Maynard, 1988). Over a longer time scale and extending the
scope of the problem into Europe, attention has also been given to real
wage inflexibility (Casson, 1983), the conflict between 'insiders' and
'outsiders' (Flanagan, 1988), and the endemic problem of hysteresis
(Lawrence and Schultz, 1987). One author has recently argued that the
trend increase in unemployment in many European countries over the
last two decades has been inevitable, given that the labour force was
growing at a faster rate than previously at a time when growth was
slowing down (Aldcroft, 1993b).

Evidence for many Western and European countries has also shown
how unemployment is related to the real wage (Layard and Nickell,
1985b; Artus, 1984). When we consider the relationship between wage
rigidity, the 'non-accelerating inflation rate of unemployment' (NAIRU)
and unemployment, we can gain a better understanding of the inefficient
labour market in the UK, at least for the early 1980s. The wage explosion
in the 1970s was certainly worst in the UK, where the incompatibility
between high employment in manufacturing and high real wages was
reflected in the rising inflation rate throughout the period. However, the
classical view of the labour market did not seem to work in practice up to
1986, namely that rising unemployment would increase the flexibility of
the real wage. This can be explained by two factors.

First, studies have shown that a massive rise in unemployment is
required to achieve a significant fall in the real wage. Some authors
have even shown that the *more* unemployment there is, the *less* real
wages become responsive (Carruth and Oswald, 1986). Second, the
substantial increase in the NAIRU since 1979 has meant that expanding
aggregate demand to increase employment will ultimately lead to an
increase in inflation. Conversely, a further decline in the rate of inflation
would require a further rise in unemployment.

Maynard (1988, pp. 126–7) is one writer who has sought to explain
the rise in the NAIRU through the 'insider/outsider' theory. He argues
that insiders gained higher real wages without losing their jobs to the

outsiders because they had trade unions and employers on their side. The long-term unemployed from this latter group eventually become demoralized and deskilled, and effectively withdraw from the labour force. Only the short-term unemployed have an impact on settlements, so the trade-off between inflation and unemployment applies to these people only and not to the long-term unemployed. From this, it can be seen how short-term unemployment would have to be increased to bring inflation down: as the proportion of the long-term unemployed in the total rises, the influence of unemployment on the real wage and inflation declines – in other words, the NAIRU rises.

Maynard provides empirical evidence that this occurred when examining the long-term unemployment rate between 1979 and 1986. The number of men who were unemployed for more than 12 months rose by 759 000, while those unemployed for more than 24 months rose by 522 000. The proportion of total unemployment represented by those unemployed for more than a year rose from 29 per cent to nearly 55 per cent.

Margaret Thatcher's first autobiography contains few references to unemployment, but she does note that at press conferences in the run-up to the 1983 General Election, ministers were forced on the defensive as they attempted to convince the electorate that unemployment should be seen in the 'new light' which Tomlinson noted above (Thatcher, 1993, p. 292).

However, what is surprising, in the written accounts of both Margaret Thatcher and Nigel Lawson, is the lack of emphasis given to the NAIRU. As far back as January 1985 on the Channel Four programme *A Week in Politics*, Mrs Thatcher was asked by Peter Jay about the natural rate of unemployment (recalled in Smith, 1987, p. 122):

> Monetarist economists again believe in something called the natural rate of unemployment, which is supposed to be the rate at which inflation stops or ceases to accelerate. Now do you think that we, Prime Minister, with all-time record unemployment figures this week, have yet reached that natural rate, even though inflation is still proceeding sufficiently to halve the value of money every fifteen years?

Mrs Thatcher's reply was surprising, given her penchant for Friedman: 'It's not a doctrine to which I've subscribed. ... I used to look at it, I used to look at it and not adopt it. It's a theory to which I've never subscribed.'

Nigel Lawson refers to the NAIRU only once in his autobiography, and then it is relegated to a mere footnote:

> Some economists would say that during my period as Chancellor, unemployment started off above the so-called NAIRU and ended

up below it. ... But since we do not have much idea of what the
NAIRU is, I do not find it a helpful concept.

(Lawson, 1992a, p. 435)

Given the enormous amount of political rhetoric delivered on the
subject of 'pricing oneself out of work', and the voluminous literature
and academic attention that had been devoted to the NAIRU, it may
seem rather odd that a prime minister and a former chancellor could
both dismiss so readily a concept that had played a central part in the
monetarist cannon. Coupled with other developments in policy from
1985, it suggests that the government continued to shift from its earlier
dogmatic views on economic policy-making.

The 1984 Mais Lecture did not mark a change in government policy
on unemployment. This was reflected in the emphasis given to
microeconomic policy and the word 'conditions' from the lecture. Given
the creation of a stable inflation environment (as a result of sound
monetary and fiscal policies) the *conditions* would then be in place for
growth and employment creation. It was then up to individuals to help
themselves into work, assisted by government reforms of the 'supply
side' of the economy.

Indeed, the Conservative government believed that a number of supply-side problems had led to unemployment: skills shortages, an excessive ratio of benefits to wages, too much taxation of employers and
employees and a high union density. While some of the reforms introduced between 1983 and 1986 appeared as if they were designed to
appease the political right, their aim, *pari passu*, was to reduce rigidities
in the labour market.

In May 1982, a House of Lords committee (1982) recommended that
the government should introduce a series of job creation measures.
While the government balked at the estimated cost (some £5 billion), it
did begin to introduce a series of special employment and training
schemes.

Table 5.1 summarizes the numbers covered by such schemes between
1981 and 1987. Between 1981 and 1982 there was a 57 per cent
increase in numbers taking up special employment and training schemes,
which increased by a further 28 per cent, 1.2 per cent, 1.4 per cent, 9.4
per cent and 7.5 per cent for the years 1982/83, 1983/84, 1984/85,
1985/86 and 1986/87, respectively. Thus the government could point to
the figures and claim that by 1983, there had been an over 100 per cent
increase in the number of participants from 1981. However, even after
a report by the Employment Committee of the House of Commons
(House of Commons, 1986) called for a greater emphasis on long-term
unemployment, critical studies have continued to argue that many of

Table 5.1 Number covered by special employment and training schemes in Great Britain, 1981–87 (December each year, 000s)

	1981	1982	1983	1984	1985	1986	1987
Community Programme	24	32	115	130	174	248	221
Young Workers Scheme	0	130	105	63	57	2	0
Youth Opportunities Programme	240	260	25	0	0	0	0
Youth Training Scheme	0	0	290	340	329	340	417
Job Release Scheme	54	77	88	79	48	27	19
Enterprise Allowance Scheme	0	2	20	39	52	74	96
New Workers Scheme	0	0	0	0	0	31	19
Jobstart Allowance	0	0	0	0	0	0	4
Total	318	501	643	651	660	722	776

Source: Trinder (1988, p. 18)

the special schemes introduced did not adequately address the skills shortfall of many young people (Gregg, 1990; Trinder, 1988).

Although it has not been the intention to cover all the issues surrounding unemployment, this section has provided a basic account of the policy difficulties facing the Conservatives. The task for the Thatcher government of the mid-1980s was to try to persuade their critics that they did not want to be judged on the success or failure of a macroeconomic policy to ameliorate unemployment, because at the macroeconomic level, they did not believe that they had the solution to the problem. Rather, the Conservatives wanted to silence their critics by setting in place macroeconomic conditions which would allow the establishment of sustained non-inflationary growth.

Leaving aside any long-term pronouncements on the success or failure of the 1980s microeconomic policies (which are worthy of separate investigation), it is time to account for the problems associated with the exchange rate in more detail.

Problems with sterling

From 1982 onwards concerns were expressed by monetary officials at the high level of the exchange rate, and disquiet grew outside the Treasury as political minds turned towards a General Election in 1983. It was even suggested by the government's chief economic adviser that a fall in the pound would not be seen as a monetarist policy retreat. Sir Terence Burns's (1982, p. 12 *et seq.*) evidence on the 1982 Autumn Statement to the Treasury Select Committee was a clear indication that the government recognized that manufacturers were having difficulty in coming out of the recession, and were being forced to compete with an inappropriate exchange rate. Events between 1982 and 1985 (particularly during July 1984 and January 1985) began to encourage Chancellor Lawson to shift away from money targets to exchange-rate targets.

For about 12 months following the 1983 General Election, foreign exchange intervention was minimal and officials obtained some stability in economic policy. Unfortunately, this benign position did not last. By July 1984 sterling's effective index had fallen to 78 (1975 = 100), which resulted in interest rates rising by almost three percentage points between Monday 9 July and Thursday 12 July. The causes of this increase were three-fold.

The first explanation can be found in the rapid rise of the dollar between 1983 and 1984. Both years witnessed a rapid pace of economic growth in the USA, accompanied by a loose fiscal policy (and large budget deficit) and a gradual tightening of monetary policy (particularly between May and July 1984). Secondly, the financial markets became worried about the miners' strike, which had begun on 8 March 1984, and the prospect of a national dock strike. Finally, the £M3 figures for June 1984 showed an upward jump of 1.7 per cent, which increased nervousness within the City.

While the Bank of England had seen the unease build in the markets during June, its response was to issue a statement on the twenty-fifth of that month designed to play down the fears that interest rates would be raised. This proved to be ineffective: by 9 July this call for calm was replaced with direct action and base rates were increased by 0.75 points as the dock strike was called and the money supply figures released; a 2-point rise on top of this on 12 July came as the Bank of England sought to steady the market further.

By the end of November rates had fallen to where they been in early July, notwithstanding a weak pound and broad money continuing to grow at the top of its target range. Indeed, the reason why rates were cut in November is puzzling, given these two developments. In his autobiography, Lawson (1992a, p. 466) acknowledges that he had misgivings about advice from the Treasury that interest rates could be cut, 'based partly on a general sense that we were being imprudent, but more particularly because sterling was continuing to slide – something to which I felt the Treasury mandarins gave too little weight'.

If Lawson was concerned with the prospect of a sterling slide, he could have vetoed the decision to cut interest rates. Perhaps the reason for not disagreeing with official advice from the Bank and the Treasury was that narrow money was now the chancellor's prime concern: M0 was in the centre of its target range. Moreover, if Lawson believed that credibility could be gained if attention were focused on the exchange rate the next episode involving the exchange rate which occurred in January 1985, was a clear sign of the growing contradictions in the government's economic strategy.

The ambiguities over exchange-rate policy reached their zenith on Friday, 11 January 1985, when Mrs Thatcher's press secretary remarked to a weekly meeting of journalists that the government would be unconcerned if parity with the dollar were reached. In reality, the Treasury, Bank, prime minister and chancellor were not prepared to see the pound slide on the foreign exchange markets, and contacted Sunday newspapers to deny reports to the contrary. Their joint statement came too late to halt the pound's slide to $1.10 at one point on Monday, 14 January. It had only been the *Observer* (1985) that had correctly reported the government's concern and its intention to raise interest rates if the situation deteriorated.

The 1985 exchange-rate crisis had numerous origins. It is clear that the London markets had become jittery by early January following rumours that the chancellor was proposing £3 billion of tax cuts for his March Budget. These stories stemmed from signs of broad monetary laxity which have been outlined earlier and which added to an overall lack of confidence in the government's monetary policy. Undoubtedly, the most important cause of the sterling crisis was, however, the confusion in the government's economic policy.

In all fairness to Lawson, the confusion between Numbers 10 and 11 Downing Street over the government's plans for the exchange rate was caused by a genuine misunderstanding between the prime minister and her press secretary. Equally, though, if Lawson had been more explicit about his intentions for the exchange rate, then the situation would not have assumed the political consequences that it did. Foreign exchange markets become jittery over confusion in governmental policy and, faced with the conflicting reports from the Treasury and the prime minister's press office, chose to believe the latter.

The MTFS of 1980 had made no reference to the exchange rate as a monetary indicator, and Lawson's attitude was expressed vividly in 1983 when he retorted to a Treasury Select Committee's second question:

> We decided right from the beginning not to have an exchange-rate target whereas we have always had monetary targets. Equally, we have always taken the exchange rate into account trying to assess the underlying financial and monetary conditions ... that is a summary of the position as it always has been and as it remains.
>
> (Lawson, 1984b, p. 2)

In private correspondence with the author in January 1992, Lawson claimed that there was a 'gradual increase in the importance attached to the exchange rate' (Lawson, 1992b). Later on in his evidence to the Treasury Select Committee, Lawson wavered and claimed that 'we are not indifferent to the exchange rate', believing that any sterling misalignment then (late 1983) was 'something of a metaphysical question' (Lawson, 1984b, p. 3).

Yet when the pound began its downward slide in January 1985, the chancellor saw little problem in telling another Treasury Select Committee that sterling was undervalued 'against the dollar and therefore against the basket of currencies because that is heavily weighted to the dollar' (Lawson, 1985a, p. 9). Moreover, in his Mansion House speech of 18 October 1984, a few months after the July hike in interest rates, Lawson was careful to rehearse the 'standard Treasury line' for his audience, even though he now admits that it was 'fiction' (Lawson, 1992a, p. 464):

It is the monetary aggregates that are of central relevance to judging monetary conditions and determining interest rates. That has always been our policy and it remains so. We take the exchange rate into account when its behaviour suggests that the domestic monetary indicators are giving a false reading, which they are not. Provided monetary conditions are kept under firm control, excessive movements, whether in the money or exchange markets in response to outside influences, will tend to correct themselves relatively quickly.

(Lawson, 1984c)

While Lawson's candid admission that these four sentences are fictitious might not excite much interest among some economists now, several years after the event, we cannot dismiss them lightly. For instance, we have noted that the financial markets in January 1985 saw the inconsistencies in government policy, and by the end of the year several monetarist economists began to register concern about the direction of the government's economic policy.

The few economists who did see through Lawson's speeches during this period, and predicted that the economy would suffer from poor direction, were remarkably perceptive. The economists (mainly the broad monetarists) who understood the implications of Lawson's actions were at first accused of scaremongering by mainstream economists, whose warnings were largely ignored by the monetary authorities and the chancellor of the exchequer. The irony was that when the apologies did arrive from those responsible for policy errors from 1985 onwards, they gave little credit to the broad monetarists: moreover, the authorities continued to make mistakes in policy based on an incorrect understanding of what had gone wrong in the first half of the 1980s!

There were three legacies of the January 1985 débâcle that shook Lawson and firmly shifted the policy balance in favour of exchange-rate targets. The first legacy was the review on whether Britain should go into the ERM. The second was when Lawson became drawn into 'global' meetings to bring stability to the international currency markets. The third legacy was the abandonment of monetarism later on in 1985. The first two legacies will be discussed in the remainder of this section, while the third will be reserved for the final section.

When Sir Alan Walters (1992) was asked about the mini-sterling crisis of 1985, he suggested that it could not really have been avoided, but policy confusion could have been minimized:

There was certainly confusion over the rationalization of policy. The view that is put that 'can we stand idly by while the pound falls?', well, you *can* stand idly by if you have your monetary conditions right. You have to have great confidence, and of course, the chancellor ... was switching over to becoming an exchange-rate targeter, above all, his enthusiasms for the ERM waxed above everything. By November of that year, he was convinced of the ERM.

When asked whether policy-makers had realized by 1985 that theoretically a truly floating pound was ideal with a money supply target, but in practice it was far better to have a (dirty) managed exchange rate and less firm monetary rules, Sir Alan replied:

> I think it was all mixed up with the EMS issue, because the EMS issue was fought out in 1985, as indeed it was in 1981. I think that they [the policy-makers] formed a view then that they should have an exchange-rate-targeting regime if they intended, as the policy was ultimately to join the ERM. But, motives differed among the people concerned. Motives are difficult to discern and difficult to understand.
>
> (Walters, 1992)

Trying to disentangle the EMS issue is, as Sir Alan hints, rather messy. We can at least gauge the motives and desires of the main protagonists, even if the Treasury's remain clouded in secrecy.

For instance, Nigel Lawson's interest in joining the ERM grew steadily from 1981, although it was not until 11 January 1985 that there was an internal Treasury meeting on the issue (Lawson, 1992a, p. 484). It was rather ironic that the subject of this meeting – whether sterling should be placed back into a fixed exchange-rate system – was held against the backdrop of the run on the floating pound. But was it timely?

In her account, Margaret Thatcher acknowledges that she agreed to a seminar (which was held on 13 February 1985) where the issues over membership could be discussed further. However, she disagrees with the four reasons listed in Lawson's account in favour of joining, namely: that the markets were unclear about the government's exchange-rate policy; that many Conservative MPs wanted closer union with Europe; that it would provide a discipline on MPs overspending and borrowing; and that £M3 was becoming 'increasingly suspect as a monetary indicator' (Lawson, 1992a, p. 488). For Margaret Thatcher, who 'was not convinced on any of these counts, with the possible exception of the last' (Thatcher, 1993, p. 695), the timing of entry was not right.[2] This also happened to be the consensus at the February meeting.

When considering Walters' assertion that by November Lawson was 'hooked' on the ERM, we should add that, by that date, both the Bank and the Treasury were in favour of it, and by the end of the year Samuel Brittan was supporting entry (Brittan, 1985).[3] Thompson has commented that the conversion of the senior officials reflected the dominance of Lawson and his views within the Treasury. According to a former senior official:

> If he says, I want to join the ERM, you talk about it to him, all the
> rest of it, but you're not going to say no, you don't think so.
> You've got to try and help him do it. ... He was a permanent
> problem from then on. He basically lost interest in the way we
> were running economic policy and proceeded to try to run it in a
> different way, based primarily on the exchange rate.
>
> (Thompson, 1996, p. 46)

The support from the Bank and the Treasury had become clear at a
meeting between all the monetary officials, the chancellor, the foreign
secretary and the prime minister on 30 September 1985. This second
meeting in eight months did little to persuade Margaret Thatcher of the
merits of membership, and it was left to a wider ministerial meeting in
November to consider a list of objections which had been raised in both
meetings.

As William Keegan recounts (1989, p. 181), a vote was taken at the
November meeting on whether to enter the ERM. Mrs Thatcher turned
to Lord Whitelaw (the deputy prime minister): 'He said: "All seven of
your advisers have voted 'aye'." "Yes," she said, echoing Abraham
Lincoln, "Ayes seven, noes one, the noes have it."'

The prime minister's views were distinctly coloured by Sir Alan Walters
who, although never present during the ERM meetings in 1985, had
argued quite forcibly in his 1986 book (via the now notorious 'Walters's
Critique') of the shortcomings of the ERM (Walters, 1986, pp. 126–
7).[4]

The Plaza meeting of 1985 and the Louvre Accord of 1987 were the
most infamous of several attempts by Lawson to become a central
player on the world's currency markets and to reduce global trade
imbalances. Lawson (1992a) provides a detailed chronicle of these epi-
sodes in his autobiography, and it would be unproductive to dwell at
length on the history of these meetings.[5] The essential facts are as
follows.

On 17 January 1985, the Group of Five (G5) finance ministers committed themselves to co-ordinated intervention in the foreign exchange
markets when it was considered necessary. This arose from the discom-
fort experienced by some member countries following the rise in the
American dollar over the preceding eight months. On 22 September
1985 at the Plaza Hotel in New York – mainly at the instigation of
James Baker, the US Treasury secretary – the G5 finance ministers
agreed to co-operate further on currency misalignments.

By the time of the Louvre Accord on the 21 and 22 February 1987,
fears had been expressed by some countries over the slide in the dollar.
These had been made most forcefully by Germany and Japan at the
Tokyo summit in May 1986, but a year later this concern was more

widespread. Concomitantly, the communiqué issued by the G6 on the 22 February pledged further international co-operation to 'foster stability of exchange rates around current levels' (Funabashi, 1989, p. 280).

It is worth noting the change in Lawson's position by the time of the Louvre Accord in 1987 as seen by a French delegate:

> I believe that intellectually and ideologically, Mr Lawson was perhaps most reluctant in the group towards this approach [reference range]. He tended to be more skeptical. Yet there was a change in Great Britain in favor of more concerted management of exchange rate fluctuations and it developed up to the Louvre Agreement. In fact, they were anxious for stability between pound sterling and European currencies.
>
> (Quoted in Funabashi, 1989, p. 175)

From the original architect of the MTFS who had told the Newspaper Society in January 1985 that he had 'never believed in intervention in the foreign exchange market as a way of life, still less as a substitute for firm fiscal and monetary action' (Congdon, 1989b, p. 20), this decision was puzzling. Perhaps such a statement could be reconciled by arguing that in the Louvre Accord, Lawson had promised that the UK would continue to follow firm fiscal and monetary action.

However, any consistency between monetary policy in January 1985 and February 1987 was chimerical. By this latter date, Lawson was about to shadow the Deutschmark, an action which had an abstruse effect on the direction of UK monetary policy. Before this is considered, it is time to examine an issue that was an important prelude: the abandonment of monetarism in October 1985.

Whatever happened to money?

In Chapter Four, it was suggested that the initial broad monetary aggregate chosen as an intermediate target (£M3) was not conforming to official expectations from an early stage in the government's monetarist experiment. In particular, it was shown that when the government did manage to target this aggregate successfully, it was due to the overfunding of the PSBR. Some critics considered overfunding a distortion in two ways: to the monetarist experiment and to the financial system. By October 1985, the system of overfunding had been abandoned and broad money targets suspended. While this attracted little hostility from the bulk of the economics profession, a small group of monetarist critics predicted that this would have disastrous consequences for inflation in particular, and the direction of government policy in general.

This section will consider the political and economic decisions to end overfunding. It will also examine why other monetary aggregates were introduced between 1983 and 1985, and ask whether the targeting of M0 re-established credibility in the government's economic policy. The title of this section is particularly apt because, from the end of 1985, many commentators were left asking: whatever happened to the British monetarist experiment?

We begin with an examination of why Chancellor Lawson decided to introduce M0 in the Budget of 1984. In his 1983 Mansion House speech, Lawson (1983, p. 3) spoke about the experience gained by looking at both broad and narrow definitions of money. He argued that 'none of the Ms is a perfect guide to the underlying concept they seek to reflect' and that while £M3 remained an important indicator, it was unreliable as a guide for short-term interest-rate decisions. It was because of this that Lawson hinted the time had come to consider other aggregates, concluding that 'it does appear that M0 could have a more important part to play as a key indicator of the growth of narrow money'.

A review of monetary policy initiated by the Chancellor had led the second permanent secretary at the Treasury (Geoffrey Littler) to recommend joining the ERM. Lawson was nonplussed at this suggestion and, according to Thompson (1996, p. 38), he wanted to refocus policy on the money supply. Yet it was not clear what measure of the money supply Lawson had in mind. Urged on by most of the monetarists, with the notable exception of Tim Congdon, the argument that a broad monetary target should be abandoned and replaced by a narrow one was not initially accepted by Lawson, who realized that the financial markets would only accept £M3. However, Geoffrey Howe's last Budget in 1982 had set the tone with targets for M1 (a narrow definition) and PSL2. The latter was a broader aggregate than £M3, but both had attracted criticism from those who suggested that the additional targets meant that authorities were more likely to hit at least one target, and from those who complained that the markets would concentrate on the worst-performing targets (Goodhart, 1989).

In his autobiography, Lawson acknowledges that he carefully considered the credibility problems associated with introducing M0 and consulted monetary experts. Sir Terence Burns wanted NIBM1 (non-interest bearing M1); Eddie George, who was in charge of monetary policy at the Bank of England, was in favour of M2; and Gordon Pepper from the City University suggested that 'nothing short of full-blooded MBC would do' (Lawson, 1992a, pp. 452–3). When Lawson finally insisted on having a separate target for narrow money and selected M0, he did so because this aggregate seemed to be the least interest-rate sensitive.

The introduction of this target (which was not a move towards MBC), coupled with the commitment to reduce the growth of money GDP, was a gradual move to restore faith in the monetary aggregates. But did it all make sense?

As Lawson later acknowledged, M0 always lacked 'street credibility' and achieving an M0 target did not have any major effects on inflationary expectations (Lawson, 1992a, p. 457). One critic of this target neatly identified the central problem:

> I was extremely suspicious of narrow money, the new narrow money – M0, which I thought was pure black-box stuff. Many monetarists, including uncomprehending American observers, liked it because they thought it was monetary base control. All the official statements explained that it was not, but that it was an indicator and should be used as an indicator. It was cash, in public hands, used as a guide to total expenditure.
>
> (Brittan, 1994)

Consequently, the decision to give M0 the same importance as £M3 – which Lawson did in his 1984 Budget speech – was rather odd. Not only did it turn out to be hopeless at warning of the build-up of inflationary pressures from the late 1980s, but its introduction did not please many of the more technical monetarists who hankered after MBC; the financial markets who never really took to it; nor Lawson himself, who only felt obliged to introduce an additional aggregate following the contradictory messages of £M3. A more far-reaching decision, which Lawson took the following year, was to end the system of overfunding and suspend broad money targets.

The decision to end overfunding and to suspend targets for £M3 was decided over two seminars held at 10 Downing Street: the first held on 25 June 1985, and the second on 16 July. The published accounts of both Nigel Lawson's and Margaret Thatcher's private feelings on the decision to end overfunding during the summer of 1985 make interesting reading. While Nigel Lawson considered overfunding 'a cosmetic technique that created far more trouble than it was worth' (1992a, p. 460), the important decision to end it is glossed over by the former prime minister, who seems more involved in accounting for Lawson's obsession with the ERM (Thatcher, 1993, p. 696).

This is most frustrating. Indeed, Margaret Thatcher's account is the more worrying (and puzzling) of the two as it had become quite clear by 1985 that Nigel Lawson had lost all interest in pursuing any form of monetarist policy, while Mrs Thatcher still favoured using monetary targets to control inflation. Indeed, although noting that £M3 during 1985 was 'rising rather fast', Mrs Thatcher does not claim that the policy *per se* was wrong:

> Rather, since we had decided against a policy of overfunding as far
> back as 1981, the fact that it had been resumed on such a scale
> without authorization did not increase my confidence in the way
> policy in general was being implemented.
>
> (Thatcher, 1993, p. 696)

Her principle objection to overfunding is on the issue of *authority*. She does not question whether it was because this technique had been used on a regular basis since 1981 that inflation had been controlled. Indeed, in the very next sentence, she acknowledges that Tim Congdon had pointed out in 1985 that inflation would rise in the future (and Congdon based his explanation for this on the fact that overfunding had been abandoned), but offers a paradoxical conclusion: 'I do not believe that monetary policy in 1985 – or 1986 – was the main cause of the problems we were later to face' (Thatcher, 1993, p. 696).

There are two possibilities for Mrs Thatcher's sang-froid with overfunding. The first is that she did not understand why this technique was central to the operation of British monetarism. This would also explain her indifference to Lawson's decision to suspend £M3 targets. Yet she acknowledges that she had 'misgivings' about the way policy was being implemented – it is surprising that this did not extend to putting up a defence on the overfunding issue. Ironically, the second part of Mrs Thatcher's (1995, pp. 569–70) autobiography is more pragmatic about how other monetary aggregates were taken up in the 1980s, and yet she still argues that the greatest success with controlling inflation occurred between 1981 and 1986, when broad money was being targeted!

The second possibility, which connects to the above point, is that as Mrs Thatcher shared Alan Walters' preference for targeting M0, she could see little virtue in supporting a 'cosmetic technique' which was irrelevant if a narrow money aggregate was targeted. During mid-1985 most of Mrs Thatcher's advisers believed that the growth of M0 showed that monetary policy was tight (Minford, 1985b, p. 45; Thatcher, 1993). To such advisers, the argument that broad money would accelerate following the ending of overfunding was of little interest, which would have no bearing on the growth of nominal GDP.

A similar line was adopted in the official announcement to end overfunding, made by the chancellor of the exchequer on Thursday 17 October 1985. In the Mansion House speech, Lawson still seemed to accept that broad money measured the liquidity of the economy, and that 'an excessive build of liquidity ... provid[es] an undesired boost to the growth of money GDP and hence to inflation', but 'the question, however, is what is excessive' and this 'inevitably involves an element of judgement' (Lawson, 1985b, pp. 10–11). The judgement would be based on monitoring M0, the exchange rate, £M3, and 'If the performance of one indicator were to deteriorate we would need convincing evidence from the other indicators before concluding that this was acceptable' (Lawson, 1985b, p. 13).

This was an explicit announcement which made clear that rules had finally been discarded for discretion and monetarism had been relegated behind pragmatism. The final nail in the monetarist coffin was the first sentence of the fifth paragraph of the speech: 'Accordingly, we are no longer seeking to control the recorded growth of £M3 by systematic overfunding' (Lawson, 1985b, p. 15).

Lawson did not believe that the recent behaviour of £M3 or his new aggregate, M0, indicated that there was trouble ahead for the British economy. But looking at where these aggregates stood in October 1985 and claiming that there was no cause for alarm was to miss the point completely. It would only be when overfunding was abandoned that £M3 would expand and provide a guide to the economy's future. M0 could only ever show what was happening in the economy at present, and did not predict what was going to happen in the economy in the future (Congdon, 1986a). As for Lawson's penchant with the exchange rate, this flew in the face of the evidence given by Friedman (1980) to the Treasury and Civil Service Committee in 1980, and had more in common with James Tobin's pragmatism.

Eight years later, in an appendix to Chapter 36 of his autobiography (poignantly entitled 'The Myth of the Monetarist Golden Age'), Nigel Lawson (1992a) effectively blows the cover on the whole concept of overfunding as detailed (and supported) by the governor of the Bank of England in his University of Kent lecture of 26 October 1984 (Bank of England, 1984a). Perversely, while Lawson and the monetary authorities have never challenged Congdon's (1990a) devastating critique on the decision to suspend overfunding in the mid-1980s, they have not denied that higher rates of broad money growth after 1985 should have been avoided.

To draw this chapter to a close, it is worth noting Lawson's criticism of a CPS publication, *Whither Monetarism?* in 1985. In this, three monetarists analysed the 1985 Mansion House speech and concluded with their slightly different but broadly similar contributions that Lawson had abandoned monetarism (Bruce-Gardyne, Congdon and Minford, 1985). For the contributor in the volume who had argued that ignoring broad money would lead to future problems, Lawson was dismissive of the argument thus: 'For Congdon it was the downgrading of broad money which was the act of rank treason – as if the mere publication of unattained, and to all practical purposes unattainable, numerical targets had some profound significance' (Lawson, 1992a, p. 482).

Not only did this reject outright the *raison d'être* of targets which had been established on so many occasions by Conservative government ministers since 1979, but it also largely rejected John Fforde's earlier argument that although money targets might not be precisely hit, it was their credibility which was important (Fforde, 1983). After effectively dismissing broad monetary targets in his 1985 Mansion House speech, two very important questions remained. What instrument was Chancellor Lawson now going to use to control inflation, and how credible would his lodestar be?

Notes

1. However, although we should not deny the pejorative role played by overmanning in perennial declining industries such as iron, steel and ship-building, low labour and capital productivity rates eventually forced a much needed 'shake-out' of labour.
2. As is widely known, Mrs Thatcher was privately opposed to any fixing of the exchange rate. This point is amplified in Chapter 24 of her autobiography, which contains many passages which are heavily influenced by the monetarists who advised her during the 1980s.
3. Two years earlier, Samuel Brittan (1983) had been scathing of the EMS, describing it as a 'mere crawling peg'.
4. 'Walters's Critique' argues that the convergence of nominal interest rates within the EMS results in real interest rates that are perversely low in high-inflation countries where demand should be reduced and perversely high in low-inflation countries where demand could be allowed to increase.
5. An excellent behind-the-scenes account is given by Funabashi (1989).

CHAPTER SIX

The return to discretion: 1986–92

> Arguably, of course, a continuation of the monetarist policies would
> have been better than the Lawson boom and slump.
>
> (Gilmour, 1992, p. 68)

Between 1986 and 1992, the Conservative's macroeconomic and political strategy lost all semblance to its earlier vintage. The unity of purpose (Burch, 1983) which had characterized and driven policy since 1979 had all but fizzled out by the end of the 1980s, amid policy disagreements within the monetarist camp, between senior Conservative politicians over Europe, and by a series of poor Treasury forecasts which severely underestimated the state of the economy.

The internal disputes in the cabinet over policy towards Europe and economic management spilt over into the public arena with particular ferocity by 1990. Between 1986 and 1990, the number of resignations rose steeply, with the majority of these associated with economic issues. In 1989 the country lost the longest-serving chancellor of the century (Lawson) and economic adviser to the prime minister (Walters). In 1990, trade and industry secretary (Ridley), the deputy prime minister (Howe) and first lord of the treasury (Thatcher) resigned, forcing the divisions within the Conservative Party out into the public arena.

It is fair to say that any disagreements over Europe which had been suppressed from mainstream public view until 1986 – with considerable adroitness by the Thatcher cabinets – were not minimal, as is now recognized widely (Stephens, 1996). Such disputes form an important backdrop to this chapter and highlight the fragility of Mrs Thatcher's economic leadership by 1990.

There are three broad developments which will be considered in this chapter. The first section examines some of the explanations for the Lawson boom. Integral to the boom is the depreciation of sterling in 1986 and the period of 'currency shadowing' between 1987 and 1988. These are both dealt with in a separate section. The final section of this chapter will account for developments between 1990 and 1992, when we examine why entry into the ERM, with its supposed elixir of low inflation for member countries, refused to quell the British monetarists' call for a return to domestic monetarism.

Some explanations for the 'Lawson boom'

Writing on the period 1986–87 for a study on macroeconomics commissioned by the NIESR, Britton (1991, p. 75) has observed:

> The narrative of economic events from the early 1970s to the mid-1980s in Britain has been, in the main, a story of problems, difficulties, setbacks and policy failures. It is a relief, therefore, to be able to end this part of the study by describing a year or two when the economy seemed to be performing really well. The recovery in output, which appeared at one time to be faltering, instead gathered pace; unemployment at last turned down and fell very rapidly; inflation remained low. For once the British economy was admired and applauded by commentators worldwide. Even at home there was more than a hint of euphoria in the air. It did not last; but let us remember that it was good at the time!

Had Britton's account finished in 1990, rather than 1987, then the verdict on the state of the economy during Lawson's latter years as chancellor would have been far less agreeable in tone. This period has received extensive critical coverage in journal papers by the Bank of England, Treasury and NIESR, along with first-hand accounts by Lawson (1992a), Thatcher (1993) and Walters (1990a) and numerous secondary sources (C. Johnson, 1991a; Smith, 1992; Stephens, 1996). However, it is the litany of explanations given for the boom which needs to be addressed here, and it should be possible to emphasise the predominance of some over others. As in previous chapters, the emphasis will be on policy decisions and why they were taken, rather than an econometric account of economic policy-making.

It will be recalled from Chapter Three that, when the Conservatives took office in 1979, they had considered the question of economic management at some length. The central economic objective was eliminating inflation, in which 'proper monetary discipline is essential, with publicly stated targets for the growth of the money supply. At the same time, a gradual reduction in the size of the Government's borrowing requirement is vital' (Conservative Party, 1979, p. 8).

By the time of the 1985 Budget, Chancellor Lawson had shifted from this earlier position. In a passage of which the first sentence managed to upset a number of monetarists, Lawson observed:

> There is nothing sacrosanct about the precise mix of monetary and fiscal policies required to meet the objectives of the medium-term financial strategy. But this is not the year to make adjustments in either direction. The wisest course is to stick to our pre-announced path.
>
> (*Parliamentary Debates*, 19 March 1985, vol. 75, col. 786)

In his autobiography, Lawson (1992a, p. 477) claims that this was inserted because:

> Subconsciously, I may have been to some extent reflecting the received wisdom of the official Treasury, which did indeed hold, at least up to a point, that in the battle against inflation there was a choice between fiscal and monetary tightening. I did not.

Like many of Lawson's reflections on the 1980s, there is some ambiguity in these two sentences.

The Treasury has always held the view that government borrowing was unwelcome, and while policy-makers were never sure of the exact harm inflicted by budget deficits, they did recognize that higher deficits drove up the rate of interest. It is apparent, however, that Lawson did not share the Treasury view in its entirety. He notes that throughout his time as chancellor, the Treasury 'greatly exaggerated the extent to which reducing or eliminating the budget deficit could bring down domestic interest rates' (Lawson, 1992a, p. 478). Yet as Congdon (1989b, p. 22) has suggested, the analytical basis of the MTFS implied that a contracting budget deficit was essential in reducing the rate of growth of the money supply.[1] Moreover, the first paragraph in Part Two of the *Financial Statement and Budget Report, 1985/86* was at odds with Lawson's Budget statement to the House of Commons: 'The MTFS ... is designed to achieve falling inflation, with the ultimate objective of stable prices, through a progressive decline in monetary growth supported by lower public sector borrowing' (HM Treasury, 1985, p. 5).

The annual *Financial Statement and Budget Report* is the official document which sets out the government's economic strategy, and its content is heavily influenced by senior Treasury officials. From the extract given above, there does not appear to be any ambiguity in the purpose of the MTFS as envisaged by the Treasury and chancellor of the exchequer. It seems odd that Lawson introduced an element of confusion into his 1985 Budget speech and later tried to justify this by claiming that it reflected Treasury thinking, when clearly it did not.

From the brief discussion above about the 1985 Budget, it would appear that Lawson was prepared to relax fiscal policy on an *ad hoc* basis. This was not the case, however. In Lawson's (1992a, p. 73) own words, 'the fiscal side of the MTFS wore better than the monetary side'. This also seems to be the general consensus among economists (Allsopp, Jenkinson and Morris, 1991; Congdon, 1992a). Indeed, during the Budgets of 1987 and 1988, Lawson introduced two new fiscal directives: first, the '1 per cent borrowing rule' in 1987 (where a PSBR forecast for 1987/88 was given as 1 per cent of GDP); and second, a commitment made in 1988 to balance the budget over the medium term.

A view which has found its way into some accounts of this period is that the tax cuts in the Budgets of 1986, 1987 and 1988 were overgenerous and fuelled the boom of the late 1980s (see Smith, 1992). This is incorrect. Far from fiscal policy being loosened in the latter half of the 1980s, OECD calculations have shown that policy was *tightened* (Table 6.1).

Table 6.1   Indicators of fiscal stance, 1980–91 (change in general government financial balance as a percentage of GDP)

Year	Actual	Cyclically adjusted
1980	−0.1	+1.3
1981	+0.7	+2.2
1982	+0.2	+0.8
1983	−0.9	−1.2
1984	−0.6	−0.6
1985	+1.1	+0.7
1986	+0.5	−0.3
1987	+1.0	0.0
1988	+2.4	+1.7
1989	+0.1	0.0
1990	−2.0	−1.4
1991	−1.4	+0.2

Notes: + = tightening; – = loosening.

Source: Lawson (1992a, p. 810)

The tenor of Sargent's (1991, p. 87) account is that the enthusiastic announcements from government ministers that tax cuts were a way of life added to 'exaggerated expectations', with the effect that: 'the public generally became converted rather prematurely and precipitately in the 1980s to a belief in economic miracles, and literally took the credit before it was clearly due'. More recent analysis by Attanasio and Weber (1994) has tended to support the view of Sargent and also that of King (1990), by suggesting that the consumption patterns of younger cohorts in the late 1980s were influenced by expectations of continuing rapid economic growth.

Chapter Two discussed the United Kingdom's output cycle between 1950 and 1979, and it was noted that the length of each cycle in the

1950s and 1960s (from peak to peak) was roughly four years. The pre-Thatcher cycle (from the third quarter of 1973 to the second quarter of 1979) was the longest in the series and was followed by an even longer cycle, again measured from peak to peak. Between the second quarter of 1979 and the third quarter of 1988, the length of the cycle was 37 quarters. Moreover, the longevity of the upturn between 1981 and 1988 'encouraged the rash belief that the cycle had been abolished' (Martin, 1990, p. 84). It is easy to cite numerous speeches made by Chancellor Lawson during the late 1980s, which are over-bullish about the strength of the British economy. Three will suffice. First, in a speech to the Edinburgh Chamber of Commerce on 23 June 1987, Lawson (1992a, p. 804) said:

> As this upswing goes on, more and more people, at home and abroad, are realizing that what we are seeing is much more than a recovery from recession, or than the operation of the normal cyclical pattern. ... Instead of wondering whether the recovery will last, people are asking what has caused this transformation.

Secondly, in his 1988 Budget speech, Lawson told a restless House of Commons that:

> The plain fact is that the British economy has been transformed. Prudent financial policies have given business and industry the confidence to expand, while supply-side reforms have progressively removed the barriers to enterprise.
> (*Parliamentary Debates*, 15 March 1988, vol. 129, col. 993)

Finally, during the summer of that year, he told the IEA that:

> I believe there can be no doubt that the transformation of Britain's economic performance during the 'eighties, a transformation now acknowledged throughout the world, is above all due to the supply-side reforms we have introduced to allow markets of all kinds to work better.
> (Lawson, 1988b, p. 7)

In his autobiography, Lawson admits he overemphasized the extent of the supply-side improvements during the latter half of the decade, thereby fuelling 'the excessive optimism that characterized the climate of the time' (1992a, p. 632).

Yet however much 'excessive' or 'exaggerated' optimism there existed in the economy – and there is an obvious problem of measuring such an elusive concept – this alone could not generate a boom, particularly on the scale of 1986–88. Indeed, the earlier quotation from Sargent, with its dual meaning, points to a real cause of the boom, namely, the surge in consumer credit.

Many monetarists feel uncomfortable with the credit growth of the 1980s, and it is easy to see why. There was a paradox from the beginning of the decade, as the Thatcher government's emphasis on 'sound money' jarred with its commitment to deregulate the financial system. Those who supported money targets have been forced to admit that:

> The removal of controls was likely to lead to an acceleration in credit growth and faster credit growth would in turn result in higher monetary growth. In effect, the objectives of financial liberalization and monetary control were on collision course.
>
> (Congdon, 1990b, p. 7)[2]

The growing deregulation in the credit market over the 1980s (Table 6.2) made it easier for the corporate and personal sectors to borrow. As Cobham (1997a, p. 76) notes:

> Financial liberalisation ... was clearly at the very least an important permissive factor in the late 1980s' boom. Total consumer credit rose annually at rates of 17 per cent and more between 1985 and 1988, loans for house purchase increased more rapidly, while the growth of lending to industrial and commercial companies accelerated to rates of 18–20 per cent over the period 1986–88.

The association between financial liberalization and the British housing market merits a particular mention. Warning had been given by Congdon (1982b) about the diversion of housing loans into consumer expenditure in the early 1980s, which was followed by articles in the *Bank of England Quarterly Bulletin* (1982a; 1982b; 1985). In contributions to the *Financial Times* which began in 1986, Muellbauer (see 1986; 1988; 1989) argued that financial liberalization and distortions in the housing market drove up house prices. According to Muellbauer and Murphy (1990, p. 350), the surge in house prices during the mid-1980s brought about a decline in personal saving rates through wealth effects: 'With the sharp rise in house prices, residential property became more than half of personal-sector wealth. Financial liberalization allowed households to cash it in as consumer expenditure financed by borrowing.'

In a 1986 lecture to the Loughborough University Banking Centre, the governor of the Bank of England noted how financial innovation had led to changes in the financial system which in turn led to distortions in the relationship between broad money and national income. The governor suggested that:

> it is perfectly fair to ask whether in these circumstances a broad money target continues to serve a useful purpose. ... Two years ago ... I envisaged the possibility that the unpredictability of the relationship between money and nominal incomes could reach a point

Table 6.2 Main financial innovations in the UK, 1980–90 (classified by main area of direct impact, with date of major expansion/change)

Banks

- (i) automated teller machines – late 1970s, early 1980s
- (ii) banks' entry to mortgage credit market – 1981–82
- (iii) interest-bearing retail sight deposits – 1983–84
- (iv) debit cards – 1987
- (v) EFTPOS – ?

Building societies

- (i) automated teller machines – early 1980s
- (ii) end of interest-rate cartel – 1983
- (iii) use of wholesale money markets as source of funds – domestic 1983, euro 1986
- (iv) unsecured personal loans – 1986
- (v) transfer to bank/plc status – 1988–89

Money market

- (i) reduction of privileges of discount houses – 1980s
- (ii) sterling commercial paper market – 1986

Domestic capital markets

- (i) Unlisted Securities Market – 1980
- (ii) London International Financial Futures Exchange – 1982
- (iii) Stock exchange: end of dual capacity and minimum commissions, opening up of membership, move to screen market – 1986
- (iv) Third Market – 1987

International capital markets in London

- (i) fixed-rate eurobonds (origin 1960s) – early 1980s
- (ii) international equity trading – early 1980s
- (iii) swaps market – 1982
- (iv) floating-rate notes (origins early 1970s) – 1982–83
- (v) euronotes – 1984
- (vi) eurocommercial paper – 1986

Source: Adapted from Cobham (1989b, p. 248)

– as in some other countries – at which we would do better to
dispense with monetary targetry altogether.

(Bank of England, 1986d, p. 507)

Writing in the same year, Charles Goodhart examined the process of
financial innovation and monetary control during the 1980s and reached
a similar conclusion: 'In a world of rapid structural change there may
be no alternative to muddling through in a discretionary, but unrigorous,
manner' (Goodhart, 1986, p. 101).

However, the issue of financial innovation and the effects of this on
monetary policy during the 1980s cannot be dismissed so readily. For
instance, Congdon's earlier assertion – that financial liberalization and
money controls were incompatible – needs to be considered alongside
the other issue which he raises, namely, that although money is created
by credit, it is money and not credit which really matters in the final
analysis. In other words, while financial change may have led to an
increase in the money supply via faster credit growth, it is ultimately
excessive money growth which has important implications for the real
economy (see Congdon, 1986c). This ties in with Congdon's wider
arguments, discussed in Chapter Five, that the monetary effects of
credit growth during the early 1980s (particularly between 1983 and
1985) were neutralized by overfunding, while credit growth after 1985
was not.

A more rigorous approach to arguments over financial innovation
and money supply targets can be found in Cobham (1989b). He argues
that the overshooting of money targets can only be explained by unanticipated financial innovation in 1981/82 and 1986/87 (and by this later
date broad money targets had been abandoned), while for 1980/81,
1984/85 and 1985/86, overshooting can only be partly explained by
financial innovation. Moreover, for 1982/83 and 1983/84, he argues
that 'financial innovation actually facilitated their [the authorities'] at-
tainment' of money targets (Cobham, 1989b, p. 261). The conclusions
of this research (Cobham, 1989b, p. 263), that 'financial innovation
implies a need not to abandon but to modify the practice of monetary
targets', is slightly at odds with a consideration of the money supply
process given in Cobham (1991, p. 69), when it is suggested that:

> More specifically, the processes of financial innovation have ir-
> reparably blurred the boundary between money and other financial
> assets, so that any analysis of the money supply process must now
> be situated within a broader context of non-monetary as well as
> monetary assets and liabilities.

In the absence of any conclusion on this debate at this stage, it is
difficult to disagree with Gowland's (1991, p. 108) view that 'the potential impact of financial innovation on the case for monetary targets is

clearly enormous but equally clearly controversial'. Equally contentious to the debate on the Lawson boom is the role of currency depreciation and currency shadowing. This is examined below.

Depreciation and currency shadowing

Chapter Five examined the arguments within the Thatcher cabinet about the ERM, and it was observed that Nigel Lawson opposed the decision not to join the mechanism in 1985. On the day Britain actually joined the ERM, on 8 October 1990, Lawson wrote in the *Financial Times* that, had Britain joined the mechanism in 1985, 'the subsequent sharp fall in sterling in 1986 would not have occurred, and we would have avoided the levels of inflation we have today' (Lawson, 1990a, p. 17).

However, this is not the most compelling of arguments, not least because it assumes that the *only* successful policy for the UK to pursue would have been for the country to join the ERM. While there are many examples in twentieth-century British economic history where similar counterfactuals might be raised, they are invariably economic culs-de-sac. David Cobham, for instance, has commented that he found it 'impossible' to construct a model showing what would have happened to the UK had it entered the ERM in November 1985 (Cobham, 1994, p. 20).

Walters (1990a, pp. 100–101) has calculated what would have happened if Britain had joined the ERM in November 1985 at around DM3.75. Using the '4 to 1' rule (where a 4 per cent depreciation in the exchange rate is matched by a 1 per cent increase in base rates), he claims that because of the 27 per cent depreciation in the sterling/mark parity between November 1985 and December 1986, it would have been necessary to have raised interest rates from the 10 to 12.5 per cent range in this period to between 17 and 20 per cent in order to maintain sterling at around DM3.75. This would have led to a severe monetary squeeze and to a devastating recession in 1987 and 1988. While Lawson has dismissed Walters's calculations as 'spurious', his own calculations (also assuming ERM entry in November 1985) indicate that 'some increase in interest rates would almost certainly have been required' to steady sterling within the ERM (Lawson, 1992a, p. 503).

Per contra, a more detailed analysis of the 'Walters's Critique' by Pill (1996) has suggested that entry into the ERM in 1985 would not have prevented the credit boom of the late 1980s. Coupled with this, the Panglossian view expressed by Lawson and later by Howe (1994, p. 451) also looks vulnerable when earlier discussions which traced the performance of the economy after the ERM veto in 1985 suggested that

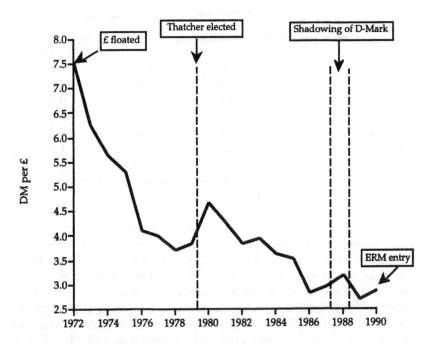

6.1 Nominal exchange rate, end years, 1972–90 (DM per £)

Source: *Bank of England Quarterly Bulletin*, various issues

the causes of the late 1980s boom are complex in nature and multi-causal in character. In short, the boom cannot be explained away simply because the United Kingdom failed to enter a semi-fixed exchange rate during the mid-1980s (Wolf, 1990). Moreover, as this section will make clear, Lawson failed to consider the decisions taken by policy-makers in the external arena (most of which were under his initiative): namely, the depreciation of 1986 and the shadowing of the Deutschmark from 1987 through to 1988. It will be argued in this section that both these occurrences contributed to the inflation of the late 1980s and were a product of the confusion in economic policy-making which followed the abandonment of monetarism.

It is important to set the context within which the depreciation of sterling occurred (Figure 6.1 provides nominal exchange rate figures since 1972). Until 1985, the United Kingdom had enjoyed an oil bo-nanza, as can be seen from Table 6.3. During the second half of the 1980s, however, the United Kingdom's income from oil fell. In the spring of 1986, oil prices had fallen considerably from their 1985 peak, and the value of oil output for 1986 as a whole averaged 2.2 per cent of GDP as against 5 per cent between 1981 and 1985.

Table 6.3   Output and price of North Sea oil

Year	Output (m. tonne)	Price (£/tonne)	Value (£bn)	% GDP
1976	12	14	0.5	0.4
1981–85	112	37	15.5	5.0
1986	128	18	8.6	2.2
1987–91	102	22	7.9	1.6
1992	91	20	9.9	1.7

Source: Robinson (1994, p. 101)

The United Kingdom had enjoyed an improvement in its terms of trade since the early 1980s, but in 1986 this was reversed (Table 6.4). As the oil price fell, the Bank of England signalled that a nominal exchange-rate depreciation was required to improve the competitiveness of the non-oil sector (Bank of England, 1986a, p. 6). This was a stance which Chancellor Lawson had taken in a lecture in 1984 (Lawson, 1992a, p. 650) and one which was endorsed by Forsyth and Kay (1980). Indeed, it was even predicted by Robinson and McCullough (1986) that a fall in oil income would lead to an expansion of manufacturing at the expense of services. As was noted earlier, while there was a reduction in the share of GDP accounted for by imports of manufactures, the current account moved into deficit after 1986.

The authorities made it clear on numerous occasions throughout 1986 that they were unconcerned with the fall in the exchange rate (Bank of England, 1986b, pp. 27–8). This was followed by a detailed passage about oil in the March Budget, when the chancellor told the House of Commons that:

Table 6.4   Terms of trade and competitiveness, 1976–92 (1985 = 100)

Year	Terms of trade (1985 = 100)	Competitiveness	
		Relative costs	Relative prices
1976	88	88	84
1981–85	100	106	101
1986	96	95	97
1987–91	100	100	104
1992	106	107	107

Source: Robinson (1994, p. 106)

> If we can survive unscathed the loss of half our North Sea oil revenues in less than 25 weeks, the prospective loss of the other half over the remainder of the next 25 years should not cause us undue concern.
>
> (*Parliamentary Debates*, 8 March 1986, vol. 94, col. 168)

Finally, the July–August depreciation of sterling was seen by the Bank of England as 'not ... sufficiently large ... to offset the beneficial effects on the near-term outlook for inflation of the fall in oil prices that has occurred over the past year' (Bank of England, 1986c, p. 333).

However, Lawson now admits that he regrets the speed at which sterling fell and wishes that he had raised interest rates higher (Lawson, 1992a, p. 651). The response by the Bank of England was to raise interest rates in January and October, when the decline in the effective exchange rate appeared too excessive. While he says that he was concerned with the weakness of sterling by September 1986, Lawson (1992a, p. 639) claims that it was 'not until the summer of 1987 that the Bank began to worry that monetary conditions may not be tight enough'.

This quotation echoes a general query Lawson raises in his autobiography, as to whether the Bank withheld information on monetary conditions occasionally. Although he dismisses this because it 'would have amounted to a dereliction of duty so grave as to be unthinkable' (Lawson, 1992a, p. 639), it is strange that Lawson mentions this. The Bank could scarcely be blamed for failing to admonish Lawson of the deleterious effects of currency shadowing, even if the ex-chancellor ignored such warnings.

Lawson also asserts in his autobiography that *both* the Bank and Mrs Thatcher were unhappy with his proposal to raise interest rates again, between November and December 1986. He records that, while he eventually managed to persuade the governor of the Bank of England to agree to this decision in a joint note to Mrs Thatcher, the prime minister only agreed to sanction a rise in interest rates during a meeting on 10 December 1986 if there was 'a clear trigger' for an increase (Lawson, 1992a, p. 667).

Even the government's chief economic adviser (Sir Terence Burns) is not immune from blame in Lawson's memoirs over the depreciation of sterling. According to Lawson (1992a, p. 651), Burns had advised against monetary and fiscal tightening in January 1986 and argued that the adverse effects of a lower pound on inflation would be offset by lower oil prices.

It may be true that, in the absence of a sterling target and with a prime minister hostile to rises in interest rates, Lawson could do little to halt sterling's slide once it had begun in the second half of 1986. Yet Lawson's account of the depreciation issue is profoundly one-sided, with only modest echoes of *mea culpa*. Indeed, there is no account in either Mrs Thatcher's autobiography or the *Bank of England Quarterly Bulletin* of the December 1986 meeting.

If anything, the depreciation of the pound suggests that the trust Lawson had in the Treasury's advice was misplaced. The chancellor would have done well to recall the 'international' monetarists at the Manchester University Inflation Workshop and LBS, who had warned, via their monetary approach to the balance of payments in the late 1970s, of an inflationary build-up following an exchange-rate depreciation. The irony was that it was Sir Terence Burns who was encouraging both Lawson and Sir Peter Middleton (the permanent secretary at the Treasury) to adopt a lax policy stance – Burns had been a one-time staunch advocate of this internationalist school (see Ball, Burns and Laury, 1977).

If allowing the excess depreciation was the first post-monetarist mistake by the chancellor, the more costly error was to shadow the Deutschmark between March 1987 and March 1988. From the experience of the UK in 1977 and the writings of Keynes (1923) 50 years earlier, it had been made clear to the authorities that some form of money supply targeting was essential under a floating exchange rate, and that any attempt to pursue exchange-rate targets under a floating rate would result in unstable monetary growth and possibly higher inflation. So why, by 1987, had Nigel Lawson forgotten the lessons of history and the wisdom of John Maynard Keynes?

It will be recalled from Chapter Five that, following the Louvre Accord in February 1987, Lawson's attitude to stabilizing exchange rates had changed. After the G6 communiqué was issued on 22 February, confidence grew in sterling. By the time of the Budget on the 17 March, the pound had risen by 16 pfennigs on its 22 February level and stood at DM2.95. As the pound appreciated between the Louvre and the Budget, Lawson cut interest rates by one percentage point, in two stages. According to Lawson (1992a, p. 682), the sentiment of the markets was such that they believed the intention of the chancellor was to keep the sterling/Deutschmark rate below DM3.00. On 18 March, at a regular markets meeting, Lawson told Treasury and Bank officials that 'this market view was useful, and ... we should validate it, by being ready to intervene as and when necessary, making sure that the intervention [is] sterilized in order to neutralize any monetary consequences' (Lawson, 1992a, p. 683).

So began a policy which became known as 'shadowing the Deutschmark'. Why the Mark was chosen to be the shadowed currency is fairly simple to explain. If the government had been intending to go into the ERM, then the Mark was undoubtedly the most suitable currency to trail. After all, it was the linchpin of the ERM, and it was far better to follow this than taking a basket of currencies such as the ECU, which had an enormous over-representation of the smaller currencies. As Lawson acknowledged to a Treasury Select Committee just after the 1988 Budget, the choice of currency was not politically significant (Lawson, 1988a, p. 36).

The level at which the shadowing was chosen and maintained by the chancellor for a year – between DM2.95 and DM3.00 – also requires an explanation. It has been suggested by Sir Alan Walters (1992) that this rate was selected because sterling happened to be at that point when the shadowing began. As noted above, Lawson's autobiography has confirmed this. When asked by this author why the DM3.00 ceiling was introduced, Samuel Brittan (1994) replied:

> What I don't know myself is why there had to be a ceiling of *exactly DM3*, which was really too easy a target for speculators. In my more malicious moments, I suspect that the Bank of England hardened to that policy in order to test it to destruction. In my more realistic moments, I think that people are harassed and they don't have time to plot anything in detail. I was a bit surprised that we did not have an indeterminate of say, around 2.95 to 3.05.

In evidence to a Treasury Select Committee, given in the same month as that by Lawson, the governor of the Bank of England readily admitted that 'as far as possible, we have attempted to keep the pound not at 2.80, but somewhere between there and in the 2.90s' (Leigh-Pemberton, 1988, p. 28).

There is general agreement that Lawson embarked on the shadowing as he wished to show how the economy could perform if it had the stability of the ERM (Keegan, 1989, p. 193; Lawson, 1992a, p. 783; Thatcher, 1993, p. 701; Walters, 1992). Yet not everyone was happy with this policy: Walters (1990a, p. 137) and Keegan (1989, p. 198) note that Treasury officials were surprised with the chancellor's decision; Peter Middleton (1995) has commented that it 'wasn't a well worked out policy, but one we drifted into'; and as will be detailed below, Mrs Thatcher remained sceptical during the entire shadowing episode.

Walters (1990a, p. 137) asserts that the policy received 'offstage assistance from that most distinguished of financial journalists, Mr Samuel Brittan'. Yet when asked by this author whether he knew about the shadowing, Sir Samuel replied:

> Yes, not because he said to me 'we are shadowing the Mark' but because everyone who followed financial affairs knew about it. If he had denied it, I would not have believed it. But he didn't find it necessary to tell me.
>
> (Brittan, 1994)

It is clear that by maintaining a rate of DM3 to the pound, Lawson was forced to keep interest rates low to prevent the exchange rate from rising. This was accompanied by massive interventions by the Bank in the foreign exchange markets, which ultimately grew to such a level that Treasury and Bank officials were becoming worried about sustaining them. Indeed, Lawson (1992a, p. 788) notes how Mrs Thatcher was 'agitated and aggressive' at a meeting on 8 December 1987, when it was observed that $27 billion had been purchased since April.

From Lawson's account, it appears that Mrs Thatcher had two worries about the intervention. First, she believed that the scale of the intervention increased monetary growth and ultimately inflation. Although Lawson argued that the intervention was sterilized, Mrs Thatcher's (1993, p. 702) account of the meeting on the 8 December suggests that she did not find this a satisfactory answer from her chancellor. When Mrs Thatcher next queried the scale of the intervention, on 4 March 1988, Lawson suggests that he could 'detect ... the influence of Alan Walters' (Lawson, 1992a, p. 796). Alan Walters confirmed in his interview with this author in 1992 that he had been worried about the scale of the intervention throughout the shadowing exercise because:

> I think that it was perfectly clear that the intervention became enormous towards the end of 1987. There was no way that you could keep monetary growth down. It was bound to bounce back, and when we reduced interest rates in May 1988, this was quite dreadful.
>
> (Walters, 1992)[3]

It is recorded by Smith (1992, p. 135) that, in the first four days of March 1988, more than $4bn was spent on keeping sterling down, causing consternation within the Number 10 policy unit, with officials urging Lawson to abandon targeting.

The second worry the prime minister had, according to Nigel Lawson (1992a, pp. 788–9), was that she was unhappy with the accumulation of dollars because they 'depreciated in value'. Under the auspices of the Louvre Accord, the G6 had agreed to support the dollar; yet, as it was Lawson's intention to maintain the DM3 parity, it made sense to purchase Deutschmarks and 'in a sense the smaller the market the better, since it might mean that a given amount of intervention would have greater immediate effect' (Lawson, 1992a, p. 787). Concomitantly, at the meeting on 8 December, Lawson successfully managed to persuade Mrs Thatcher that the Deutschmark was the better currency to buy.

For Walters (1990a, p. 112), the (inappropriate) low interest rates during the shadowing period were 'critical in exacerbating the inflationary pressure' within the British economy. Monetary policy was loosened following the Black Monday crash of 17 October 1987, which in retrospect was not a wise response.[4] While the Federal Reserve tightened monetary policy in 1987, the shadowing exercise being pursued by the British chancellor effectively ruled out higher interest rates.

The effects that cuts in interest rates were going to have on monetary growth and on inflation were only too obvious to those who had read Friedman's (1980, p. 59) evidence to a Treasury Select Committee in 1980. He had asserted that 'the lag between a change in monetary growth and output is roughly six to nine months, between the change in monetary growth and inflation, two years'.

Indeed, the growth of real GDP was faster in 1988 than 1987 and the pace of inflation also quickened between 1989 and 1990. Thus it is very plausible to argue that the boom of the late 1980s can be located to the exchange-rate targeting (see Cobham, 1997a), although in correspondence with this author and in recent evidence given to the Treasury Select Committee, Lawson (1992b, 1996) makes it clear that shadowing the Deutschmark was 'analogous' to membership of the ERM and had nothing to do with the overheating of the British economy in 1988.

One of the most fascinating issues to arise from the shadowing exercise is Mrs Thatcher's claim that she did not realize that Lawson was shadowing the Deutschmark until told by two journalists from the *Financial Times* in November 1987. In her autobiography she addresses this directly:

> It may be asked how he [Lawson] could have pursued this policy since March without it becoming clear to me. But the fact that sterling tracks the Deutschmark (or the dollar) over a particular period does not necessarily mean that the pursuit of a particular exchange rate is determining policy. ... There are so many factors involved in making judgements about interest rates and intervention that it is almost impossible at any particular time to know which factor has been decisive for whoever is in day-to-day charge.
> (Thatcher, 1993, p. 701)

Nevertheless, it may seem strange that she had not realized sooner what Lawson was doing. Alan Walters acknowledged in his June 1992 interview with this author that he kept Mrs Thatcher informed about the shadowing exercise from an early stage, and it would have been clear from the scale of the intervention over the year that this was not merely a policy of 'taking in reserves for a rainy day'.

Nigel Lawson is adamant that the prime minister was aware of the policy:

> It was always an implausible insult to her formidable intelligence to suggest that she could possibly have been unaware of it, even if I wished to keep her in the dark, which, of course, I did not. In fact

we discussed it openly on a number of occasions, of which the 8
December bilateral is merely one instance. What is true is that
there was no meeting at which the DM3 ceiling was formally
agreed.

(Lawson, 1992a, p. 789)[5]

Yet Lawson does not provide any more information about the 'number
of occasions' when the policy was discussed. It was obvious that at the
meeting on the 8 December, Mrs Thatcher would have been aware of
the shadowing exercise and she acknowledges this. However, this raises
a supplementary question: once the prime minister made her feelings
known on 8 December, why did she allow the chancellor to continue
with a policy which she was unhappy with? There were several different
things Mrs Thatcher could have done once she had been made aware of
Lawson's policy.

First, she could have sacked her chancellor. This would have been the
most controversial and also the most difficult, as we shall discuss in
Chapter Seven.

Second, she could have chosen to ignore entirely what her chancellor
was doing, but this would have been a negation of her responsibilities
as first lord of the treasury. Mrs Thatcher's approach to any aspect of
policy, particularly economic policy, was to take charge.

Third, it has been suggested by Alan Walters (1992) that the prime
minister was so engrossed in other business of state that she did not
have the time to become involved with her chancellor's disparate agenda.
This is plausible but unlikely: as noted above, she always took her
position as first lord of the treasury seriously. The intervention figures
were sent to Number 10 every evening and, even if there was little time
to consider them in detail, it would have been obvious when
Deutschmarks were purchased on a large scale.

Fourth, the prime minister could have agreed to Nigel Lawson's
policy. According to Lawson's account, this is what she did. It may be
recalled from the discussion about the scale of intervention and the
prime minister's worries that Lawson states that Mrs Thatcher agreed
to the purchase of Deutschmarks rather than dollars. Yet there is no
mention in Mrs Thatcher's account which confirms that this was the
product of her meeting on 8 December with Lawson. Moreover, a
close reading of Nigel Lawson's autobiography implies that all the
prime minister apparently agreed was 'that it would be worth attempting in the *first instance* to hold sterling below the DM3 ceiling
by intervening in Deutschmarks' (Lawson, 1992a, p. 879; emphasis
added). Precisely how long the 'first instance' would last is never
mentioned, but if the prime minister made this remark on 8 December
and the policy of shadowing the Deutschmark was not abandoned

until some three months later, this appears to be a protracted preliminary exercise.

Finally, and picking up on the third and fourth points, perhaps Mrs
Thatcher refused to become involved in Lawson's Herculean efforts on
the foreign exchange markets until the scope of intervention became
unacceptable, as it did during the first week of March 1988. As she
notes:

> I sought to discourage too much exchange-rate intervention, but
> without much success. ... I knew that once I exerted my authority
> to forbid intervention on this scale it would be at the cost of my
> already damaged working relationship with Nigel.
>
> (Thatcher, 1993, p. 702)

It seems that from the time she discovered Lawson had been shadowing the Deutschmark, Mrs Thatcher began to rely frequently on Sir
Alan Walters when she sought independent economic advice (Walters,
1992). A corollary was that this then isolated the prime minister from
Lawson, which further strained what had once been an excellent working relationship.

The final point to mention is that, even after the official ending of the
£/Mark target, Lawson was determined to maintain some form of tracking on the pound's rise. As Walters notes (1990a, p. 109), the band was
moved to between DM3.10 and DM3.30 and kept there until September 1989. This was really unforgivable, as the market became convinced that it was the Mark which was again the bulwark of British
economic policy. With a prime minister who was unconcerned (at least
in public) if the pound continued to rise and a chancellor determined to
keep the currency down, British economic policy was at its most contradictory for the whole decade.

Inside and outside the Exchange-Rate Mechanism

As this book has suggested, Mrs Thatcher was opposed to membership
of the ERM. There are two reasons for this. First, as a monetarist, she
preferred floating rates to fixed rates; and second, she felt that membership was another move towards Britain losing sovereignty to Europe.
Consequently, the decision to join the ERM was an important ideological concession by Mrs Thatcher and, given the political fallout which
had occurred over this issue, it was also an expedient manoeuvre for her
political survival.

According to Thompson's account, a senior Treasury official recalls
that on Thursday 4 October 1990 a group of officials went to see
Thatcher for an informal discussion about joining the ERM later in the

year. It is quite poignant to read that Thatcher sanctioned one of the most important acts of her premiership when 'she was going out to dinner somewhere; she had to get into a long dress, so the whole thing was punctuated by this changing' (Thompson, 1996, p. 172). After all the discussions and ructions of the 1980s, permission to join the ERM was given apparently without any qualms (Thatcher apparently asking whether entry the next day was feasible).

The decision to join had important implications for the conduct of British economic management: since the floating of the pound in 1971, in theory at least, policy-makers had scarcely needed to give the exchange rate a second thought (although, as this study has demonstrated, this was not the case in practice). Now that the pound was set to return to a fixed rate of exchange, it implied that greater restrictions would be placed on domestic monetary policy, along similar lines to how policy operated during membership of the Bretton Woods system. Yet Mrs Thatcher made it clear upon entry that membership would not be 'at the expense of domestic monetary conditions' (Thatcher, 1993, p. 723), and upon joining the mechanism interest rates were cut by one percentage point. Ironically, this reduction threw into question the seriousness of the United Kingdom's membership from the start. The cuts in interest rates were probably made to placate Mrs Thatcher's unease over joining the ERM, and have parallels with those which had accompanied the 1981 Budget. But was Mrs Thatcher's sanction of membership – almost her last important decision made in high office – to become a poisoned chalice for her chancellor?

Whereas Nigel Lawson had inherited an economy which was about to enjoy several years of growth, Mr Major's inheritance as chancellor was not so fortuitous. Indeed, following the Lawson boom, Chancellor Major faced several unpleasant tasks, both economic and political. First, he had to negotiate with the prime minister over the timing and level of entry into the ERM. Second, because of his desire to find a compromise between the pro- and anti-European factions within the Conservative Party (Thatcher, 1993, p. 721), Major was restricted in discussions over European monetary union (EMU) with European Community finance ministers. Third, the British economy entered a sharp recession in the second quarter of 1990 (Table 6.5). Finally, there was a leadership challenge to Mrs Thatcher which succeeded in displacing Britain's longest-serving prime minister this century and elevating John Major from chancellor of the exchequer to prime minister, first lord of the treasury and minister for the Civil Service.

On becoming prime minister, John Major might have adopted a more pro-European stance than his predecessor, thereby successfully uniting the fissure in the Conservative Party. The reality, after six and a half

Table 6.5   Actual and potential GDP volumes, 1977–93

	GDP at factor cost		Potential GDP 1977= 100	Output gap in per cent	RPI rise in per cent
	Level 1977=100	Change in per cent			
1977	100.0	—	100.0	0.0	15.9
1978	102.7	2.7	102.2	0.5	8.2
1979	105.5	2.7	104.4	1.0	13.4
1980	103.4	–2.0	106.7	–3.2	18.0
1981	102.2	–1.2	109.1	–6.4	11.9
1982	104.0	1.8	111.5	–6.7	8.6
1983	107.9	3.7	113.9	–5.3	4.5
1984	110.1	2.0	116.5	–5.5	5.0
1985	114.5	4.0	119.0	–3.8	6.0
1986	119.1	4.0	121.6	–2.1	3.4
1987	124.6	4.6	124.3	0.2	4.2
1988	130.8	5.0	127.0	2.9	4.9
1989	133.6	2.2	129.8	2.9	7.8
1990	134.4	0.6	132.7	1.3	9.5
1991	131.6	–2.1	135.6	–3.0	5.9
1992	130.9	–0.5	138.6	–5.5	3.7
1993	133.6	2.1	141.6	–5.7	3.0

Note: Potential output growth = 2.2 per cent a year.

Source: Johnson (1995, p. 121)

years of hindsight, was that nothing presented Mr Major with more difficulties than holding the Conservative Party together over European issues. Indeed, since Britain's entry into the ERM on the 9 October 1990, the Conservative Party has appeared to have bifurcated, in much the same way as it did earlier in the century. Nor did Britain's abrupt exit from the ERM make life any easier for Major – his economic credibility vanished completely with the decision to leave the mechanism on 16 September 1992, coupled with earlier, overoptimistic forecasts about the state of the economy.

The debate over entry had raged for some considerable time both inside and outside Westminster. Supporters of the ERM at the NIESR, who had been urging membership from the mid-1980s, commented in the late 1980s that 'it is regrettable that the opportunity for full membership has not so far been taken' (*National Institute Economic Review*, 1988, p. 6). In a different tone to Mrs Thatcher, the *Review* also implied that membership did not necessarily mean total subservience to the Bündesbank. When the UK joined, the *Review* noted that 'it would have been better to join earlier in the year when the exchange rate was lower and the markets relatively calm' (*National Institute Economic Review*, 1990, p. 5).

Whether the pound was overvalued when it entered the ERM is a moot point which has already led to several academic studies into the question. In the year leading up to entry, work carried out at the NIESR and published in a discussion paper used the concept of FEERs to suggest that a lower entry rate might have been appropriate (Wren-Lewis, 1990; Wren-Lewis, Westaway, Soteri and Barrell, 1990). This analytical framework was developed by John Williamson (1983), who used it to support the arguments of the NIESR team that sterling was between 10 to 15 per cent overvalued upon entry into the ERM (see Williamson, 1991; Wren-Lewis, Westaway, Soteri and Barrell, 1991).

Those who opposed this view argued that analysis based on purchasing power parity (PPP) indicated either that sterling had entered at the 'right rate' (Davies, 1990), or that sterling was undervalued when it joined the ERM (Brittan, 1995). When challenged about the rate of entry by a member of the Treasury and Civil Service Committee on 5 December 1990, Chancellor Lamont defended the rate of entry and argued that 'the 2.95 rate is, of course, very close to the average real exchange rate against the Deutschmark over the last 10 years' (Lamont, 1990, p. 30). The Treasury also justified the rate of entry to the same Treasury Committee (Burns, 1990, p. 16) and later discussed at length their reasons for this (HM Treasury, 1991).

Such arguments, using either PPP or FEER, are never fully resolved. As Thatcher (1993, p. 722) comments, the decision to join the ERM was influenced by several factors:

> First, the rate chosen had to be credible in the light of recent exchange-rate movements. Second, it should not be so low that it weakened the fight against inflation, by requiring imprudently low interest rates to keep sterling down. Third, and by contrast, it must not be so high that it imposed unnecessary pressure on industry, both through high interest rates which made borrowing expensive and a high exchange rate which made our goods uncompetitive.

The trouble with Britain's sortie into the ERM was that industry was soon wrestling with a major recession and, while inflation was brought down, the rate of entry ultimately proved unsustainable. Ironically, given the success of lower inflation over the ERM period, the strongest critics of the ERM episode were the monetarists.

Initially, the trepidation of the monetarists was lost in the euphoria surrounding entry. Indeed, one former monetarist was so optimistic about the level of entry that he suggested that it would be a few months before Britain moved to the narrow bands of the mechanism (Budd, 1990). However, by January 1991 the monetarists began their fiercest attack on government policy since the 1970s and returned to the pages of *The Times* to conduct it. On 2 January, Alan Walters (1991) argued that membership of the ERM was exacerbating a recession and that 'the only feasible, let alone humane, policy is to engineer a substantial devaluation of sterling'. A few days later, Budd (1991) shifted slightly from his earlier position and, while conceding that the ERM was causing economic distress, he suggested that 'membership is proving painful because there are questions about our commitment'.

The monetarists were quick to respond to Budd's article. In a letter to *The Times* on 13 February 1991, Tim Congdon, Bill Martin, Patrick Minford, Gordon Pepper, Alan Walters and Peter Warburton urged the government to cut interest rates so as to avoid a 1930s-style slump (Congdon et al., 1991).

As Wickham-Jones (1992) has argued, the monetarist protest of 1991 was similar to the 1981 protest to *The Times* by the 364 economists. Patrick Minford refused to sign the 1981 letter and claimed at the time that 'the economist who downs tools to sign petitions for apparently political ends is playing a dangerous and dishonest game' (quoted in Wickham-Jones, 1992, p. 183). Yet Minford's protest at the government's policy in 1991 could hardly be described as non-partisan, even though Congdon claimed in a interview with this author that the letter had 'got mixed up with this kind of vague Conservative Party argument about the right wing and Mrs Thatcher and the whole debate on Europe' (Congdon, 1991).

The letter also failed to stop some critics from noting that:

> The former advocates of sound money are now proposing devaluation at a time when we still face an underlying inflation rate of some 7.5 per cent. The solid supporters of the intense squeeze of 1979–81 are now proclaiming their concern for the impact of draconian deflationary discipline on the British economy.
>
> (Stevens, 1991)

The monetarist protest about the ERM is also ironic for two further reasons. First, the demur from the monetarists in 1991 was as vociferous as that of the unreconstructed Keynesians who warned of a slump (Godley 1991; Godley and Rowthorn, 1991). Second, the letter from Congdon et al. was followed by an interest rate cut of half a percentage point. Although this gave the appearance that the monetarists were (once again) influencing policy, Keegan (1991) was quick to point out that government officials had used market conditions to determine the cut.

By Wednesday 16 September 1992, economic policy in the United Kingdom had been dominated, *de jure*, by a fixed exchange rate for almost two years and, as this study has argued, *de rigueur*, for almost eight. By this date, however, it was clear that Britain was finding the restrictions of the fixed exchange rate too much to bear and had to pull out of the ERM rather unceremoniously. The ignominious exit from the system was a mixed blessing. On the one hand, it appeared to release the British economy from the straitjacket of high interest rates and an uncompetitive exchange rate for a more accommodating monetary policy. To this extent, exit from the ERM was indeed to be welcomed. But on the other hand, it left policy-makers with a credibility and policy gap.

The government had placed Britain's membership of the ERM at the fulcrum of economic policy-making and had made it clear on several occasions that:

> the government's policy is that we intend to stick within our ERM bands. We believe that the benefit of the discipline of the ERM, the benefits of sticking to the existing parity, are paramount. We have no intention whatsoever of altering the parity.
>
> (Lamont, 1991, p. 50)

After devaluation, Lamont (1992, p. 6) told the Treasury Select Committee that:

> The Italians had devalued on the Monday and had been under intense pressure ever since and, frankly, the game was up by Wednesday and we had no option but to withdraw [however] ... I had always made it clear that we did not think devaluation was the right policy for this country. I remain convinced that within a fixed exchange-rate system my judgement on that was right.

With hindsight, it is difficult to envisage what other policy the government could have implemented other than withdrawal from the ERM in the autumn of 1992. During the summer of 1992, the pound was not that far off the central rate within the mechanism (DM2.90 – 2.91/£) and there was widespread agreement that interest rates were too high. Although Cobham (1997b) has suggested that a rise in UK interest rates in mid-July would have indicated unequivocally the UK's commitment to the mechanism, such a decision would have been overzealous. Given that the economy was in recession, higher interest rates would have been politically insensitive and economically absurd. After all, over the period since October 1990 inflation had fallen from nearly 11 per cent to under 4 per cent, interest rates had been cut from 15 per cent to 10 per cent, and Britain's trade performance had improved.

Against this background, Chancellor Lamont had justified Britain's continuing membership of the ERM and had set out the government's options in a speech to the European Policy Forum on 10 July 1992. The five alternatives were: to cut interest rates within the ERM and to pull the economy out of recession; to seek a general realignment of the ERM based on a revaluation of the Deutschmark; devaluation within the ERM; to cut interest rates and leave the ERM; and finally, to reintroduce domestic monetary targets. Lamont ruled out the first and third options, arguing that the currency markets would force interest rates up. Nor did he consider it fair that Britain's European partners should 'sacrifice their hard-won credibility by allowing their currencies to be devalued against the Deutschmark' (Stephens, 1996, p. 213). Moreover, Britain would lose its anti-inflation credibility if it did leave the ERM which Lamont argued could not be restored by domestic monetary targets.

Lamont's speech was exquisitely double-edged, for within eight weeks he had abandoned the central tenet of the government's economic policy and had found new faith in monetary targets. The 'new monetary' framework set out by the chancellor in a letter to the chairman of the Treasury and Civil Service Select Committee made it clear that the objective would be to keep underlying inflation within a range of 1–4 per cent for the remainder of the parliament. This would be attained through a monetary policy directed by a 'wide range of factors' (Lamont, 1992, p. 2). In practice, this meant taking into account the level of the exchange rate, adopting a number of monetary indicators (M0 would be targeted, M4 would have a monitoring range) and examining the behaviour of asset prices (particularly house prices).

As Cobham (1996) has argued, the adoption of an inflation target can be questioned. Even if monetary targets are unviable because of velocity changes, arguably nominal income targets are superior to inflation targets because they lead to less variability of real output in response to adverse supply shocks. Moreover, Simpson's (1994, p. 25) criticism (echoing Friedman's (1960) argument that a central bank cannot control the price level) is that to target inflation 'is to target the *objective* of policy, rather than an instrument such as the money supply or the exchange rate. By so doing, it is implied that policy will be determined pragmatically; thus there is a theoretical vacuum at the heart of monetary policy-making.'

Perhaps the vacuum which Simpson refers to has resulted from something more fundamental which occurred during the 1980s: the downgrading of the quantity theory of money. For example, when Chancellor Major (1989, p. 42) was asked about the quantity theory of money while appearing at a Treasury Committee, he noted that 'it used to be the theory ... the government may have followed some time ago. It certainly has not been the theory that the government have followed during any period I have been in the Treasury.' Major's omission is very informative, for it demonstrates unequivocally that the wrong lessons have been drawn from the monetary theory.

In Chapter Three, it was stated that the quantity theory of money is the essence of monetarism, and monetarists have claimed that money demand functions were stable over long periods. It was this which convinced the authorities that money targets were appropriate for the British economy from the 1970s.

However, the work of Friedman and Schwartz (1982) – which confirmed the assumption that money was related in a stable way to income – was challenged by Hendry and Ericsson (1983). Yet using the same econometric methods as Hendry and Ericsson, Holly and Longbottom (1985) supported the earlier work of Friedman and Schwartz. Not deterred, Hendry and Ericsson (1991) pursued further econometric tests on one of the equations used by Friedman and Schwartz and still rejected the arguments of the monetarists. In a reply, Friedman and Schwartz (1991) argued that the one regression on which Hendry and Ericsson had concentrated could not support an anti-monetarist conclusion and if anything, tended to support the monetarist case.

Furthermore, Wood (1995) has argued that the erratic movements in the velocity of circulation over the 1980s due to financial innovation had been recognized in pre-econometric based versions of the quantity theory developed by Hume and Thornton. This supports the argument first made in Chapter Five that, although financial innovation might have unsettled some monetarist supporters, it did not 'discredit the quantity theory' (Wood, 1995, p. 110) or disprove monetarism. Perhaps if the authorities had been more aware of their monetary history, then the abandonment of monetarism would not have happened.

Lawson's embrace of the ERM and support for currency stabilization from the mid-1980s has led some observers to suggest that he was still committed to controlling inflation but through a more pragmatic approach (Willetts, 1994). The analysis presented so far has stressed the opposite to this view: namely, that Lawson sacrificed lower inflation in pursuing a discretionary policy and that, as one of the original architects of the MTFS, he should have realized the problems with pragmatism. While Lawson could claim in the early 1980s that if 'discretion is being exercised by those whose commitment to the policy and to the overriding need to maintain financial discipline is beyond doubt, then there is no cause for such misgivings' (Lawson, 1982, p. 5), this did not hold true by the end of the decade as the *theoretical* structure of government policy had moved away from monetarism. Ironically, even if the strict discipline of the ERM offered policy-makers an effective means of controlling inflation, the UK was forced to relinquish its membership of the mechanism faster than it had abandoned the monetarist experiment during the 1980s.

Notes

1. Indeed, it may be recalled that this was the fourth defining characteristic of the MTFS which was discussed in Chapter Three.
2. British Keynesians have argued that credit controls (or some form of credit management) would have served the British economy better during the 1980s (Hutton, 1991). However, when the present author interviewed Tim Congdon and asked whether, as a monetarist, he would prefer credit controls or high interest rates as a weapon of monetary restraint, Congdon (1991) rebutted the suggestion of credit controls firmly: 'I prefer to manage credit via variations in interest rates. I think that credit controls are very damaging to public efficiency and it is possible to do it through interest rate variations – as indeed the Bank did it through decades in the nineteenth century.'
3. Pepper (1990, p. 48) notes that although the monetary authorities did not sterilize the intervention completely during 1987, they had managed to do so by the first quarter of 1988.
4. Lawson also feared a slump due to a decline in wealth, which implied lower consumption, and so he loosened monetary policy. In fact, the decline in consumption did not occur.
5. Lawson (1992a, p. 789) also claims in a footnote that Mrs Thatcher 'publicly admitted that she had known about my policy of shadowing the Deutschmark' in an interview in June 1991. All she admits in the interview is that it was a mistake to allow Lawson to shadow the Deutschmark and put 'exchange-rate stability above monetary indicators' (Thatcher, 1991). There is no time-scale mentioned in this interview and, as was noted in the main text, she claimed in 1993 that she was aware of the shadowing only from November 1987 (Thatcher, 1993, p. 701).

Learning from the past?

It is necessary to note that over the past two decades the UK has tried almost every macroeconomic strategy, and has failed at each. The credibility of UK macroeconomic policy-making is largely non-existent.

(Currie and Dicks, 1993, p. 34)

There is a distinct amount of irony to be found in the observation that, whereas politicians clamoured to take kudos for the 1981 Budget, few wished to be associated with the macroeconomic decisions from the mid-1980s. Undoubtedly, the late 1980s boom was much more effective at destroying the credibility of the Thatcher government's economic strategy than the missed monetary targets of the early 1980s. In the former period inflation fell (from 22 per cent in 1980 to 4.5 per cent in 1984), whereas in the last few years of the final Thatcher administration, inflation rose (from 4.2 per cent in 1987 to 9.5 per cent in 1990).

As economic policy shifted over the 1980s – becoming more discretionary and relying less on rules – the end result was greater confusion in policy. Lawson has argued that at the heart of the discretion versus rules debate was monetary policy, and that is why he came to regard 'an external monetary discipline, such as the gold standard, [as] the best practicable monetary rule. In modern circumstances, this in practice meant adherence to the Deutschmark standard via membership of the Exchange Rate Mechanism of the EMS' (Lawson, 1992a, p. 1022).

Yet Lawson's tinkering with ERM membership in 1987 and 1988 was highly discretionary with unpleasant results. This does not necessarily imply, *inter alia*, that the ERM lacks firm rules or cannot be an effective anti-inflationary discipline. It simply means that Nigel Lawson was playing the wrong game for Britain when he shadowed the Deutschmark between 1987 and 1988.

The introduction of monetary targets by Mrs Thatcher's administration in 1979 marked a firm belief that inflation could be controlled via intermediate targets, and that the most suitable monetary aggregate was £M3. The subsequent abandonment of these targets, and the adoption of narrow money, might be viewed as the British government pragmatically accepting Goodhart's Law. However, this is one step removed from the change in attitude which the authorities expressed during the 1980s over the relationship between broad money and money GDP. It would have been far better if the chancellor and Treasury officials had stuck to domestic monetary rules after 1985. According to Goodhart, quoted in Congdon (1989b, p. 50):

> The capacity of the present Conservative government, and of the Treasury, to move from an (invalid) viewpoint that the growth of broad money is an exact determinant of the growth of nominal incomes to the (invalid) viewpoint that the growth of broad money has no relationship at all with the growth of nominal incomes is staggering with respect to its speed and the comprehensive nature of the intellectual somersault involved.

Specifically, this study has emphasized that two things in particular which happened during the 1980s were crucial in explaining the fragmentation of macroeconomic policy. First, that many of the decisions taken in the monetary and exchange-rate domain were highly questionable, such as the abandonment of broad money targets, the ending of overfunding, the excess depreciation, the currency shadowing and the overvaluation of sterling in the ERM. Second, there was growing dissension at a political and economic level over a number of issues between a variety of protagonists. This included the deterioration in the personal relationship between Nigel Lawson and Mrs Thatcher, the disagreements within the cabinet over Europe, rivalry between Lawson and Walters, and the unease between officials in the Treasury and Bank of England over the direction of economic policy. These developments, together with the other issues which have been raised, provide a *Gestalt* within which policy evolution can be explained.

This final chapter will suggest that, through the social learning model, it is possible to account for the shifts in macroeconomic policy during the 1980s. It will attempt to address the four questions which Hall (1993, p. 276-7) raised in his article and which were mentioned in Chapter One. These were:

> How should we understand the relationship between ideas and policy-making? How do the ideas behind policy change course? Is the process of social learning relatively incremental, as organization theory might lead us to expect, or marked by upheaval and the kind of 'punctuated equilibrium' that often applies more generally to political change? Are bureaucrats the principal actors in social learning, or do politicians and societal organizations also play a role?

The first section will examine whether the policy paradigm shifted during the 1980s and early 1990s and will address the third and fourth questions raised by Hall. The crucial issue of fourth-order learning will then be addressed, which will allow us to consider how ideas and policy-making interact. This is followed by some conclusions about macroeconomic policy-making during the 1980s, a reassessment of Hall's model and the implication of this for the policy transfer debate.

A case of third-order change?

Thus far, this book has supported much of Hall's (1993) theoretical model, first discussed in Chapter One, by drawing on empirical evidence from the 1970s and 1980s. Yet in Chapter Four, it was noted that some of the seemingly routine first-order changes (instrument settings) in economic policy during the early 1980s were part of a wider dissatisfaction with the policy instruments, and this led to the adoption of alternative instruments. It was also argued that the changes in the instruments (second-order change) led to the abandonment of the strict monetarist framework by 1981.

Hall (1993, p. 282) notes that between 1981 and 1985 there were several second-order changes. He does not expand upon this but merely acknowledges that there was a gradual move 'away from a monetary policy oriented primarily to rigid targets for the rate of growth of £M3'. Chapters Four and Five proceeded to outline how the instruments themselves changed between 1981 and 1985 and discussed the introduction of M0, the greater emphasis put on the exchange rate by Chancellor Lawson and the ending of overfunding in 1985.

Chapter Six argued that, between 1985 and 1992, macroeconomic policy exhibited all the old tendencies of discretionary management: a variety of targets, poor forecasts and disagreements over policy. From 1985 and until the government joined the ERM in October 1990, policy wavered between pragmatism and eclecticism. Finally, the UK's experience of the ERM was short-lived and, although policy became less pragmatic, economic credibility was lost when sterling left the system in 1992.

In toto, there appear to have been some important changes in policy during the first part of the 1980s, although it was only post-1985 that some of these changes became more fundamental. What is unclear from the discussion presented so far in this study is whether by 1990 there was a new paradigm in place as a result of these policy changes.

Hall (1993, p. 280) offers three guidelines about the movement from one policy paradigm to another which ought to be considered carefully. First, he suggests it is likely to be more sociological than scientific, encompassing judgements that are not formed on the basis of pure economics alone. Second, the issue over which person or group is the most authoritative on the technicalities of policies is very important because this will determine whom politicians choose to listen to. Third, for the paradigm to shift, there has to have been a process of policy experimentation and failure. In short:

> the movement from one paradigm to another that characterizes third-order change is likely to involve the accumulation of anomalies, experimentation with new forms of policy and policy failures

that precipitate a shift in the locus of authority over policy and initiate a wider contest between competing paradigms. This contest may well spill beyond the boundaries of the state itself into the broader political arena.

The developments which have been discussed in Chapter Six undoubtedly qualify as third-order change under these three guidelines – but does the evidence suggest that there was a paradigm shift in British economic policy between 1985 and 1990?

To examine third-order change in more detail, it will be instructive to focus on the conflicts in authority and the disagreements between Walters, Lawson and Mrs Thatcher (the shifts 'in the locus of authority') and how the prime minister and her chancellor came to rely on advice from economic specialists ('the broader political arena').

By March 1988, the disagreements between Lawson and Mrs Thatcher over entry into the ERM were evident in public (Jones and Smallwood, 1988). In July 1988, Lawson learnt that Professor Sir Alan Walters was going to return to act as personal economic adviser to the prime minister. Lawson viewed the return of Walters with dismay (Lawson, 1992a, p. 842). While both men had shared a similar economic philosophy in the early 1980s when Walters had last advised Mrs Thatcher, by end of the decade the situation had changed.

In his book *Britain's Economic Renaissance*, Walters (1986, p. 127) had suggested that the ERM was flawed. Between 1986 and 1989, Walters's hostility towards the mechanism hardened further so that, by the time he returned as economic adviser to the prime minister, he firmly opposed Britain's entry. On 18 October 1989, the *Financial Times* reported that Walters had written a biographical essay for the *American Economist*, in which he described the ERM as 'half baked' (Holberton, 1989; Walters, 1989, p. 24).

While the article was written before Walters rejoined British Government employment, it rankled considerably with Nigel Lawson. Lawson opposed Walters's view not only because he was a major proponent of ERM entry, but also because the chancellor realized that Walters's opinion would be favoured by the prime minister, who would further delay Britain's entry into the ERM. In his resignation speech on 31 October 1989, Lawson noted that 'the article written by my right honourable friend's former economic adviser was of significance only inasmuch as it represented the tip of a singularly ill-concealed iceberg, with all the destructive potential that icebergs possess' (*Parliamentary Debates*, 31 October 1989, vol. 159, col. 208).

Just after Lawson resigned, he was asked by Brian Walden to outline his disagreements with Walters. Politically, he responded that:

> The art of economic management, conducting of economic policy, to a very considerable extent, is credibility and confidence: the credibility of the minister who is charged with the responsibility of carrying out the policy, and the confidence, both of business and industry, and of the financial markets, in what he is doing, and what he is saying. And ... it was ... the diminution of credibility and therefore the lack of confidence which was doing the great damage.
>
> (Cox, 1990, p. 62)

He explained that the economic difference was:

> where does the exchange rate fit in? Is it part of the market freedom, let it go where it will, wherever the markets are going to push it? Or should it be, as I believe – and I don't think Alan Walters does, I feel sure he doesn't – should it be part of the financial discipline to bear down on inflation?
>
> (Cox, 1990, p. 62)

Lawson's (1992a) autobiography details several allegations against Walters, but is relatively silent on how he countered any disagreements with the former economic adviser. However, in an interview with this author, Walters has stated that:

> After the 1985 débâcle, I tried to engage Lawson in discussions on the exchange-rate, right through to 1989. He never would discuss it with me. Never discuss exchange rate policy, never the arguments, the 'Walters's Critique', and all the other aspects. When I came back in 1989, I went to make my peace with him and I started trying to introduce a discussion of exchange rates: the EMS, ERM and so on at that time, but he would never discuss it with me or at meetings if I brought it up. He would go off on another topic, or change it.
>
> (Walters, 1992)[1]

Undoubtedly the hostility between the chancellor and Professor Walters led to politicians and the financial markets questioning the instruments and objectives of policy, as Lawson notes (1992a, p. 957).[2] Indeed, in his letter of resignation to the prime minister on 26 October 1989, Lawson made it clear that he could not proceed as chancellor 'so long as Alan Walters remains your personal economic adviser' (Lawson, 1992a, p. 964).[3]

While Walters had been based in Washington since he left British government employment in the mid-1980s, he continued to be highly influential on Mrs Thatcher. By the time of the Deutschmark shadowing, the prime minister was using Walters's advice over that of her chancellor (Walters, 1992). Concomitantly, at the time of Lawson's resignation, it appears Mrs Thatcher would rather have lost her estranged chancellor than her personal economic adviser. The exchanges between Brian Walden and Margaret Thatcher in *The Walden Interview* on Sunday 29 October 1989 – just after Lawson's resignation – are particularly revealing:

> *Brian Walden:* A last question: do you deny that Nigel would have stayed if you had sacked Professor Alan Walters?
>
> *Margaret Thatcher:* I don't know. I don't know.
>
> *Brian Walden:* You never even thought to ask him that?
>
> *Margaret Thatcher:* I … that is not … I don't know. Nigel had determined that he was going to put in his resignation, I did everything possible to stop him.
>
> *Brian Walden:* But …
>
> *Margaret Thatcher:* I was not successful. No, you're going on asking the same question …
>
> *Brian Walden:* Of course, but that's a terrible admission, Prime Minister.
>
> *Margaret Thatcher:* I have nothing further … I don't know … of course I don't know.
>
> *Brian Walden:* You don't know, you could have kept your chancellor, possibly, if you had sacked your part-time adviser?
>
> (Cox, 1990, p. 36; ellipses in original)

Coats (1981a, p. 356–57) has suggested that an economic adviser:

> can preserve his integrity only by remaining silent when faced with official policies of which he strongly disapproves, and if his silence proves embarrassing or unacceptable to his employers, he should resign. … But resignation, however conducted, is a once-for-all decision, a confession of failure, and a gesture unlikely to have any effect on policy.

For the Lawson–Walters confrontations, Coats's comments require some modification. Arguably, Walters had no need to resign or stay silent if he disapproved of UK policy on Europe, because his scepticism was shared by the prime minister. When a member of the Treasury Select Committee recently suggested that Walters had allowed the prime minister to undermine Lawson, Walters replied:

> as an adviser it is my job to advise on what I believe to be true. It may undermine a minister, or it may cause all sorts of trouble, but my job as an economic adviser is to produce logical arguments and empirical evidence to show what is true. If it undermines a minister, so be it. … Lord Lawson took the view that what I said was not true, that ERM was splendid and it would not blow up and it was not perverse. I appeal to history to see which of us was right on the issue.
>
> (Walters, 1996, p. 121)

It was Chancellor Lawson, repeatedly told by the prime minister that Britain would join the ERM when the 'time was ripe' (Lawson, 1992a, p. 485), who resigned. The main reason that Mrs Thatcher did not *sack* her chancellor after his illicit moonlighting with the ERM between 1987 and 1988 was because of the support he commanded in the House of Commons, a point acknowledged by Mrs Thatcher (1993, p. 703). While Lawson's resignation was a genuine admission of failure in persuading Mrs Thatcher to enter the ERM, Walters's resignation was no more than a token political gesture. As we saw in Chapter Six, government policy on the ERM changed within twelve months.

While Alan Walters appears to have had more influence on the prime minister after 1987 than Nigel Lawson, who was affecting Nigel Lawson's decisions?

From the beginning of his chancellorship in 1983, Lawson relied on several different economic voices (Lawson, 1992a, p. 264). Among the most prominent were Samuel Brittan from the *Financial Times*; Peter Middleton, permanent secretary at the Treasury; Terry Burns, chief economic adviser; Robert Culpin, press secretary to Lawson and, from 1986, a group of outside independent economists ('Gooies').[4]

This last group were economists who broadly espoused the 'New Right' view of the 1980s, although the participants did not always agree on government policy. Peter Middleton (1995) has suggested that, as a whole, this group did not have much authority in policy decisions, and Lawson (1992a, p. 390) acknowledges that the group was 'illuminating rather than operationally useful'. However, given Nigel Lawson's 'restless search for policy frameworks' (Stephens, 1996, p. 277), the 'Gooies' were a useful conduit for frank and open discussions on economic policy. Lawson was known to favour Patrick Minford's view that the growth of narrow money was a better guide to future inflation than broad money and Samuel Brittan's view that the ERM was the best way of controlling inflation. Not only were Brittan and Minford vehemently opposed to what each of the other was arguing, but they sought to influence government policy in different ways. Brittan's highly influential column in the *Financial Times* became increasingly pro-ERM from 1985 and strongly supported Lawson's private desire to take the pound into the ERM (see Brittan, 1985).

The product of all these factors is not difficult to disaggregate. The narrow monetarists (represented by Minford) were arguing for a policy which the broad monetarists (represented by Congdon) opposed on technical grounds. The chancellor did not have one broad monetarist in the 'Gooies', but had narrow money followers (Minford and Pepper) and an influential ERM supporter in Brittan. The narrow money followers did not want either ERM entry or targets for the exchange rate.

They were supported by a prime minister who opposed the ERM for economic and political reasons and who had in Alan Walters, her economic adviser, a narrow monetarist who was very anti-ERM. Lawson intensely disliked the presence of Walters (the 'unelected chancellor') due to his ready access to the prime minister with his alternative views on economic policy.

Consequently, from the mid-1980s, Lawson's views were slowly isolated from the broad monetarists, the narrow monetarists, the prime minister's economic adviser and the prime minister. It is clear that Lawson's proclamations about inflation control in 1979 seemed to be lost, and in the words of once economic critic:

> In truth, Mr Lawson saw no virtue in price stability as an objective of official policy ... deep down, he had always been a 'growthman' of 1960s vintage, someone who wanted the government to push Britain higher up the international league tables of economic growth.
>
> (Congdon, 1992a, p. 65)

However, although there were numerous first- and second-order changes in the first half of the decade, and despite the main ingredients for a paradigm shift being in place post-1985, it cannot be convincingly argued that such a shift did occur. As Rose (1993, p. 26) has noted, 'A paradigm shift involves a major intellectual reorientation that has a pervasive effect on the way in which many problems and programs are viewed.'

Clearly, despite the accumulation of anomalies, experimentation, fragmentation of authority and contestation in the 1980s, there was not an institutionalization of a wholly new paradigm by the end of the decade. Although money supply targets had been abandoned, the Conservative government continued to eschew direct controls on wages and prices as a means to control inflation and to emphasize that unemployment could not be eradicated by government action (the antithesis of Keynesianism).

Moreover, there is an important caveat to the third-order change argument: namely, over the ultimate goal of policy as *presented* by the government. Lawson's enthusiasm for the ERM as an anti-inflation discipline was set out clearly on many occasions, not least in his autobiography. The arguments made in favour of the mechanism by Chancellor Major when Britain joined in October 1990 were that Britain could lock itself into a fixed exchange-rate system which would secure a lower inflation rate for the UK. As such, inflation still appeared the most important goal of policy and joining the ERM was merely a process of second-order change.

The *reality* of government policy, echoed in part by Congdon's quotation above, was that the control of inflation had been lost by lax

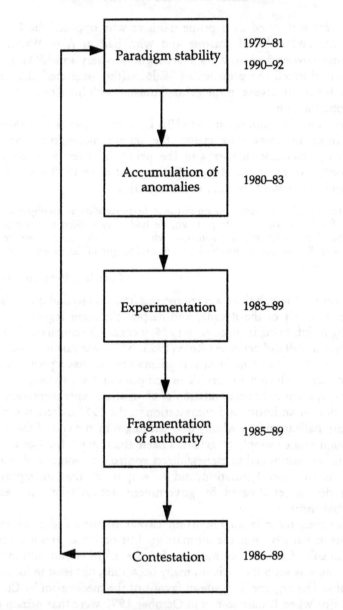

7.1   The policy paradigm in the 1980s

monetary discipline, and that ERM entry was a *volte face* to appease
the growing unease in the Conservative Party over the Thatcher government's anti-European stance.[5] Every *Financial Statement and Budget
Report* began with a firm commitment towards reducing inflation, even

though the assurances of this goal were wafer thin by the end of the decade.

It would be wrong to conclude from the preceding analysis that Hall's description of third-order change is incorrect because the paradigm did not shift in the 1980s. In the 1970s, first-order change plus second-order change equalled third-order change (1+2=3), but Hall has warned that this process is not necessarily mechanical: 'first- and second-order changes in policy *do not automatically* lead to third-order changes. As in the case of scientific change, normal policy-making can proceed for some time without necessarily precipitating a paradigm shift' (Hall, 1993, pp. 279–80; emphasis added).

The discussion in Chapter One also suggested that there was a six-stage process to the paradigm shift in the 1970s. Figure 7.1 illustrates that during the 1980s there was only a five-stage process, with 'contestation' being followed by 'paradigm stability' rather than the 'institutionalization of a new paradigm'. Figure 7.1 also illustrates that the nexus between the five stages during the 1980s was not as orderly as in the 1970s. For example, 'experimentation' was simultaneous with the 'fragmentation of authority' and 'contestation' stages.

Fourth-order learning

In the previous section, it was suggested that it is possible to use the social learning model to identify a relationship between first-, second- and third-order change during the 1980s. What was not discussed was the facilitating mechanism through which fluctuations in one order of change affect another order of change. It is suggested here that fourth-order learning was simultaneous with first-, second- and third-order change during the 1980s and early 1990s, and that as dissatisfaction occurred with the basic settings of instruments (and later with the instruments themselves), lessons were drawn from policy failures and successes. A consideration of fourth-order learning will address Hall's first two questions on how ideas and policy-making interact.

Apart from a footnote in Hall's (1993, p. 293) article, there are no explicit references to fourth-order change in the academic literature, although Argyris and Schön (1978) and recent work by Dodd (1994) have attempted to extrapolate the idea of 'deutero-learning' from Bateson (1972). With some careful reasoning, it is possible to envisage how fourth-order learning can be applied to the subjects under discussion in this study so that it becomes a dynamic tool and central feature of the social learning process.

For Peter Hall (1993, p. 293), fourth-order learning is where 'policy-makers learn how to learn'. For our purposes, this should also incorporate learning by politicians. As Mrs Thatcher (1993, p. 715) has argued, in the 1980s it was advisers who gave advice but it was ministers who decided policy. Equally, in his role as permanent secretary to the treasury, Burns (1994, p. 50) notes that it is 'ministers who design and execute policy, and are accountable'.

None the less, as discussed in earlier chapters, there does appear to have been some occasional obfuscation over who was forming macroeconomic policy during the 1980s, in particular between the prime minister and Chancellor Lawson. The implications of this for fourth-order learning will become clear in the following discussion.

There are three questions about 'learning to learn' which will be considered in this section. First, what factors influence how a politician will learn? Second, when do politicians learn how to learn? Third, when do societies learn?

The first question has been addressed by Dodd (1992, p. 10) in a review essay on the careers of US senators during the 1980s. Dodd argues that, to some extent, it is possible to see in the careers of some senators a degree of 'learning to learn':

> they (and we) come to believe in their inner resources and intuitive capacities – to believe that they can learn through experience to respect the open and serendipitous nature of politics and to reassess their political preconceptions in the light of new conditions and expanding awareness. Such politicians ... may not be the most immediately successful ... , but they may ultimately become the most 'real', the best 'tested', the most genuine or empathetic, the sort of leader one would 'trust'.

There are three particular factors which influenced the learning of US senators which can be applied to the British context. First, Dodd notes that the senators who take the time to reflect and reassess new ideas and information will enjoy a fair amount of developmental learning. The two main protagonists of the 1980s both acknowledge that their years in opposition between 1974 and 1979 were crucial for the development of post-1979 policies (Lawson, 1992; Thatcher, 1995). Once in power, it became more costly for both politicians to experiment, fail and reassess. Moreover, Nigel Lawson was more keen to flirt with other money aggregates and explore currency shadowing in 1987 and 1988, while Mrs Thatcher (1993, p. 14) saw any deviation in economic policy as a sign of failure and wished to avoid the policy reversals which had beleaguered her predecessor in the 1970s.

Dodd's first point also addresses *when* lessons may be sought, by suggesting that it is only when a political party is in opposition (the

Conservatives between 1974 and 1979; the Labour Party between 1979 and 1997; the Republicans since 1992) that they can conduct a wholesale review of policy. Once elected, it is more difficult to pursue or to change policy dramatically without losing the support of the electorate.

Second, Dodd (1992, p. 11) argues that those politicians who exhibit reflective self-awareness 'are prepared to listen to their intuitive feelings, to re-examine their personal and political preconceptions, and thus to learn and change'. Lawson undoubtedly adjusted his mindset throughout the 1980s (from floating to fixed rates; from rules to discretion) while keeping a core of central beliefs (inflation could be controlled; unemployment was decided by the market). On Dodd's definition, it is more difficult to label Mrs Thatcher 'self-aware': as the 1980s unfolded the prime minister refused to shift from her conviction beliefs and in particular how her economic vision could be attained.

A third factor which is central to the success of a politician is facilitative personal circumstances. If a politician is surrounded by informed staff, who are 'in touch with reality' they are much more likely to learn. In the early 1980s, Mrs Thatcher was surrounded by monetarist advisers such as Keith Joseph, Alan Walters and Brian Griffiths who guided and developed her thoughts. But as these advisers either left office or became minority voices, then their ability to influence the prime minister weakened. Howe (1994, p. 146) also suggests that the resignation of Ian Gow as the prime minister's parliamentary private secretary 'may be seen in retrospect as one of the prime causes of her slowly developing isolation'.

It is interesting to note that when Alan Walters returned to advise Mrs Thatcher in May 1989, he did so in a part-time capacity and after spending a considerable amount of time in the United States, where he was impervious to developments in European integration and currency alignment. Thus even before his return to the United Kingdom, Walters was in a different mindset and thus in conflict with Lawson, who was surrounding himself with pro-ERM advisers while distancing himself from the monetarist experiment.

However, even if these are some of the prerequisite factors which need to be in place before learning begins, there is still no guarantee that politicians will learn how to learn. Nor is there any guarantee that politicians will automatically learn the right lessons over time. Indeed, the analysis presented in Chapters Two and Three suggested that for much of the post-war period, ignorance about monetary policy, persistence of a 'stop-go' mentality and supply-side problems continued perennially until the underlying Keynesian paradigm collapsed. Furthermore, even when it appeared that the authorities had learnt something from monetarism in the early 1980s, they forgot the most fundamental lessons by the end of the decade. It is appears that even if we can identify *where* policymakers might be able to learn, it does not give any sort of guarantee as to *when* they may learn.

Consequently, any analysis which merely sees fourth-order change as a process which involves the techniques of learning does not utilize the concept particularly well. What happens after an individual or group learns *how* to learn? In what follows, we extend the discussion by suggesting that, after learning to learn, there is a process of 'learning by doing' (Coats, 1981a, p. 345). To consider learning by doing a specific analogy can be made with learning to drive.

Assume that an individual wishes to learn to drive. After taking a number of lessons, the individual will put in for his test. Let us assume that he successfully passes his test, thereby fulfilling his ambition of 'learning to drive'. A few weeks after passing his test, while out driving in the city, the driver ignores a speed restriction. In failing to heed this, he crashes into another vehicle. Our new driver forgot a basic lesson: heed speed restrictions. Just because he has learnt how to drive does not mean that he will never make mistakes. He will always be vulnerable to accidents, either because of mechanical failure, but more likely because he will occasionally forget his Highway Code, however many times it was drilled into him in his driving lessons.

The point of such a laborious example can be seen when we consider the evolution of British macroeconomic policy since 1970. In the mid-1970s, the Conservatives were learning about monetarism. By the early 1980s, they could put into practice the lessons of Milton Friedman. As Minford (1979, p. 29) argued, the first Thatcher budget was 'the first ... drawn up explicitly according to monetarist principles', and Pratten (1982, p. 36) commented that 'the nearest approach to an experiment occurs when a government adopts new policies. ... Mrs Thatcher's policies, which are based ... on monetarist theories of how the economy operates are therefore of special interest to economists.'

Yet instead of following Friedman to the letter, the Conservatives combined a mixture of theoretical and political monetarism. In a way, they were like a driver who has passed his test, but who has yet to experience the 'real-world' situation on the roads, where other people's driving and the odd hazard force him to modify his driving skills. As in our earlier example, however, there are some lessons which a driver must never forget. This study has suggested that the policy-makers and politicians who learnt and applied monetarism to the UK hit upon several 'hazards' (financial liberalization, currency problems, etc.) and ended the experiment. It was questionable whether the hazards really did require that the experiment should be terminated; but once ended, policy-makers forgot even the basic lessons of monetarism, which had severe repercussions for the British economy.

Conclusions

The Conservative government elected in 1979 was committed to what has been described as a 'monetarist' economic policy. While the debate continues over whether any such experiment was really undertaken in the British economy, it is clear that there were several important changes to the formulation of economic policy during the 1980s.

In the initial policy framework of the early 1980s, it was believed that the authorities' ultimate target (price stability) would be best achieved by adopting an intermediate target (broad money). However, over the course of the decade this money aggregate was gradually rejected and eventually replaced with an exchange-rate target. This led to a conflict in economic policy which by 1987 had set the economy on a traditional 'stop-go' path and lost the government its reputation for sound finance.

This book has examined macroeconomic policy since 1979 and has suggested why, as the decade unfolded, certain policy instruments were abandoned and others were adopted. It is now quite clear why the monetarist experiment was jettisoned when inflation fell after 1983 and why officials did not readopt similar monetarist techniques at the end of the 1980s when the economy began to overheat: the goals, instruments and instruments settings had been gradually changed. With monetary policy in particular, officials had thrown the baby out with the bath water by the late 1980s and it would have been impossible to return to the hard-line monetarist approach of the early 1980s.

A crucial element in the 1980s learning process was trying to maintain economic credibility within the monetarist paradigm. £M3 was not a credible indicator of the monetary conditions between 1980 and 1981, and when this aggregate indicated that monetary policy was loose the opposite applied. M0 was then introduced, to accord with the facts. The problem with M0 was that it did not really say much about inflation and was merely a nod towards monetary targets to give a public appearance that the monetarist experiment was still 'on course'. Consequently, the monetarist paradigm was only really credible when broad money targets were being pursued; the authorities might have argued that they did not reflect the UK's economic position accurately, but their downsizing led to a loss of credibility in the overall policy framework.

Thain (1984) has suggested that senior officials could have been responsible for the disintegration in government policy at the start of the 1980s. More than a decade on, there is enough evidence to corroborate this claim and to support a case which places several senior politicians at the centre of the policy disintegration. Yet these politicians did not act in a vacuum, and it is clear that the media, outside advisers and the pattern of events all contributed to the policy changes. Indeed, from the mid-1980s, some of these agents began to cause friction post-1985, so that by the time Alan Walters returned to Downing Street in May 1989 tensions between the prime minister and her chancellor were considerably strained.

One detailed investigation into macroeconomic policy during the 1974–87 period has noted that 'Macroeconomic policy was conducted in a pragmatic, atheoretical fashion ... with much apparent success. Neither the monetarists nor the Keynesians were happy with the situation, but ministers were most of the time, and so was much of the general public' (Britton, 1991, p. 110).

This study has attempted to analyse why such pragmatism set in, and in so doing has suggested that the monetarist experiment did bring success between 1983 and 1986. The book has argued that from 1985, both Nigel Lawson and Mrs Thatcher were unhappy with policy implementation and examined why this was so. Furthermore, this volume has also tried to explain why policy, which was essentially monetarist at the start of the 1980s, became a curious mixture of 'Thatcherite Keynesianism' (Congdon, 1986b) by the mid-1980s and then a hybrid of 'exchange-rate monetarism' by the early 1990s.

The model chosen to examine the policy changes since 1979 was taken from the work of Peter Hall (1993). Following a more detailed examination of the 1980s, this volume has supported the thrust of Hall's main argument, although it has been argued that early first- and second-order changes led to a movement towards third-order change. This study has suggested that variations in the three orders of change are part of a wider learning experience, and that fourth-order learning is integral to the other orders of change (Figure 7.2).

After examining fourth-order learning in more detail, it could be argued that lesson-drawing is the *sine qua non* of the social learning model. Yet the fundamental question raised by fourth-order learning – when do policy-makers actually learn lessons? – has a parallel with the wider question thrown up by the policy transfer literature – at what stage does policy transfer occur? Although Rose (1993, pp. 132–4) lists the factors which may constrain policy transfer, he does not discuss this question directly. When policy-makers draw on similar policies in other countries, what combination of ideas, instruments and goals do they borrow? If a policy paradigm is taken from one country and it fails to work abroad, does this imply that the policy paradigm is wrong *per se*, or that, for example, some of the instruments or instrument settings need to reflect the different economic, social and cultural environment? More fundamentally, even if policy-makers learn lessons from other countries, how do they educate the public (if they need to at all)?

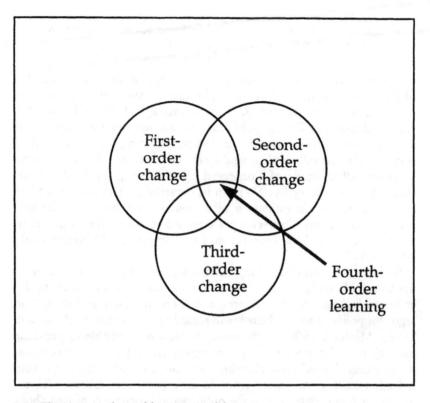

7.2 The integrated social learning model

Consequently, one of the wider questions that all these learning models need to address is: what do societies learn?

If we return to the example of recent UK economic policy-making it is possible to offer a mixed assessment of what lessons have been drawn. During the 1980s, there were numerous oral and written contributions from politicians and policy-makers, reflecting on what they believed they had learnt from a particular economic encounter and how policy pursued at time-1 would now work in the light of knowledge gained in time-0 (see Bank of England, 1990; Burns, 1988; Middleton, 1989). *Plus ça change* for the 1990s. Following the decisions made on 16 October 1992, there have been similar noises from the authorities which have echoes with the past (Bank of England, 1993).

A survey of the state of the economic consensus among academic, business and government economists was clear that since 1979:

> the overall weight of opinion amongst respondents was against
> reductions in the level of government spending ... that the Euro-

> pean Monetary System is superior to a floating-exchange-rate
> régime, and was against the view that the prime concern of macro-
> economic policy should be to eliminate inflation.
>
> (Ricketts and Shoesmith, 1990, p. 86)

Equally, it is not easy to prove (or conclude) that the average member
of the British public has developed a heightened awareness of trade-offs
in economic policy since 1979. Dennis Kavanagh (1994, p. 8) has even
suggested that the British public moved against key elements of the
Conservatives' programme in the 1980s, including the 'disavowal of
responsibility for full employment' by the government. Moreover, Philip
Norton's (1990) study of Conservative MPs during the 1980s shows
that only one in every five MPs can be regarded as Thatcherite, and an
even more recent investigation into Conservative Party membership
suggests 'grassroots Conservatives opposed many of the policy posi-
tions taken up by Mrs Thatcher and her supporters' (Whiteley et al.,
1995, p. 197).

Within the monetarist camp, the civil war of the early 1980s continues to rumble on between those who argue for decisions on monetary
policy to be based on the performance of broad money and those who
argue for policy to be conducted with regard to narrow money (Congdon,
1996a; Minford, 1996). If the policy experts were unable to persuade
the majority of politicians to accept monetarism, it was inevitable that
the electorate would view Thatcher's economic agenda with scepticism.
Indeed, recalling the quote from Samuel Brittan in Chapter Three,
perhaps it was inevitable that the public would become confused about
the government's economic strategy, given the inherent contradictions
in policy post-1979.

The obvious question is whether officials have now learnt the right
lessons on how to conduct monetary policy after withdrawal from the
ERM and whether they have returned credibility to economic policy-
making generally.

It was suggested earlier in the chapter that one reason why the United
Kingdom joined the ERM in October 1990 was to appear more 'European'. As Chapter Six has discussed, on economic grounds, two further
reasons included securing greater policy credibility and a tighter discipline on inflation. It also appears that the UK authorities had reconsidered the lessons of the 1970s and 1980s on the exchange rate versus the
money supply when they decided to opt for a fixed exchange rate. Yet
the speculative attacks leading to the withdrawal of the pound from the
ERM in less than two years showed that credibility was not achieved
(Masson, 1995).

At such an early stage, it is unclear what lessons have been drawn by
the authorities. On a positive note, Chancellor Clarke's (1994) Mansion

House speech stressed that he had learnt from post-war economic history and would take precautions to avoid the 'boom and bust' of the past. Ironically, Nigel Lawson (1994) has queried this commitment. In contrast to Clarke, Lawson's contribution to the debate about learning from the past is more interesting because of what it leaves out: there is no reference to the erratic monetary policy from the mid-1980s which caused the boom of the late 1980s.

Yet there are two broad lessons from the 1980s and early 1990s that have been carried over into the mid-1990s by the government and policy-makers. First, that a policy of benign neglect towards unemployment is not necessarily an electoral handicap. This was learnt following the Conservatives' victory at the polls in 1983 and has not been forgotten since. Second, the government continues to eschew direct controls on wages and prices as a means to control inflation.

On the issue of credibility, Mervyn King (1995, pp. 90–91) has recently argued that:

> Credibility can be enhanced by a policy framework based on an inflation target, and by institutional changes such as the degree of openness and transparency embodied in the Bank's *Inflation Report* and in the publication of the minutes of the monthly monetary meetings between governor and chancellor. The key to building credibility lies in the maxim, 'say what you do, and do what you say'.

The relationship between the Treasury and the Bank since the implementation of the post-1992 monetary framework heralds a new attempt to foster credibility in economic policy-making. Since February 1993, the Bank has produced a quarterly *Inflation Report* which includes its forecast of inflation over the next two years. From the autumn of 1993, this report has been shown to the Treasury in its final form only, precluding any direct censorship by Treasury officials. Coupled with this, the monthly monetary meetings between the chancellor and the governor have been formalized, and since April 1994 have been published about six weeks after the meeting. While this greater transparency might highlight the extent to which policy decisions are taken on political grounds, and frustrate the attempts by politicians to hijack the economic policy-making process for fear of unfavourable publicity, the framework has been pejoratively described as 'elusive' (Walters, 1996, p. 120). Bearing this in mind, Cobham (1996) is right to caution against judgements for or against this new framework because, up to mid-1997, the new system had not been subjected to pressures of the kind experienced in the Lawson boom.

In toto, the social learning process since 1979 has been a mixed affair. The 1980s were a time of policy experiments at both the macro

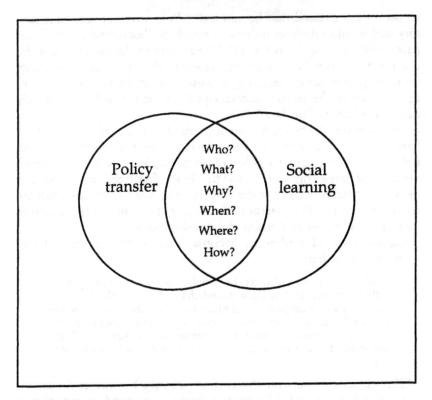

7.3 Policy transfer and social learning

and micro level, and officials encountered a combination of old and new problems when attempting to achieve economic targets. While it would be wrong to see policy as an unqualified successes in the 1980s, it would be equally incorrect to conclude that nothing positive has come from the past 16 years. There is at present a greater consensus between Keynesian and monetarist economists about how economies operate, and a growing scepticism on both sides of the Atlantic that econometric modelling is the philosopher's stone. Indeed, given the failure of economic forecasters to predict the Japanese recession of 1993, the boom of the late 1980s in the UK, the depth of recession in the German economy following unification and the problems of the ERM since 1992, some members of the economics profession realize that the consequences of econometrics can no more be undone than the furies returned to Pandora's box (Mayer, 1993; Ormerod, 1994).

This study has extended the social learning model, and in so doing has exposed the differences between social learning and policy transfer. In contrast, Figure 7.3 lists six factors where both models overlap, taken from Table 1.1. Through a detailed case study, it has been shown how these factors can be applied to social learning. Because the social learning model is of an interdisciplinary nature, all writers now have an opportunity to use this approach to analysing the past. It is refreshing to find that social learning is now being discussed in City and academic publications (Congdon, 1996b; Stone, 1996), and is being considered alongside policy transfer as a way of explaining change over time (Oliver, 1996a).

Given that an explicit model now exists, social learning could be applied to the evolution of education, foreign and welfare policy-making. It would certainly give a renewal to the debate on the shift from the Treasury view to Keynesianism in the 1940s which has so far been conducted through a heuristic framework. Moreover, given the method of application in this study, economic historians might find that they need to spend more time studying institutions and individuals as political sociologists: looking at how staff are recruited, the social and educational backgrounds of policy-makers and politicians, and the role of interest groups and ideology in policy-making.

The social learning model serves to highlight two things above all else: first, that economic policy-making cannot be fully understood by recourse to current time periods alone; second, that the role of the politician in the policy-making process is crucial. In the final analysis, if the social learning model has anything to offer to help explain policy-making and policy changes, then it is important to remember that new policies develop from both past successes and past failures, aided by the diversity of institutions within and outside the state.

Notes

1. While Lawson may have refused to get drawn into arguments with Walters on the exchange rate, his autobiography (Lawson, 1992a) does contain a three-page appendix to Chapter 40 which addresses the 'Walters's Critique'.
2. The animosity between Lawson and Walters continued even after Mrs Thatcher's resignation. In an article for *The Times* in December 1990, Walters (1990b) claimed that Nigel Lawson and Geoffrey Howe had played a part in a conspiracy to depose the prime minister. In reply, Lawson (1990b) refutes this theory, and claims instead that Mrs Thatcher was undermined by the return of Walters in May 1989.
3. In his autobiography, Lawson is vitriolic that although he was unable to persuade the prime minister to join the ERM, Mrs Thatcher was forced to swallow the bitter pill a year later (8 October 1990), and that within a month she had resigned (21 November 1990).
4. The group of outside independent economists comprised Alan Budd, Samuel

Brittan, Walter Eltis, Mervyn King, Geoffrey Maynard, Patrick Minford, John Muellbauer, Gordon Pepper and Harold Rose.

5. Nigel Lawson (1992a, p. 504) notes that the economics of ERM membership became slightly subsumed under the wider debate over Europe in the Conservative Party during 1990.

Bibliography

Aldcroft, D. H. (1992), *Education, Training and Economic Perform-ance, 1944 to 1990*, Manchester: Manchester University Press.

—— (1993a), *The European Economy, 1914–1990*, London: Routledge.

—— (1993b), 'Why Has Unemployment Remained so High in Eu-rope?', *Current Politics and Economics of Europe*, vol. 3, no. 3/4, pp. 277–91.

Alford, B. W. E. (1996), *Britain in the World Economy since 1880*, London: Longman.

Allsopp, C. (1985), 'The Assessment: Monetary and Fiscal Policy in the 1980s', *Oxford Review of Economic Policy*, vol. 1, no. 1, pp. 1–20.

Allsopp, C., Jenkinson, T., and Morris, D. (1991), 'The Assessment: Macroeconomic Policy in the 1980s', *Oxford Review of Economic Policy*, vol. 7, no. 3, pp. 68–80.

Alt, J. E. and Chrystal, K. A. (1983), *Political Economics*, Brighton: Wheatsheaf.

Anderton, B. (1996a), 'Trade performance and the role of R&D, pat-ents, investment and hysteresis: an analysis of disaggregated bilateral import volumes for the UK, Germany and Italy', *National Institute Discussion Paper*, no. 101.

—— (1996b), 'UK Trade performance and the role of product qual-ity, innovation and hysteresis: some preliminary results', *National Institute Discussion Paper*, no. 102.

Argyris, C. and Schön, D. (1978), *Organizational Learning: A Theory of Action Perspective*, Reading, MA: Addison-Wesley Publishing Co.

Artis, M. J. and Bladen-Hovell, R. (1987), 'The UK's Monetarist Ex-periment, 1979–84', *International Review of Applied Economics*, vol. 1, no. 1, pp. 23–47.

Artis, M. J. and Cobham, D. (eds) (1991), *Labour's Economic Policies 1974–1979*, Manchester: Manchester University Press.

Artis, M. J. and Lewis, M. K. (1991), *Money in Britain*, Hemel Hemp-stead: Philip Allan.

Artis, M. J., Bladen-Hovell, R., Karakitsos, E. and Dwolatzky, B. (1984), 'The Effects of Economic Policy 1979–82', *National Institute Eco-nomic Review*, no. 108, pp. 54–67.

Artis, M., Cobham, D., and Wickham-Jones, M. (1992), 'Social De-mocracy in Hard Times: The Economic Record of the Labour Gov-ernment 1974–1979', *Twentieth-century British History*, vol. 3, no. 1, pp. 32–58.

Artus, J. R. (1975), 'The 1967 Devaluation of the Pound Sterling', *IMF Staff Papers*, vol. 22, no. 3, pp. 595–640.

—— (1984), 'The Disequilibrium Real Wage Hypothesis: An Empirical Evaluation', *IMF Staff Papers*, vol. 31, no. 2, pp. 249–302.

Attanasio, O. P. and Weber, G. (1994), 'The UK Consumption Boom of the Late 1980s: Aggregate Implications of Microeconomic Evidence', *Economic Journal*, vol. 104, no. 427, pp. 1269–302.

Ball, R. J. (1978), *Report of the Committee on Policy Optimization*, London: HMSO.

Ball, R. J., Burns, T. and Laury, J. S. E. (1977), 'The Role of Exchange Rate Changes in Balance of Payments Adjustment – the United Kingdom Case', *Economic Journal*, vol. 87, no. 345, pp. 1–25.

Bandura, A. (1977a), 'Towards a unifying theory of behavioural change', *Psychological Review*, vol. 84, no. 2, pp. 191–215.

—— (1977b), *Social Learning Theory*, Englewood Cliffs, NJ: Prentice-Hall.

Bank of England (1969), 'Domestic Credit Expansion', *Bank of England Quarterly Bulletin*, vol. 9, no. 3, pp. 363–82.

—— (1971), 'Competition and Credit Control', *Bank of England Quarterly Bulletin*, vol. 11, no. 2, pp. 189–93.

—— (1978), 'Reflections on the Conduct of Monetary Policy', *Bank of England Quarterly Bulletin*, vol. 18, no. 1, pp. 31–7.

—— (1979), 'Monetary Base Control', *Bank of England Quarterly Bulletin*, vol. 19, no. 2, pp. 149–56.

—— (1980), 'Methods of Monetary Control', *Bank of England Quarterly Bulletin*, vol. 20, no. 4, pp. 428–9.

—— (1981a), 'Monetary Control: Next Steps', *Bank of England Quarterly Bulletin*, vol. 21, no. 1, pp. 38–9.

—— (1981b), 'Monetary Control – Provisions', *Bank of England Quarterly Bulletin*, vol. 21, no. 3, pp. 347–50.

—— (1982a), 'Recent Changes in the Monetary and Regulatory Framework', *Bank of England Quarterly Bulletin*, vol. 22, no. 1, pp. 101–3.

—— (1982b), 'Mortgage Lending and the Housing Market', *Bank of England Quarterly Bulletin*, vol. 22, no. 3, pp. 390–98.

—— (1984a), 'Some Aspects of UK Monetary Policy', *Bank of England Quarterly Bulletin*, vol. 24, no. 4, pp. 474–81.

—— (1984b), 'Funding the Public Sector Borrowing Requirement: 1952–83', *Bank of England Quarterly Bulletin*, vol. 24, no. 4, pp. 482–92.

—— (1985), 'The Housing Finance Market: Recent Growth in Perspective', *Bank of England Quarterly Bulletin*, vol. 25, no. 1, pp. 80–91.

—— (1986a), 'General Assessment', *Bank of England Quarterly Bulletin*, vol. 26, no. 1, pp. 3–8.

—— (1986b), 'Operation of Monetary Policy', *Bank of England Quarterly Bulletin*, vol. 26, no. 1, pp. 27–37.

—— (1986c), 'Operation of Monetary Policy', *Bank of England Quarterly Bulletin*, vol. 26, no. 3, pp. 333–44.

—— (1986d), 'Financial Change and Broad Money', *Bank of England Quarterly Bulletin*, vol. 26, no. 4, pp. 499–507.

—— (1990), 'Monetary Policy in the Second Half of the 1980s', *Bank of England Quarterly Bulletin*, vol. 30, no. 2, pp. 215–20.

—— (1993), 'Ten Years On', *Bank of England Quarterly Bulletin*, vol. 33, no. 3, pp. 383–4.

Bank of England and HM Treasury (1980), *Monetary Control*, Cmnd. 7858, London: HMSO.

Bateson, G. (1972), *Steps to an Ecology of Mind*, New York: Ballantine.

Batstone, E. (1988), *The Reform of Workplace Industrial Relations*, Oxford: Clarendon Press.

Bean, C. and Crafts, N. (1996), 'British economic growth since 1945: relative economic decline ... and renaissance?', in Crafts, N. and Toniolo, G. (eds), *Economic Growth in Europe Since 1945*, Cambridge: Cambridge University Press.

Beckerman, W. (1985), 'How the battle against inflation was really won', *Lloyds Bank Review*, no. 155, pp. 1–12.

Beckerman, W. and Jenkinson, T. (1986), 'What stopped the inflation? Unemployment or Commodity prices?', *Economic Journal*, vol. 96, no. 175, pp. 39–54.

Beenstock, M. (1980), 'Memorandum', in Treasury and Civil Service Committee, *Memoranda on Monetary Policy*, HC 720–II, London: HMSO.

—— (1983), *The World Economy in Transition*, London: George Allen & Unwin.

Booth, A. (1983), 'The "Keynesian Revolution" in Economic Policy-making', *Economic History Review*, 2nd series, vol. 36, no. 1, pp. 103–23.

Brandon, H. (1966), *In the Red: The Struggle for Sterling, 1964–66*, London: André Deutsch.

Brittan, S. (1969), *Steering the Economy*, London: Secker and Warburg.

—— (1982), *How to End the 'Monetarist' Controversy*, 2nd edn, London: Institute of Economic Affairs.

—— (1983), 'How the EMS has become a mere crawling peg', *Financial Times*, 24 March.

—— (1985), 'Now, alas, it is time to join the EMS', *Financial Times*, 14 November.

———— (1994), Interview with Michael Oliver, 2 August, London.

———— (1995), *Capitalism with a Human Face*, Cheltenham: Edward Elgar.

Britton, A. (1991), *Macroeconomic Policy in Britain 1974–1987*, Cambridge: Cambridge University Press.

Broadberry, S. (1994), 'Employment and Unemployment', in Floud, R. and McCloskey, D. (eds), *The Economic History of Britain since 1700*, vol. 3, Cambridge: Cambridge University Press.

Bruce-Gardyne, J., Congdon, T. and Minford, P. (1985), *Whither Monetarism?*, London: Centre for Policy Studies.

Brunner, K. (1968), 'The Role of Money and Monetary Policy', *Federal Reserve Bank of St Louis Review*, vol. 50, no. 7, pp. 8–24.

Budd, A. (1990), 'In the band: now for the fine tuning', *The Times*, 6 October.

———— (1991), 'Why it should be a tough Budget', *The Times*, 12 January.

Budd, A. and Burns, T. (1977), 'Economic Viewpoint – How much Reflation?', London Business School, *Economic Outlook*, October, pp. 7–11.

Buiter, W. H. and Miller, M. (1981), 'The Thatcher Experiment: The First Two Years', *Brookings Papers on Economic Activity*, no. 2, pp. 315–79.

———— (1983), 'Changing the Rules: Economic Consequences of the Thatcher Regime', *Brookings Papers on Economic Activity*, no. 2, pp. 305–79.

Burch, M. (1983), 'Mrs Thatcher's Approach to Leadership in Government: 1979–June 1983', *Parliamentary Affairs*, vol. 36, no. 4, pp. 399–416.

Burk, K. and Cairncross, A. (1992), *'Goodbye, Great Britain': The 1976 IMF Crisis*, London: Yale University Press.

Burns, T. (1981), 'Economic Policy and Prospects', *Public Money*, vol. 1, no. 3, pp. 45–52.

———— (1982), 'Minutes of Evidence', in Treasury and Civil Service Committee, *Autumn Statement*, First Report, HC 49, London: HMSO.

———— (1988), 'The UK Government's Financial Strategy', in Eltis, W. and Sinclair, P. (eds), *Keynes and Economic Policy: The Relevance of the General Theory after Fifty Years*, Basingstoke: Macmillan.

———— (1990), 'Evidence' in Treasury and Civil Service Committee, *The 1990 Autumn Statement*, First Report, HC 41, London: HMSO.

———— (1994), 'Some reflections on the Treasury', in Holly, S. (ed.), *Money, Inflation and Employment: Essays in Honour of James Ball*, Aldershot: Edward Elgar.

Burton, J. (1982), 'The varieties of Monetarism and their implications', *Three Banks Review*, no. 134, pp. 14–31.

Butler, R. A. (1971), *The Art of the Possible*, London: Hamish Hamilton.

Cairncross, A. (1985), *Years of Recovery: British Economic Policy, 1945–51*, London: Methuen.

—— (1992), *The British Economy since 1945*, Oxford: Blackwell.

Cairncross, A. and Cairncross, F. (eds) (1992), *The Legacy of the Golden Age: The 1960s and their Economic Consequences*, London: Routledge.

Canterbery, E. R. (1987), *The Making of Economics*, Belmont, CA: International Thompson Publishing.

Caporaso, J. A. and Levine, D. P. (1992), *Theories of Political Economy*, Cambridge: Cambridge University Press.

Carruth, A. and Oswald, A. (1986), 'Wage Inflexibility in Britain', *London School of Economics Discussion Paper*, no. 258.

Casson, M. (1983), *Economics of Unemployment: An Historical Perspective*, Oxford: Martin Robertson.

Castles, F. (1982), 'The Impact of Parties on Public Expenditure', in Castles, F. (ed.), *The Impact of Parties: Politics and Policies in Democratic Capitalist States*, London: Sage.

Central Statistical Office (1993), *Economic Trends: Annual Supplement*, London: HMSO.

—— (1994), *Economic Trends: Annual Supplement*, London: HMSO.

Chrystal, K. A. (1984), 'Dutch Disease or Monetarist Medicine? The British Economy under Mrs Thatcher', *Federal Reserve Bank of St Louis Review*, vol. 66, no. 5, pp. 27–38.

Cipolla, C. M. (1991), *Between History and Economics: An Introduction to Economic History*, Oxford: Basil Blackwell.

Clarke, K. (1994), 'Mansion House Speech', 15 June, HM Treasury press release.

Coats, A. W. (1981a), 'Introduction', *History of Political Economy*, vol. 13, no. 3, pp. 341–64.

—— (1981b), 'Britain: the Rise of the Specialists', *History of Political Economy*, vol. 13, no. 3, pp. 365–404.

Cobham, D. (1989a), 'UK Monetary Targets 1977–86: Picking the Numbers', in Cobham, D., Harrington, R. and Zis, G. (eds), *Money, Trade and Payments*, Manchester: Manchester University Press.

—— (1989b), 'Financial Innovation and the Abandonment of Monetary Targets: the UK Case', in O'Brien, R., and Datta, T. (eds), *International Economics and Financial Markets*, Oxford: Oxford University Press.

—— (1991), 'The Money Supply Process', in Green, C. J. and Llewellyn, D. T. (eds), *Surveys in Monetary Economics, Volume 2: Financial Markets and Institutions*, Oxford: Blackwell.

—— (1994), 'The Lawson Boom: Excessive Depreciation versus Financial Liberalisation', *University of St Andrews Discussion Paper Series*, no. 9411.

—— (1996), 'Bounded Credibility: the post-ERM Framework for Monetary Policy in the UK', *University of St Andrews Discussion Paper Series*, no. 9602.

—— (1997a), 'The Lawson Boom: Excessive Depreciation versus Financial Liberalisation', *Financial History Review*, vol. 4, no. 1, pp. 69–90.

—— (1997b), 'Inevitable disappointment? The ERM as the Framework for UK Monetary Policy, 1990–92', *International Review of Applied Economics*, vol. 12, no. 2, pp. 213–28.

Cockett, R. (1995), *Thinking the Unthinkable: Think-Tanks and the Economic Counter-Revolution, 1931–1983*, rev. edn, London: HarperCollins.

Congdon, T. (1978), *Monetarism: An Essay in Definition*, London: Centre for Policy Studies.

—— (1982a), 'Winning the Economic War', *Spectator*, vol. 248, no. 8029, 29 May.

—— (1982b), 'The Coming Boom in Housing Credit', *Research Report*, London: L. Messel and Company.

—— (1986a), 'Time to Take a Broader View of Money', *Financial Times*, 16 April.

—— (1986b), 'Will the House-buying Boom Save Thatcher?', *The Times*, 17 June.

—— (1986c), 'Why Lawson must stick to his target', *The Times*, 31 October.

—— (1987), 'British and American Monetarism Compared', in Hill, R. (ed.), *Keynes, Money and Monetarism*, Basingstoke: Macmillan.

—— (1989a), 'Credit, Broad Money and the Economy' in Llewellyn, D. (ed.), *Reflections on Money*, London: Macmillan.

—— (1989b), *Monetarism Lost and why it must be Regained*, London: Centre for Policy Studies.

—— (1990a), 'The Case for a Resumption of Overfunding, Continued', *Gerrard and National Monthly Economic Review*, no. 11, May.

—— (1990b), 'The End of the Great Credit Boom', *Gerrard and National Monthly Economic Review*, no. 9, March.

—— (1991), Interview with Michael Oliver, 23 February, Gloucestershire.

—— (1992a), *Reflections on Monetarism*, Aldershot: Edward Elgar.

—— (1992b), 'The Exchange Rate in British Economic Management: Where British Economics Went Wrong', *Discussion Paper Series in Financial and Banking Economics*, FABER/92/1/1/A, University of Wales College at Cardiff.

—— (1996a), 'In defence of the broad money school of thought', *Daily Telegraph*, 15 July.

—— (1996b), 'An Open Letter to Professor Minford', *Gerrard and National Monthly Economic Review*, no. 85, July.

—— (1998), 'Fiscal Policy in the UK Since the Second World War', in Maloney, J. (ed.), *Debt and Deficits*, Cheltenham: Edward Elgar.

Congdon, T. et al. (1991), 'Urgent need for interest-rate cut', Letters, *The Times*, 13 February.

Conservative Party (1979), *The Conservative Manifesto 1979*, London: Conservative Central Office.

Coutts, K., Godley, W., Rowthorn, B., and Zezza, G. (1990), *Britain's Economic Problems and Policies in the 1990s*, London: IPPR.

Cowart, A. (1978a), 'The Economic Policies of European Governments Part I: Monetary Policy', *British Journal of Political Science*, vol. 8, no. 3, pp. 238–311.

—— (1978b), 'The Economic Policies of European Governments Part II: Fiscal Policy', *British Journal of Political Science*, vol. 8, no. 4, pp. 425–34.

Cox, D. (1990), *The Walden Interviews*, London: Boxtree.

Crafts, N. F. R. (1991), 'Economic Growth', in Crafts, N. F. R. and Woodward, N. W. C. (eds), *The British Economy since 1945*, Oxford: Oxford University Press.

Crafts, N. F. R. and Woodward, N. W. C. (1991), 'Introduction and Overview', in Crafts, N. F. R. and Woodward, N. W. C. (eds), *The British Economy since 1945*, Oxford: Oxford University Press.

Craig, F. W. S. (1990), *British General Election Manifestos 1959–1987*, Aldershot: Parliamentary Research Services.

Currie, D. A. and Dicks, G. (1993), 'Economic Viewpoint: UK Economic Prospects and Policy Dilemmas', London Business School, *Economic Outlook*, vol. 17, no. 5, pp. 30–35.

Davies, G. (1990), 'Memorandum: The Autumn Statement' in Treasury and Civil Service Committee, *The 1990 Autumn Statement*, First Report, HC 41, London: HMSO.

Denham, A. and Garnett, M. (1996), 'The Nature and Impact of Think Tanks in Contemporary Britain', *Contemporary British History*, vol. 10, no. 1, pp. 43–61.

Dimsdale, N. H. (1991), 'British Monetary Policy since 1945', in Crafts, N. F. R. and Woodward, N. W. C. (eds), *The British Economy since 1945*, Oxford: Oxford University Press.

Dodd, L. C. (1992), 'Learning to Learn: The Political Mastery of US Senators', *Legislative Studies Section Newsletter*, Extension of Remarks, November.

—— (1994), 'Political Learning and Political Change: Understanding Development across Time', in Dodd, L. C. and Jillson, C. (eds), *The Dynamics of American Politics: Approach and Interpretations*, Boulder, CO: Westview Press.

Dolowitz, D. and Marsh, D. (1996a), 'Who Learns What from Whom: a Review of the Policy Transfer Literature', *Political Studies*, vol. 44, no. 2, pp. 343–57.

—— (1996b), 'What is this thing called policy transfer and why is it a good comparative technique?', paper presented to the 1st Policy Transfer Conference, 26–27 October, Birmingham.

Dornbusch, R. (1976), 'Expectations and Exchange Rate Dynamics', *Journal of Political Economy*, vol. 84, no. 6, pp. 1161–76.

Dornbusch, R. and Fischer, S. (1984), *Macroeconomics*, 3rd edn, London: McGraw-Hill.

Dow, J. C. R. (1964), *The Management of the British Economy, 1945–1960*, Cambridge: Cambridge University Press.

Dow, S. C. (1985), *Macroeconomic Thought: A Methodological Approach*, Oxford: Basil Blackwell.

Ellison, G. and Fudenberg, D. (1993), 'Rules of Thumb for Social Learning', *Journal of Political Economy*, vol. 101, no. 4, pp. 612–43.

Eltis, W. (1976), 'The Failure of the Keynesian Conventional Wisdom', *Lloyds Bank Review*, no. 121, pp. 1–18.

Emminger, O. (1983), 'Minutes of Evidence', in Treasury and Civil Service Committee, *International Monetary Arrangements*, 4th Report, HC 21–II, London: HMSO.

Etheredge, L. (1981), 'Governmental Learning: An Overview', in Long, S. (ed.), *Handbook of Political Behaviour*, vol. 2, New York: Plenum Press.

—— (1985), *Can Governments Learn?*, New York: Pergamon.

Evans, M. K. (1983), *The Truth about Supply-side Economics*, New York: Basic Books.

Fellner, W. (1976), *Towards a Reconstruction of Macroeconomics – Problems of Theory and Policy*, Washington, DC: American Enterprise Institute for Public Policy Research.

—— (1979), 'The Credibility Effect and Rational Expectations: Implications of the Gramlich Study', *Brookings Papers on Economic Activity*, no. 1, pp. 167–90.

—— (1980), 'The Valid Core of Rationality Hypotheses in the Theory of Expectations', *Journal of Money, Credit and Banking*, vol. 12, no. 4, pp. 763–87.

Fforde, J. (1983), 'Setting Monetary Objectives', *Bank of England Quarterly Bulletin*, vol. 23, no. 2, pp. 200–208.

Fisher, N. (1973), *Iain Macleod*, London: André Deutsch.

Flanagan, R. J. (1988), 'Unemployment as a Hiring Problem', *OECD Economic Studies*, no. 11, pp. 123–54.

Fleming, J. M. (1962), 'Domestic Financial Policies under Fixed and Floating Exchange Rates', *IMF Staff Papers*, vol. 9, no. 3, pp. 369–80.

Foreman-Peck, J. (1991), 'Trade and the Balance of Payments', in Crafts, N. F. R. and Woodward, N. W. C. (eds), *The British Economy since 1945*, Oxford: Oxford University Press.

Forsyth, J. (1980), 'Public Borrowing and the Exchange Rate', *Morgan Grenfell Economic Review*, March.

Forsyth, P. J. and Kay, J. A. (1980), 'The Economic Implications of North Sea Oil Revenues', *Fiscal Studies*, vol. 1, no. 3, pp. 1–28.

Friedman, M. (1953), 'The Case For Flexible Exchange Rates', in *Essays in Positive Economics*, Chicago, IL: University of Chicago Press.

—— (1956), 'The Quantity Theory of Money', in Friedman, M. (ed.), *Studies in the Quantity Theory of Money*, Chicago, IL: University of Chicago Press.

—— (1959), 'The Demand for Money: Some Theoretical and Empirical Results', *Journal of Political Economy*, vol. 67, no. 4, pp. 327–51.

—— (1960), *A Program for Monetary Stability*, New York: Fordham University Press.

—— (1966), 'Interest Rates and the Demand for Money', *Journal of Law and Economics*, vol. 9, pp. 71–85.

—— (1968a), 'Money: Quantity Theory', in Sills, D. (ed.), *The International Encyclopedia of the Social Sciences*, New York: Macmillan Free Press.

—— (1968b), 'The Role of Monetary Policy', *American Economic Review*, vol. 58, no. 1, pp. 1–17.

—— (1970a), 'A Theoretical Framework for Monetary Analysis', *Journal of Political Economy*, vol. 78, no. 2, pp. 193–238.

—— (1970b), *The Counter-Revolution in Monetary Theory*, Occasional Paper 33, London: Institute of Economic Affairs.

—— (1971), *A Theoretical Framework for Monetary Analysis*, Occasional Paper 112, New York: National Bureau of Economic Research.

—— (1972), 'Comments on the Critics', *Journal of Political Economy*, vol. 80, no. 5, pp. 906–50.

—— (1975), *Unemployment versus Inflation?*, London: Macmillan.

—— (1980), 'Memorandum', in Treasury and Civil Service Committee, *Memoranda on Monetary Policy*, HC 720–I, London: HMSO.

Friedman, M. and Schwartz, A. J. (1963), *A Monetary History of the United States*, Princeton, NJ: Princeton University Press.

―― (1982), *Monetary Trends in the United States and United Kingdom*, Chicago, IL: University of Chicago Press.

―― (1991), 'Alternative Approaches to Analysing Economic Data', *American Economic Review*, vol. 81, no. 1, pp. 30–49.

Funabashi, Y. (1989), *Managing the Dollar: From the Plaza to the Louvre*, Washington, DC: Institute for International Economics.

Gamble, A. (1980), 'Economic Policy', in Layton-Henry, Z. (ed.), *Conservative Party Politics*, London: Macmillan.

―― (1994), *The Free Economy and the Strong State*, 2nd edn, Basingstoke: Macmillan.

Gilmour, I. (1992), *Dancing with Dogma*, London: Simon and Schuster.

Glynn, A. and Booth, A. (1996), *Modern Britain: An Economic and Social History*, London: Routledge.

Godley, W. (1991), 'Terminal Decay', *New Statesman and Society*, vol. 4, no. 142, 15 March, p. 11–14.

Godley, W. and Rowthorn, R. (1991), 'The Warnings of a Coming Slump', Letters, *Financial Times*, 24 April.

Goodhart, C. (1984), *Monetary Theory and Practice*, Basingstoke: Macmillan.

―― (1986), 'Financial Innovation and Monetary Control', *Oxford Review of Economic Policy*, vol. 2, no. 4, pp. 79–102.

―― (1989), 'The Conduct of Monetary Policy', *Economic Journal*, vol. 99, no. 396, pp. 293–346.

Gowland, D. H. (1991), 'Financial Innovation in Theory and Practice', in Green, C. J. and Llewellyn, D. T. (eds), *Surveys in Monetary Economics, Volume 2: Financial Markets and Institutions*, Oxford: Blackwell.

Gregg, P. (1990), 'The Evolution of Special Employment Measures', *National Institute Economic Review*, no. 132, pp. 49–58.

Hall, P. A. (1982), *The Political Dimensions of Economic Management*, Ann Arbor, MI: University Microfilms International.

―― (1986), *Governing the Economy*, Cambridge: Polity Press.

―― (1990), 'Policy Paradigms, Experts and the State: The Case of Macro-economic Policy-making in Britain', in Brooks, S. and Gagnon, A. (eds), *Social Scientists, Policy and the State*, New York: Praeger.

―― (1992), 'The Movement from Keynesianism to Monetarism: Institutional Analysis and British Economic Policy in the 1970s' in Steinmo, S., Thelen, K. and Longstreth, F. (eds), *Structuring Politics: Historical Institutionalism in Comparative Analysis*, New York: Cambridge University Press.

―― (1993), 'Policy Paradigms, Social Learning, and the State: The

Case of Economic Policy-making in Britain', *Comparative Politics*, vol. 25, no. 3, pp. 275–96.

Hancock, W. K. and Gowing, M. M. (1949), *The War Economy*, London: HMSO.

Hansen, B. and Snyder, W. W. (1969), *Fiscal Policy in Seven Countries, 1955–1965*, Paris: OECD.

Harrod, R. (1960), 'Minutes of Evidence', in Committee on the Working of the Monetary System, *Principal Memoranda of Evidence*, vol. 3, London: HMSO.

Healey, D. (1989), *The Time of my Life*, London: Michael Joseph.

Healey, N. (1993), 'From Keynesian Demand Management to Thatcherism', in Healey, N. (ed.), *Britain's Economic Miracle, Myth or Reality?*, London: Routledge.

Heclo, H. (1974), *Modern Social Politics in Britain and Sweden*, New Haven, CT: Yale University Press.

Heller, W. W. (1982), 'Kennedy Economics Revisited', in Fink, R. H. (ed.), *Supply-side Economics: A Critical Appraisal*, Westport, CT: Greenwood Press.

Hendry, D. and Ericsson, N. R. (1983), 'Assertion without empirical basis: an econometric appraisal of *Monetary Trends in the United States and the United Kingdom*, by Milton Friedman and Anna Schwartz', *Bank of England Panel of Economic Consultants*, Monetary Trends in the United Kingdom, Panel Paper no. 22, October, pp. 45–101.

——— (1991), 'An econometric analysis of UK money demand in *Monetary Trends in the United States and the United Kingdom* by Milton Friedman and Anna J Schwartz', *American Economic Review*, vol. 81, no. 1, pp. 8–38.

Hibbs, D. A. Jr (1977), 'Political Parties and Macroeconomic Policy', *American Political Science Review*, vol. 71, no. 3, pp. 1467–87.

——— (1982), 'Economic outcomes and political support for British governments among occupational classes: A dynamic analysis', *American Political Science Review*, vol. 76, no. 2, pp. 259–79.

Higgins, T. L. (1992), Interview with Michael Oliver, 25 June, London.

HM Treasury (1959), *Committee on the Working of the Monetary System, Report* (Radcliffe Committee), Cmnd. 827, London: HMSO.

——— (1961), *The Control of Public Expenditure* (Plowden Report), Cmnd. 1432, London: HMSO.

——— (1980), *Financial Statement and Budget Report 1980–81*, HC 500, London: HMSO.

——— (1982), *Financial Statement and Budget Report 1982–83*, HC 237, London: HMSO.

—— (1985), *Financial Statement and Budget Report 1985–86*, HC 265, London: HMSO.

—— (1991), 'Measures of Real Exchange Rates and Competitiveness', *Treasury Bulletin*, vol. 2, no. 1, pp. 25–32.

Holberton, S. (1989), 'PM's Economist adds his Guarded Support', *Financial Times*, 18 October.

Holly, S. and Longbottom, A. (1985), 'Monetary Trends in the UK: A Reappraisal of the Demand for Money', *London Business School Discussion Paper*, no. 147.

Holmes, M. (1982), *Political Pressure and Economic Policy: British Government 1970–74*, London: Butterworth.

Hood, C. C. (1994), *Explaining Economic Policy Reversals*, Buckingham, Open University Press.

House of Commons (1986), *Special Employment Measures and the Long-term Unemployed*, 1st Report, HC 199, London: HMSO.

House of Lords (1982), *Unemployment: Volume One – Report*, HL 142, London: HMSO.

Howe, G. (1981), 'The Fight against Inflation', Third Mais Lecture, 12 May, HM Treasury press release.

—— (1982), 'Minutes of Evidence' in Treasury and Civil Service Committee, *The 1982 Budget*, 4th Report, HC 270, London: HMSO.

—— (1991), 'The 364 Economists: Ten Years On', *Fiscal Studies*, vol. 12, no. 4, pp. 92–107.

—— (1994), *Conflict of Loyalty*, London: Macmillan.

Hutton, W. (1991), *Good Housekeeping: How to Manage Credit and Debt*, London: IPPR.

James, H. (1995), *International Monetary Co-operation Since Bretton Woods*, Oxford: Oxford University Press.

Jay, P. (1990), 'Growth: The Elusive Target', *The Times*, 23 March.

—— (1993), Interview with Michael Oliver, 10 November, London.

Johnson, C. (1991a), *The Economy under Mrs Thatcher 1979–1990*, London: Penguin.

—— (1991b), *Monetarism and the Keynesians*, London: Pinter.

—— (1995), 'Memorandum: The November 1994 Budget', in Treasury and Civil Service Committee, *The 1994 Budget*, 3rd Report, HC 79, London: HMSO.

Johnson, H. G. (1971), 'The Keynesian Revolution and the Monetarist Counter-revolution', *American Economic Review*, vol. 61, no. 2, pp. 1–14.

—— (1972), 'The Monetary Approach to Balance of Payments Theory', in Johnson, H. G. (ed.), *Further Essays in Monetary Economics*, London: Allen and Unwin.

Johnson, M. H. (1982), 'Are Monetarism and Supply-side Economics

Compatible?', in Fink, R. H. (ed.), *Supply-side Economics: A Critical Appraisal*, Westport, CT: Greenwood Press.

Jones, M. and Smallwood, C. (1988), 'Neighbours, the Row that Split the Street', *Sunday Times*, 20 March.

Joseph, K. (1977), *Reversing the Trend*, London: Centre for Policy Studies.

—— (1987), 'Escaping the Chrysalis of Statism', *Contemporary Record*, vol. 1, no. 1, pp. 26–31.

Kaldor, N. (1980), 'Memorandum', in Treasury and Civil Service Committee, *Memoranda on Monetary Policy*, HC 720–I, London: HMSO.

Katzenstein, P. J. (1978), 'Conclusion: Domestic Structures and Strategies of Foreign Economic Policy', in Katzenstein, P. J. (ed.), *Between Power and Plenty*, Madison, WI: University of Wisconsin Press.

—— (1985), *Small States in World Markets*, Ithaca, NY: Cornell University Press.

Kavanagh, D. (1994), 'A Major Agenda?', in Kavanagh, D. and Seldon, A. (eds), *The Major Effect*, Basingstoke: Macmillan.

Keegan, W. (1989), *Mr Lawson's Gamble*, London: Hodder and Stoughton.

—— (1991), 'Strange, but not True, Bedfellows', *Observer*, 17 February.

Keynes, J. M. (1913), *How Far are Bankers Responsible for the Alternations of Crisis and Depression?*, reprinted in Moggridge, D. (ed.), *The Collected Writings of John Maynard Keynes*, vol. XIII, London: Macmillan.

—— (1923), *A Tract on Monetary Reform*, reprinted in *The Collected Writings of John Maynard Keynes*, vol. IV, Basingstoke: Macmillan.

—— (1930), *A Treatise on Money: 2. The Applied Theory of Money*, reprinted in *The Collected Writings of John Maynard Keynes*, vol. VI, Basingstoke: Macmillan.

—— (1936), *The General Theory of Employment, Interest and Money*, London: Macmillan.

—— (1940), *How To Pay For The War*, reprinted in *The Collected Writings of John Maynard Keynes*, vol. IX, Basingstoke: Macmillan.

King, M. (1990), 'Discussion', *Economic Policy*, vol. 5, no. 2, pp. 383–7.

—— (1995), 'Credibility and Monetary Policy: Theory and Evidence', *Bank of England Quarterly Bulletin*, vol. 35, no. 1, pp. 84–91.

Kirby, M. W. (1991), 'Supply-side Management', in Crafts, N. F. R. and Woodward, N. W. C. (eds), *The British Economy since 1945*, Oxford: Oxford University Press.

Krasner, S. (1978), *Defending the National Interest*, Princeton, NJ: Princeton University Press.

—— (1984), 'Approaches to the State', *Comparative Politics*, vol. 16, no. 2, pp. 223–46.

Kuhn, T. (1970), *The Structure of Scientific Revolutions*, Chicago, IL: University of Chicago Press.

Labour Party (1976), *Report of the Seventy-Fifth Annual Conference of the Labour Party*, London: Labour Party.

Laidler, D. (1966), 'The Rate of Interest and the Demand for Money: Some Empirical Evidence', *Journal of Political Economy*, vol. 74, no. 6, pp. 545–55.

—— (1977), *The Demand for Money: Theories and Evidence*, New York: Dun-Donnelly.

—— (1981a), 'Monetarism: An Interpretation and an Assessment', *The Economic Journal*, vol. 91, pp. 1–28.

—— (1981b), 'Notes on Gradualism' in Treasury and Civil Service Committee, *Monetary Policy*, 3rd Report, HC 163–II, London: HMSO.

—— (1982), *Monetarist Perspectives*, Oxford: Philip Allan.

—— (1985), 'Monetary Policy in Great Britain: Success and Short-comings', *Oxford Review of Economic Policy*, vol. 1, no. 1, pp. 35–43.

—— (1989a), 'Dow and Saville's Critique of Monetary Policy: A Review Essay', *Journal of Economic Literature*, vol. 27, no. 3, pp. 1147–59.

—— (1989b), 'Radcliffe, the Quantity Theory and Monetarism', in Cobham, D., Harrington, R. and Zis, G. (eds), *Money, Trade and Payments*, Manchester: Manchester University Press.

Lamfalussy, A. (1963), *The United Kingdom and the Six*, Homewood, IL: Irwin.

Lamont, N. (1990), 'Minutes of Evidence' in Treasury and Civil Service Committee, *The 1990 Autumn Statement*, First Report, HC 41, London: HMSO.

—— (1991), 'Minutes of Evidence' in Treasury and Civil Service Committee, *The 1991 Autumn Statement*, First Report, HC 58, London: HMSO.

—— (1992), 'Minutes of Evidence' in Treasury and Civil Service Committee, *The Future Conduct of Economic Policy*, HC 201–i, London: HMSO.

Lawrence, R. Z. and Schultz, C. L. (eds) (1987), *Barriers to European Growth: A Transatlantic View*, Washington, DC: The Brookings Institute.

Lawson, N. (1978), 'The Economic Perils of Thinking for the Moment', *The Times*, 14 September.

—— (1980a), *The New Conservatism*, London: Centre for Policy Studies.

—— (1980b), 'Britain's Policy and Britain's Place in the International Financial Community', speech at the *Financial Times* 1980 Euromarket Conference, 21 January, HM Treasury press release.

—— (1981), 'Thatcherism in Practice: A Progress Report', speech to the Zürich Society of Economics, 14 January, HM Treasury press release.

—— (1982), *Financial Discipline Restored*, London: Conservative Political Centre.

—— (1983), 'Mansion House speech', 20 October, HM Treasury press release.

—— (1984a), 'The British Experiment', Fifth Mais Lecture, 18 June, HM Treasury press release.

—— (1984b), 'Minutes of Evidence', in Treasury and Civil Service Committee, *The Government's Economic Policy: Autumn Statement*, 1st Report, HC 170, London: HMSO.

—— (1984c), 'Mansion House speech', 18 October, HM Treasury press release.

—— (1985a), 'Minutes of Evidence', in Treasury and Civil Service Committee, *Exchange Rate Policy*, 5th Report, HC 181, London: HMSO.

—— (1985b), 'Mansion House speech', 17 October, HM Treasury press release.

—— (1986), 'Monetary Policy', Lombard Association speech, HM Treasury press release, 16 April 1986.

—— (1988a), 'Minutes of Evidence', in Treasury and Civil Service Committee, *The 1988 Budget*, 4th Report, HC 400, London: HMSO.

—— (1988b), 'The State of the Market', 21 July, HM Treasury press release.

—— (1990a), 'No Quick-fix Solution to Economic Problems', *Financial Times*, 8 October.

—— (1990b), 'Was there a 1989 Press Conspiracy to "Get Thatcher?"', Letters, *The Times*, 7 December.

—— (1992a), *The View from No 11*, London: Bantam Press.

—— (1992b), Private communication with Michael Oliver on 31 January.

—— (1994), 'The Mais Lecture – Ten Years On', The Social Market Foundation/LSE lecture, 20 June.

—— (1996), 'Minutes of Evidence', in Treasury and Civil Service Committee, *Stage Three of Economic and Monetary Union*, HC 283-II, London: HMSO.

Layard, R. and Nickell, S. J. (1985a), 'The Causes of British Unemployment', *National Institute Economic Review*, no. 111, pp. 62–85.

—— (1985b), 'Unemployment, Real Wages and Aggregate Demand

in Europe, Japan and the US', *London School of Economics Discussion Paper*, no. 214.

Layard, R., Nickell, S. J. and Jackman, R. (1994), *The Unemployment Crisis*, Oxford: Oxford University Press.

Leigh-Pemberton, R. (1988), 'Minutes of Evidence', in Treasury and Civil Service Committee, *The 1988 Budget*, 4th Report, HC 400, London: HMSO.

Leslie, D. (1993), *Advanced Macroeconomics: Beyond IS/LM*, Maidenhead: McGraw-Hill.

Lewin, L. (1991), *Self-interest and Public Interest in Western Politics*, Oxford: Oxford University Press.

Longstreth, F. (1983), 'The Dynamics of Keynesian Political Economy: The British Case and its Implications', University of Bath: unpublished paper.

Maddison, A. (1991), *Dynamic Forces in Capitalist Development: A Long-run Comparative View*, Oxford: Oxford University Press.

Major, J. (1989), 'Minutes of Evidence', in Treasury and Civil Service Committee, *The 1989 Autumn Statement*, First Report, HC 20, London: HMSO.

Malabre, A. L. (1994), *Lost Prophets: An Insider's History of the Modern Economists*, Boston, MA: Harvard Business School Press.

Martin, B. (1990), 'Memorandum: 1990 Autumn Statement', in Treasury and Civil Service Committee, *The 1990 Autumn Statement*, 1st Report, HC 41, London: HMSO.

Masson, P. R. (1995), 'Gaining and Losing ERM Credibility: The Case of the United Kingdom', *Economic Journal*, vol. 105, no. 430, pp. 571–82.

Matthews, K. and Minford, A. P. L. (1987), 'Mrs Thatcher's Economic Policies 1979–87', *Economic Policy*, vol. 2, no. 5, pp. 59–101.

Matthews, R. C. O. (1968), 'Why has Britain had Full Employment since the War?', *The Economic Journal*, vol. 78, no. 311, pp. 555–69.

Matthews, R. C. O., Feinstein, C. H. and Odling-Smee, J. (1982), *British Economic Growth, 1856–1973*, Oxford: Clarendon Press.

Mayer, T. (1975), 'The Structure of Monetarism', *Kredit und Kapital*, vol. 8, pp. 191–215 and 293–313.

—— (1993), *Truth versus Precision in Economics*, Aldershot: Edward Elgar.

Maynard, G. (1988), *The Economy under Mrs Thatcher*, Oxford: Basil Blackwell.

—— (1993), 'Britain's Economic Recovery' in Healey, N. M. (ed.), *Britain's Economic Miracle: Myth or Reality?*, London: Routledge.

McCombie, J. S. L. and Thirlwall, A. P. (1994), *Economic Growth and the Balance-of-Payments Constraint*, Basingstoke: Macmillan.

Meade, J. (1955), 'The Case for Variable Exchange Rates', *Three Banks Review*, no. 27, pp. 3–27.

Meen, G. (1988), 'International Comparisons of the UK's Long-run Economic Performance', *Oxford Review of Economic Policy*, vol. 4, no. 1, pp. xxii–xli.

Mehta, G. (1977), *The Structure of the Keynesian Revolution*, London: Martin Robertson.

Middleton, P. (1989), 'Economic Policy Formulation in the Treasury in the Post-war Period', *National Institute Economic Review*, no. 127, pp. 46–51.

—— (1995), Interview with Michael Oliver, 1 February, London.

Middleton, R. (1985), *Towards the Managed Economy: Keynes, the Treasury and the Fiscal Policy Debate of the 1930s*, London: Methuen.

Minford, P. (1979), 'A Return to Sound Money?', *The Banker*, vol. 129, no. 641, July, pp. 29–31.

—— (1981), 'Minutes of Evidence', in Treasury and Civil Service Committee, *Monetary Policy*, 3rd Report, HC 163–II, London: HMSO.

—— (1985a), *Unemployment: Cause and Cure*, Oxford: Basil Blackwell.

—— (1985b), 'Consulting the Oracle', in Bruce-Gardyne, J., Congdon, T. and Minford, P., *Whither Monetarism?*, London: Centre for Policy Studies.

—— (1996), 'Why Clarke should keep on cutting away at interest rates', *Daily Telegraph*, 15 July.

Ministry of Reconstruction (1944), *Employment Policy*, Cmd. 6527, London: HMSO.

Mosley, P. (1984), *The Making of Economic Policy*, Brighton: Wheatsheaf.

Muellbauer, J. (1986), 'How House Prices Fuel Wage Rises', *Financial Times*, 23 October.

—— (1988), 'Argument and Counter-argument for Tax on the Market Value of Housing', Letters, *Financial Times*, 11 May.

—— (1989), 'The Case for a Tax on Land, *Financial Times*, 20 March.

Muellbauer, J. and Murphy, A. (1990), 'Is the UK Balance of Payments Sustainable?', *Economic Policy*, vol. 5, no. 2, pp. 348–83.

Mundell, R. A. (1963), 'Capital Mobility and Stabilization Policy Under Fixed and Flexible Exchange Rates', *Canadian Journal of Economics and Political Science*, vol. 29, no. 4, pp. 475–85.

National Institute Economic Review (1988), 'Summary and Appraisal', no. 124, pp. 3–6.

National Institute Economic Review (1990), 'Summary and Appraisal', no. 134, pp. 3–8.

Niehans, J. (1981), *The Appreciation of Sterling – Causes, Effects, Policies*, New York: Center for Research in Government Policy and Business.

Nordhaus, W. D. (1975), 'The Political Business Cycle', *Review of Economic Studies*, vol. 42, pp. 169–90.

—— (1989), 'Alternative Approaches to the Political Business Cycle', *Brookings Papers on Economic Activity*, no. 2, pp. 1–29.

Nordlinger, E. A. (1981), *On the Autonomy of the Democratic State*, Cambridge, MA: Harvard University Press.

North, D. C. (1984), 'Transaction Costs, Institutions, and Economic History', *Journal of Institutional and Theoretical Economics*, vol. 140, no. 1, pp. 7–17.

North, D. C. and Thomas, R. P. (1973), *The Rise of the Western World*, Cambridge: Cambridge University Press.

Norton, P. (1990), '"The Lady's Not for Turning" But What About the Rest? Margaret Thatcher and the Conservative Party 1979–89', *Parliamentary Affairs*, vol. 43, no. 1, pp. 41–58.

Observer (1985), 'Thatcher in U-turn to Save Pound', 13 January.

Oliver, M. J. (1996a), 'Social Learning: A Necessary Precondition to Policy Transfer?', paper presented to the 1st Policy Transfer Conference, 26–27 October, Birmingham.

—— (1996b), 'A Response to Denham and Garnett's "The Nature and Impact of Think Tanks in Contemporary Britain"', *Contemporary British History*, vol. 10, no. 2, pp. 80–86.

—— (1998), 'From Anodyne Keynesianism to Delphic Monetarism: British Economic Policy-making, 1960–1979', *Twentieth-Century British History*, vol. 9.

Olson, M. (1982), *The Rise and Decline of Nations*, New Haven, CT: Yale University Press.

Ormerod, P. (1994), *The Death of Economics*, London: Faber and Faber.

Orzechowski, W. P. (1982), 'Monetary Aspects of Supply-side Economics', in Fink, R. H. (ed.), *Supply-side Economics: A Critical Appraisal*, Westport, CT: Greenwood Press.

Panitch, L. (1976), *Social Democracy and Industrial Militancy*, Cambridge: Cambridge University Press.

Parliamentary Debates (Hansard), House of Commons Official Report, Fifth Series, London: HMSO.

—— Sixth Series, London: HMSO.

Parsons, D. W. (1989), *The Power of the Financial Press*, Aldershot: Edward Elgar.

Peden, G. C. (1988), *Keynes, the Treasury and British Economic Policy*, Basingstoke: Macmillan.

Pepper, G. (1977), 'The Uses of Monetarism for Practical Working Economists', *Business Economist*, vol. 8, no. 3, pp. 6–12.

—— (1990), *Money, Credit and Inflation*, London: Institute of Economic Affairs.

—— (1993), 'Measuring the Money Supply and Distortions to Monetary Data', *National Westminster Bank Quarterly Review*, February, pp. 40–58.

Pill, H. (1996), 'The "Walters's Critique" of the EMS: Fact or Fiction?', *Harvard Business School Working Paper*, no. 96–020.

Pliatzky, L. (1982), *Getting and Spending: Public Expenditure, Employment and Inflation*, Oxford: Basil Blackwell.

—— (1989), *The Treasury under Mrs Thatcher*, Oxford: Basil Blackwell.

Polak, J. J. (1957), 'Monetary Analysis of Income Formation and Payments Problems', *IMF Staff Papers*, vol. 6, no. 1, pp. 1–50.

Polsby, N. (1984), *Political Innovation in America: the Politics of Policy Innovation*, London: Yale University Press.

Pollard, S. (1982), *The Wasting of the British Economy*, London: Croom Helm.

—— (1992), *The Development of the British Economy, 1914–90*, 4th edn, London: Edward Arnold.

Pontusson, J. (1995), 'From Comparative Public Policy to Political Economy: Putting Political Institutions in their Place and Taking Interests Seriously', *Comparative Political Studies*, vol. 28, no. 1, pp. 117–47.

Pratten, C. F. (1982), 'Mrs Thatcher's Economic Experiment', *Lloyds Bank Review*, no. 143, pp. 36–51.

Price, R. W. R. (1978), 'Budgetary Policy', in Blackaby, F. T. (ed.), *British Economic Policy 1960–74*, Cambridge: Cambridge University Press.

Ricketts, M. and Shoesmith, E. (1990), *British Economic Opinion: A Survey of a Thousand Economists*, London: Institute of Economic Affairs.

Riddell, P. (1983), *The Thatcher Government*, Oxford: Martin Robertson.

Ridley, N. (1992), *My Style of Government*, London: Fontana.

Robinson, B. (1994), 'Structural Adjustment in the UK Economy: the Effects of North Sea Oil', in Holly, S. (ed.), *Money, Inflation and Employment: Essays in Honour of James Ball*, Aldershot: Edward Elgar.

Robinson, B. and McCullough, A. (1986), 'Economic Viewpoint: Manufacturing Prospects after OPEC III', London Business School, *Economic Outlook*, vol. 10, no. 5, pp. 20–28.

Rollings, N. (1988), 'British Budgetary Policy, 1945–1954: A "Keynesian Revolution"?', *Economic History Review*, 2nd series, vol. 41, no. 2, pp. 283–98.

Rose, R. (1993), *Lesson-drawing in Public Policy: A Guide to Learning across Time and Space*, Chatham, NJ: Chatham House Publishers, Inc.

Rowlatt, P. (1987), 'Analysis of the Inflation Process', *Treasury Working Paper*, no. 50, London: HM Treasury.

Runciman, W. G. (1993), 'Has British Capitalism Changed since the First World War?', *British Journal of Sociology*, vol. 44, no. 1, pp. 53–67.

Sacks, P. M. (1980), 'State Structure and the Asymmetrical Society: An Approach to Public Policy in Britain', *Comparative Politics*, vol. 12, no. 3, pp. 349–76.

Sargent, J. R. (1991), 'Deregulation, Debt and Downturn in the UK Economy', *National Institute Economic Review*, no. 137, pp. 75–88.

Sargent, T. (1993), *Rational Expectations and Inflation*, 2nd edn, New York: HarperCollins.

Sargent, T. and Wallace, N. (1976), 'Rational Expectations and the Theory of Economic Policy', *Journal of Monetary Economics*, vol. 2, no. 2, pp. 169–83.

Schmidt, M. (1982), 'The Role of Political Parties in Shaping Macroeconomic Policy', in Castles, F. (ed.), *The Impact of Parties: Politics and Policies in Democratic Capitalist States*, London: Sage.

Schott, K. (1982), 'The Rise of Keynesian Economics: Britain 1940–1964', *Economy and Society*, vol. 11, no. 3, pp. 292–316.

Simpson, D. (1994), *The End of Macro-Economics?*, London: Institute of Economic Affairs.

Skocpol, T. and Ikenberry, J. (1983), 'The Political Formation of the American Welfare State in Historical and Comparative Perspective', *Comparative Social Research*, vol. 6, pp. 87–148.

Smith, D. (1987), *The Rise and Fall of Monetarism*, London: Penguin.

—— (1992), *From Boom to Bust: Trial and Error in British Economic Policy*, London: Penguin.

Snowdon, B. Vane, H. and Wynarczyk, P. (1994), *A Modern Guide To Macroeconomics*, Aldershot: Edward Elgar.

Soskice, D. (1978), 'Strike Waves and Wage Explosions, 1968–70: An Economic Interpretation', in Crouch, C. and Pizzorno, A. (eds), *The Resurgence of Class Conflict in Western Europe, Volume Two: Comparative Analysis*, London: Macmillan.

Soteri, S. and Westaway, P. (1993), 'Explaining Price Inflation in the UK: 1971–92', *National Institute Economic Review*, no. 144, pp. 85–93.

Stafford, G. B. (1970), 'Full Employment since the War: Comment', *Economic Journal*, vol. 80, no. 317, pp. 165–72.

Steinbrunner, J. (1974), *The Cybernetic Theory of Decision*, Princeton, NJ: Princeton University Press.

Steinmo, S., Thelen, K. and Longstreth, F. (eds) (1992), *Structuring Politics: Historical Institutionalism in Comparative Analysis*, New York: Cambridge University Press.

Stephens, P. (1996), *Politics and the Pound: The Conservatives' Struggle with Sterling*, London: Macmillan.

Stephenson, H. (1980), *Mrs Thatcher's First Year*, London: Norman.

Stevens, J. (1991), 'Disagreements over Interest Rates and Sterling Levels', Letters, *The Times*, 15 February.

Stewart, M. (1986), *Keynes and After*, 3rd edn, Harmondsworth: Penguin.

Stockman, D. A. (1986), *The Triumph of Politics*, London: Bodley Head.

Stone, D. (1996), *Capturing the Political Imagination: Think Tanks and the Policy Process*, London: Frank Cass.

Tebbit, N. (1988), *Upwardly Mobile*, London: Weidenfeld and Nicolson.

Temperton, P. (1991), *UK Monetary Policy: The Challenge for the 1990s*, Basingstoke: Macmillan.

Thain, C. (1984), 'The Treasury and Britain's Decline', *Political Studies*, vol. 32, pp. 581–95.

—— (1985), *The UK Medium-term Financial Strategy, 1980–84: A Study in the Implementation of Macroeconomic Policy*, Ph.D. thesis, University of Manchester.

Thatcher, M. H. (1989), *The Revival of Britain: Speeches on Home and European Affairs*, London: Arum Press.

—— (1991), 'My Dash for Freedom', *The Times*, 29 June.

—— (1993), *The Downing Street Years*, London: HarperCollins.

—— (1995), *The Path To Power*, London: HarperCollins.

The Times (1968a), 'Surge in Money Supply a Blow for Managers of Economy', 24 September.

—— (1968b), 'Understanding the Role of the Money Supply', 15 October.

—— (1974a), 'Getting to Grips with the Catastrophic Effects of Inflation', 6 September.

—— (1974b), 'The Sharp Shock of Truth', 6 September.

—— (1974c), 'Ministers Move in to Condemn Speech', 7 September.

—— (1975), 'Mrs Thatcher Defines New Mood for Tory Politics', 11 October.

—— (1980), 'Intent Friedman; Result, Hayek', 31 July.

—— (1981), 'Monetarism Attacked by Top Economists', 30 March.

Thirlwall, A. P. (1979), 'The Balance of Payments Constraint as an Explanation of International Growth Rate Difference', *Banca Nazionale del Lavora Quarterly Review*, no. 128, pp. 44–53.

Thompson, H. (1994), *Joining the ERM: Core Executive Decision-making in the UK 1979–1990*, Ph.D. thesis, London School of Economics.

—— (1996), *The British Conservative Government and the European Exchange Rate Mechanism, 1979–1994*, London: Pinter.

Tobin, J. (1981), 'Minutes of Evidence' in Treasury and Civil Service Committee, *Monetary Policy*, 3rd Report, HC 163–II, London: HMSO.

Tomlinson, J. D. (1981a), *Problems of British Economic Policy 1870–1945*, London: Methuen.

—— (1981b), 'Why was there never a "Keynesian Revolution" in Economic Policy?', *Economy and Society*, vol. 10, no. 1, pp. 72–87.

—— (1984), 'A "Keynesian Revolution" in Economic Policy-Making?', *Economic History Review*, 2nd series, vol. 37, no. 2, pp. 258–62.

—— (1990), *Public Policy and the Economy since 1900*, Oxford: Oxford University Press.

—— (1994), 'British Economic Policy since 1945', in Floud, R. and McCloskey, D. (eds), *The Economic History of Britain since 1700*, vol. 3, Cambridge: Cambridge University Press.

Treasury and Civil Service Committee (1980a), *Memoranda on Monetary Policy*, HC 720–I, London: HMSO.

—— (1980b), *Memoranda on Monetary Policy*, HC 720–II, London: HMSO.

—— (1980c), *Monetary Control* (two volumes), 3rd Report, HC 713–I and HC 713–II, London: HMSO.

—— (1981), *Monetary Policy*, 3rd Report, HC 163–II, London: HMSO.

Trinder, C. (1988), 'Special Employment Measures and Registered Unemployment', *National Institute Economic Review*, no. 123, pp. 17–19.

Tufte, E. R. (1978), *Political Control of the Economy*, Princeton, NJ: Princeton University Press.

Vane, H. R. and Thompson, J. L. (1979), *Monetarism: Theory, Evidence and Policy*, London: Martin Robinson.

Walker, P. (1987), *Trust the People*, London: Collins.

—— (1991), *Staying Power*, London: Bloomsbury.

Walters, A. A. (1986), *Britain's Economic Renaissance*, Oxford: Oxford University Press.

—— (1989), 'A Life Philosophy', *American Economist*, vol. 23, no. 2, pp. 18–24.

—— (1990a), *Sterling in Danger*, London: Fontana.

—— (1990b), '"Get Thatcher", and they did', *The Times*, 5 December.

—— (1991), 'Dare Major devalue?', *The Times*, 2 January.

—— (1992), Interview with Michael Oliver, 18 June, London.

—— (1996), 'Minutes of Evidence', in Treasury and Civil Service Committee, *Stage Three of Economic and Monetary Union*, HC 283-II, London: HMSO.

Ward, R. and Zis, G. (1974), 'Trade Union Militancy as an Explanation of Inflation: An International Comparison', *Manchester School of Economic and Social Studies*, vol. 42, no. 1, pp. 45–65.

Wass, D. (1978), 'The Changing Problems of Economic Management', *Economic Trends*, no. 293, pp. 97–104.

Weir, M. and Skocpol, T. (1985), 'State Structures and the Possibilities for "Keynesian" Responses to the Great Depression in Sweden, Britain and the United States', in Evans, P., Ruescheneyer, D. and Skocpol, T. (eds), *Bringing the State Back In*, Cambridge: Cambridge University Press.

Westaway, P. and Wren-Lewis, S. (1993), 'Is there a Case for the MTFS?', *Manchester School of Economic and Social Studies*, vol. 61, no. 3, pp. 227–47.

Whiteley, P. (1986), *Political Control of the Macroeconomy*, London: Sage.

Whiteley, P. F., Seyd, P., Richardson, J. and Bissell, P. (1994), 'Thatcherism and the Conservative Party', *Political Studies*, vol. 42, no. 2, pp. 185–203.

Wickham-Jones, M. (1992), 'Monetarism and its Critics: The University Economists' Protest of 1981', *Political Quarterly*, vol. 63, no. 2, pp. 171–85.

—— (1997), 'Right Turn: A Revisionist Account of the 1975 Conservative Party Leadership Election', *Twentieth-Century British History*, vol. 8, no. 1, pp. 74–89.

Wilensky, H. L. and Turner, L. (1987), *Democratic Corporatism and Policy Linkages*, Berkeley, CA: Institute of International Studies, University of California.

Willetts, D. (1994), Interview with Michael Oliver, 23 November, London.

Williamson, J. (1983), *The Exchange Rate System*, Washington, DC: Institute for International Economics.

—— (1991), 'FEERs and the ERM', *National Institute Economic Review*, no. 137, pp. 45–50.

Wolf, M. (1990), 'The UK and the ERM: Setting the Record Straight', *Financial Times*, 21 December.

Wolman, H. (1992), 'Understanding Cross-national Policy Transfers: The Case of Britain and the US', *Governance*, vol. 5, no. 1, pp. 27–45.

Wood, G. E. (1995), 'The Quantity Theory in the 1980s', in Blaug, M. et al., *The Quantity Theory of Money from Locke to Keynes and Friedman*, Aldershot: Edward Elgar.

Worswick, G. D. N. (1971), 'Trade and Payment', in Cairncross, A. (ed.), *Britain's Economic Prospects Reconsidered*, London: Allen and Unwin.

Wren-Lewis, S. (1990), 'The Danger of a High Level Entry Level', *Financial Times*, 17 October.

Wren-Lewis, S., Westaway, P., Soteri, S. and Barrell, R. (1990), 'Choosing the Rate: An Analysis of the Optimum Level of Entry for Sterling into the ERM', *National Institute Discussion Paper*, no. 171.

—— (1991), 'Evaluating the UK's Choice of Entry Rate into the ERM', *Manchester School of Economic and Social Studies*, vol. 59, Supplement, pp. 1–22.

Wright, G. (1986), 'History and the Future of Economics', in Parker, W. N. (ed.), *Economic History and the Modern Economist*, Oxford: Basil Blackwell.

Zis, G. (1975), 'Inflation: An International Monetary Problem or a National Social Phenomenon', *British Journal of International Studies*, vol. 1, no. 2, pp. 98–118.

Subject Index

Name Index